"Unfailingly engaging and lyrical. A beautifully written love letter to the intertwining tendrils of nature and community, *Satellite* takes its rightful place among the finest work by outstanding Sonoran Desert writers including Gary Paul Nabhan, Alison Hawthorne Deming, and Alberto Ríos."

—MICHAEL P. BRANCH, author of *On the Trail of the Jackalope: How a Legend Captured the World's Imagination and Helped Us Cure Cancer*

"A beautiful book grounded in family, community, and nature to take hope and inspiration from."

—ALISON HAWTHORNE DEMING, author of *Blue Flax and Yellow Mustard Flower*

"A rich and warm and love-filled meditation...Generosity of spirit and constancy of attention imbue every one of the essays in this splendid, shining collection."

—ELIZABETH DODD, author of *Horizon's Lens: My Time on the Turning World*

"From the direct sensual pleasures of photographing wildflowers and drinking beer to the more complex pleasures and pains of fatherhood, fraught with dangers from rattlesnakes to mood swings, this beautiful and deep collection of essays covers fascinating terrain....A moving distillation of a lifetime of work and thought."

—DAVID GESSNER, author of *All the Wild That Remains: Edward Abbey, Wallace Stegner, and the American West*

"*Satellite* links us lyrically to expanses of wildness, recollections of familial experience,...orbiting an ever-revolving heartfelt artistry that takes the reader on a journey toward reverence, respect, and greater kinship with nature and humanity...An act of love."

—J. DREW LANHAM, author of *The Home Place: Memoirs of a Colored Man's Love Affair with Nature*

"Unlike so many of his predecessors, Buntin is never torn between loving the wilderness and loving his family, between wanting to explore with his camera and wanting to explore with his young daughters. The love for one increases the love for the other in a sort of whirlwind of curiosity, generosity, and deep feeling. These are thoughtful, detail-rich essays that are deeply engaged with the natural world and with humans as part of the menagerie. They model in the best way what I have lately heard called *tonic masculinity* and manage to have a great deal of fun in the process."

—PAM HOUSTON, author of *Deep Creek: Finding Hope in the High Country*

"Whether admiring the Great Orion Nebula with his daughter, chasing a rare 'explosion' of desert wildflowers along the U.S.-Mexico border, asserting craft beers as an expression of place, or meditating on individual and communal heritage, Buntin invites us to rediscover the extraordinary in the seemingly simple intimacies—with people and places, near and far. Wherever you call home, *Satellite* is a guide to belonging and cherishing 'the sheer abundance of it all.'"

—JOHN T. PRICE, author of *All Is Leaf: Essays and Transformations*

"The best personal essays offer insights into the world as well as the writer. Simmons Buntin manages that fine balance in this collection, which ranges geographically across the American West, from his Tucson backyard to the slopes of Mount Saint Helens, and ranges autobiographically from memories of growing up as the son of a troubled mother to scenes of delight and anguish as the father of two young daughters. Readers will find him an illuminating guide as he searches for beauty and spiritual grounding in nature, a search reflected in the haunting photographs that accompany each essay."

—SCOTT RUSSELL SANDERS, author of *The Way of Imagination*

"Even as naturalist and writer Simmons Buntin introduces his daughters to nature, he must come to terms with his place in the world…yielding to beauty, building wonder, and sketching out hope for our children. Here is a field guide to a father's love."
—JANISSE RAY, *Craft and Current: A Manual for Magical Writing*

"I can't think of a better guide—to whiptails, desert super blooms, craft beer, constellations, photography, fatherhood, community, and, well, *life*—than Simmons Buntin. From Denver to Tucson, the Bosque del Apache, Mount Saint Helens, and beyond, Buntin writes with equal facility about the beautiful, dynamic intricacies of the natural world and the many lovely, knee-buckling complexities of family. These wide-ranging, self-aware, astute essays will leave you enlightened and deeply glad—glad right down to your heart and bones, the feathery roots of what some of us might even call a soul."
—JOE WILKINS, author of *The Entire Sky*

SATELLITE

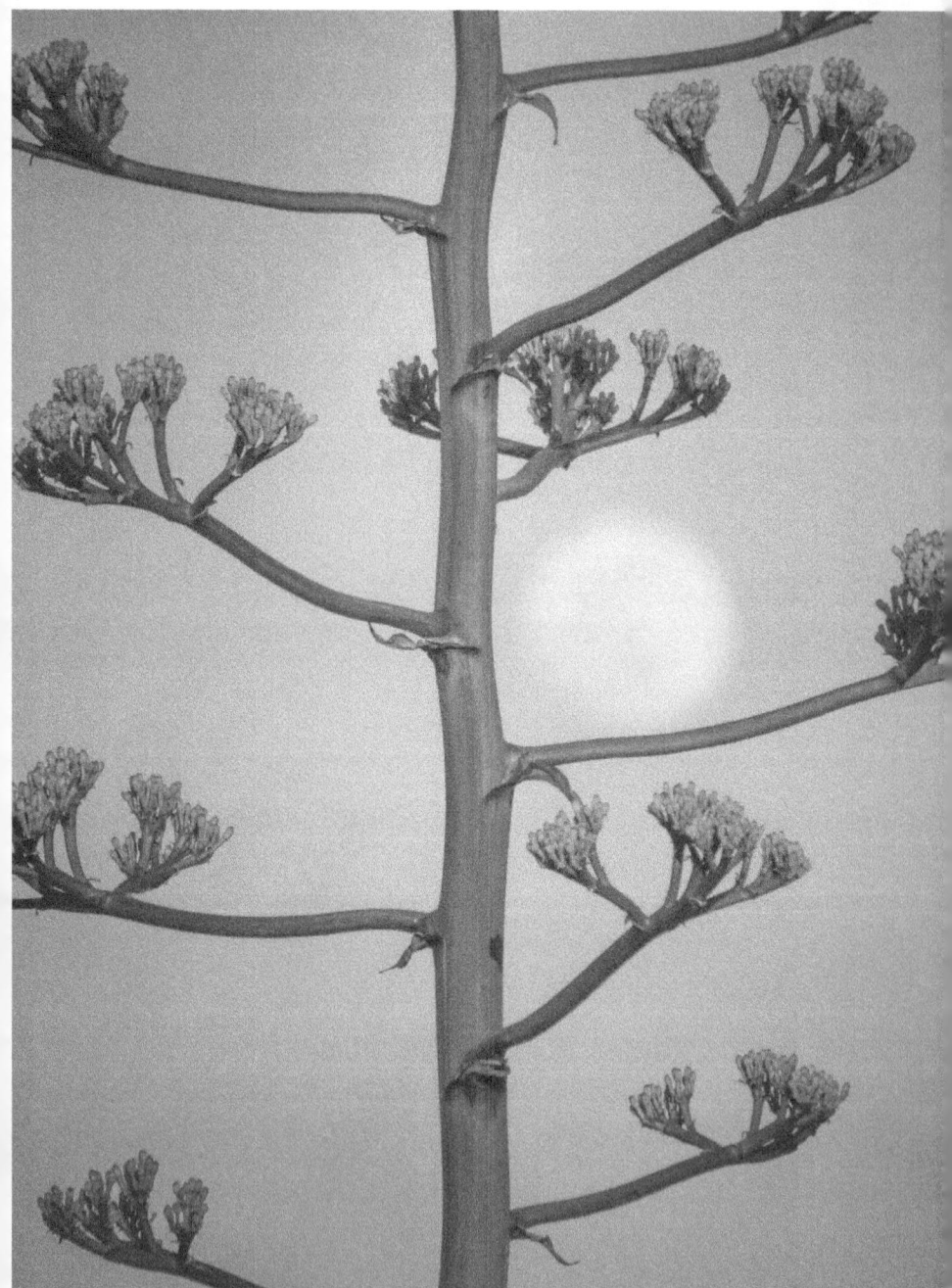

SATELLITE

*Essays on Fatherhood and Home,
Near and Far*

Simmons Buntin

TERRA FIRMA BOOKS

TRINITY UNIVERSITY PRESS

San Antonio

Terra Firma Books, an imprint of Trinity University Press
San Antonio, Texas 78212

Book design by BookMatters, Berkeley
Cover design by Anne Boston
Photographs by Simmons Buntin
Author photo by Chris Richards

ISBN 978-1-59534-311-6 paper
ISBN 978-1-59534-312-3 ebook

Page iii, Full moon and agave inflorescence, Tucson, Arizona; page 1, Ringtail
in a velvet mesquite, Civano, Tucson, Arizona; page 17, Casa Encantada,
Álamos, Sonora; page 35, Observatory atop Kitt Peak, Arizona; page 50,
Sandhill crane, Bosque del Apache National Wildlife Refuge, New Mexico;
page 73, Black River near Craftsbury Common, Vermont; page 84, Misión
San Francisco Borja de Adac, Baja California Norte; page 95, Mexican gold
poppies, Ironwood Forest National Monument, Arizona; page 105, Lagartos
Irish Red, El Paso Brewing Company, Texas; page 122, Altar along All Souls
Procession, Tucson, Arizona; page 141, Civano, Tucson, Arizona; page 154, El
Tiradito shrine, Tucson, Arizona; page 173, Harris's hawk, Arizona–Sonora
Desert Museum, Tucson, Arizona; page 181, Professor Valley, Utah; page
195, Guadalupe Mountains National Park, Texas; page 219, H. J. Andrews
Experimental Forest, Oregon; page 247, Misión de Nuestra Señora de Loreto
Conchó, Loreto, Baja California Sur

Trinity University Press strives to produce its books using methods and
materials in an environmentally sensitive manner. We favor working with
manufacturers that practice sustainable management of all natural resources,
produce paper using recycled stock, and manage forests with the best possible
practices for people, biodiversity, and sustainability. The press is a member
of the Green Press Initiative, a nonprofit program dedicated to supporting
publishers in their efforts to reduce their impacts on endangered forests,
climate change, and forest-dependent communities.

The paper used in this publication meets the minimum requirements of the
American National Standard for Information Sciences—Permanence of Paper
for Printed Library Materials, ANSI 39.48–1992.

CIP data on file at the Library of Congress

29 28 27 26 25 | 5 4 3 2 1

for Billie, Onyx (Ann-Elise), and Juliet
for beauty, family, landscape, and community

CONTENTS

THE SUM OF ALL SPECIES

These are perilous times in my neighborhood. A musky pack of javelinas—all grisly hair and yellow tusks—roams the streets after midnight. A four-foot rattlesnake tracks a rabbit through my neighbor's yard, corners it under the sumac, and strikes. On our doorstep, my flashlight reveals a black widow the size of a ripe olive, its red hourglass gleaming as the spider wraps a moth into its gauzy corner web.

Inside our house, my family meets other risks. Returning from two weeks of travel, we find that creatures have had the run of the place—not just the hermit crabs in their sandy cove or the cichlids of the aquarium—but something new and foreign. Something that doesn't dash but instead saunters across the kitchen floor, over the rug shadowed by the dishwasher, and beneath the pantry door. Though the creature moves slowly, it catches me by surprise, so I am uncertain of its intentions, cannot tell just yet if it is venomous, as so many animals in the desert are. Its tail is up, curved like the broken handle of a teacup. Is there a stinger at the end, a tiny venom-filled syringe? How many legs: four or six or more?

I grab the flashlight and swing the pantry door wide. Light blunts the small space and, between the wall and a carton, the animal stalls. I slide to my knees, within easy reach, and exhale. The lizard's body is nearly translucent among uneven stripes, darkened only by a pair of eyes that freeze, like the still legs, the tiny toes resembling the fingers of an infant's hand. My lapse is the window the gecko needs, and it darts beyond my cupped hand—into the darker spaces and out of sight.

Despite my wife's complaints, I don't chase after it. Billie's not keen on having a gecko in the house—even less so after we discover two in different rooms the next day—but lizards are lucky, I say. Mistaken first for a scorpion, a little illusion young geckos cast by curling plump tails when scared, scorpions are at the top of their diet, followed by silverfish, earwigs, and small centipedes. Natural pest control, I tell her. She's not so sure, but knowing what western banded geckos eat convinces her to let these lizards lie, at least for now. Besides, we have other matters to attend to: a palo verde borer beetle raps erratically on the glass of the back door, seeking entry. It's as thick and dense as a roll of quarters, and the pane rattles under the insect's assault.

That our house is filled with lizards is the result both of chance and circumstance. The geckos, smaller than a finger, come out at night, scouring the baseboards without a sound. They enter, I suspect, through a small gap in the weather stripping beneath our front door. Perhaps they follow less-desirable critters. So far, they are tidy, amiable housemates that give us good reason to avoid pesticides.

Other lizards come in, too. Outside, the sun-dappled yard bristles with the sudden scrambling of whiptail lizards, their body-length stripes providing odd camouflage among lantana and sage. Given my ten-year-old daughter Ann-Elise's affinity for tracking small animals, she soon catches a young specimen, which she subdues by stroking its head and body. Within minutes, it comfortably scales her hand and arm, weaving through her hair, never trying or at least succeeding in escape.

Escape is not a part of my daughter's plans; it rarely is. In the seven years we've lived in the master-planned community of Civano in southeast Tucson, a pell-mell pile of plastic bug jars, terrariums, and butterfly baskets has found a permanent home in our garage. None are used lightly. After summer rainstorms, Ann-Elise and her seven-year-old sister, Juliet, race to the temporary ponds at the end of our street to collect tadpoles, scooping the rainwater and savoring the cloudy concoction with its teaming pollywogs as if it were a succulent stew. When the girls return home, they place a rock in the stained and shallow box so that, as the water evaporates, the morphing tadpoles can crawl from the water. The girls have no intention of returning the tadpoles to the ponds, both because the thirsty ground drinks the ponds down and because the excitement is in watching them become frogs. Or die trying.

Ann-Elise's excitement about the whiptail is evident not only in the new home she has created in the largest of the portable terrariums—sand substrate, cholla skeleton, sprig of chuparosa—but in the way she carries the lizard throughout the day. They are inseparable, and any hopes of regular hand-washing after handling the reptile (what with pet store warnings of salmonella) are lost in the first hour of their acquaintance. Initially, I encourage her to return the lizard to the wild—its wild, anyway, for our yard is not so much wild as it is purposefully tangled, with layers of prickly pear, Mexican bird-of-paradise, and desert willow. How else to attract and admire the family of quail at sunrise, the comical cactus wrens at the other end of the day? But I can only relent, both in the knowledge that she has wanted and asked for a pet lizard for years, and because at that age I had collected, and kept, my own community of desert critters, from centipedes to scorpions, field mice to king snakes.

Perhaps, then, I am more intrigued by my daughter's passion than I should be. Yet as a father, I cannot help but consider the educational value of caring for this small and common creature. From this perspective, I'm less concerned with the relationship's academic profits than with its importance in establishing her sense of connection to the natural world. It is all too easy, for children and adults alike, to move through the day conscious and yet still ignorant of the complexity and importance of the natural world.

Raising a single lizard will not teach my daughter the desert's intricacies, of course, but it can teach her about community, just as her family's relationship with human neighbors teaches her about social and political community. And appreciating community is central to learning about and caring for the habitat both outside her door and across the globe. In his 1949 classic, *A Sand County Almanac*, conservationist Aldo Leopold writes, "We abuse land because we regard it as a commodity belonging to us. When we see land as a community we belong to, we may begin to use it with love and respect." It is not too much to hope, I think, for a lizard to further imbue my child with love and respect—even as I acknowledge that removing an animal from its habitat raises its own questions of ethics, its own lessons of humans taking and dominating nature once again. What, then, will the experience teach her, and in turn teach me?

Ann-Elise waits eagerly for me as I return from work. Squeaky, the name she gives the whiptail, is curled beneath a smooth rock in the terrarium. Soon we'll be on our way to the local pet store for the essentials, which we're vague on but undoubtedly include food and some device to warm the cold-blooded reptile. Before we depart, however, I urge my daughter to learn a bit more about the lizard, to ensure that we can in fact meet its needs as a pet. "Dad," she says, frowning, "what do you think I've been doing all day?" She lowers the clear, lidded box, walks to the den, and returns with a dozen pages of whiptail lizard information she's gathered off the internet.

"It's a western whiptail lizard," she announces, eyes flitting between the sheets of paper. "Or maybe a New Mexico whiptail, since the stripes are so bright." I nod, and encourage her to tell me what they eat.

"Bugs, Dad. What'd you think?" Which is her way of saying, *Would you quit asking me stupid questions so we can get going?*

"Hmm," I say. "Maybe rocks and flower pots and, let's see, small children?" I grab her wrist and start gnawing on it. She giggles for a moment but then straightens up. There are serious matters at hand, and she crosses her arms.

"Okay, okay. Anything else we need to know?" I ask.

"I did see something weird, but I don't know what it means. What's this?" She points to a page she pulls from the middle of the collection, to the word *parthenogenesis*. Sounds familiar, I tell her, and it does, but I must read the full passage to take in its meaning. "In fifteen of the *Cnemidophoros* species there are no males," it begins. "They reproduce without fertilization, a process known as parthenogenesis, or 'virgin birth.' Parthenogenesis is well known in lower animals, such as aphids, bees, and *Daphnia*, but is rare in vertebrates."

From my copy of the *Natural History of the Sonoran Desert* I then read aloud: "In Arizona approximately 60 percent of whiptail species are *parthenogenetic*, meaning that they reproduce asexually. These species…consist entirely of genetically identical females that lay unfertilized eggs, creating a population of clones. Oddly enough, many of the behaviors exhibited by sexually reproducing species are expressed by these parthenogenetic lizards. Females will engage in pseudocopulation and mount and bite other females. Apparently, this triggers hormonal changes necessary for ovulation and egg laying."

I hadn't intended for this conversation to morph from lizards to the birds and the bees, so when she asks me what *pseudocopulation* is, I look at my watch and say, "We'd better get going." Now she stalls, until I tell her that a girl lizard pretends she's a boy lizard to encourage mating that isn't really mating, to fertilize the eggs.

"Dad," she says, "that's just gross." Because I don't have to further explain, and because she's already in fifth grade, when some might not think that copulation of any kind is so vulgar, I'm relieved.

An hour and a half later, we're back at home with a ten-gallon tank, sand, warming stone, and a foam-topped tube of flightless fruit flies that may or may not be parthenogenetic. No one asks, least of all Squeaky, who once in her new home races after the clueless flies, reminding us of the frenzied way whiptails dash through the leaf litter beneath the bushes of the yard.

Beyond our yard, beyond the length of the lushly landscaped street, the times are perilous indeed. At the northern edge of Civano, Mexican laborers risk the heat of August to blade the shallow bluffs that separate the subdivision from Pantano Wash, a wide, seasonal streambed that serves as wildlife highway. The wash tracks down from the Rincon Mountains east of Tucson and then flows, during violent summer thunderstorms, northeast into the city. This area is the neighborhood's final—and most controversial—development, where concrete replaces the natural grades and vegetation of arroyos in a move that is antithetical to Civano's environmental upbringing, let alone common desert sense. Instead of dry rivulets filtered with palo verde and cholla, the neighborhood's northern boundary is now defined by high block walls and cement floodways. The area marketed as "North Ridge" was once a series of wildlife corridors, connecting the higher desert with the wash. Thorn-scrub gullies thick with barrel cactus and young saguaro tumbled to a bench of creosote before meeting the mesquite and desert willows along the wash's sandy edge. Walking the adjacent path, my daughters and I have seen coyotes, javelina, and once a silver kit fox. Neighbors have noted ringtails and bobcats. A solitary mountain lion was glimpsed in a particularly dry year.

The corridors may yet survive, as sightings of rattlesnakes and roadrunners appear to be on the rise. Yet I fear this may be the corporeal climax before the new barriers cut the animals out completely. The increase in wildlife is likely a result of this year's heavy monsoon. Wild animals, too, have been forced into the neighborhood's center by the new construction along the periphery. While it is easy to answer the question of why this scenic and biologically rich habitat is under development—the Civano master plan curiously allows for it, and the oversized, garage-dominant houses will make the builder plenty of money—the question of why wildlife is important for a community's health is less quantitative, falling largely outside the lingo of developers, builders, and many home buyers, whose communal word is *economics*.

Money talks, as they say, but wildlife cannot—though in fairness anyone who has spent an evening at Civano, an evening among the trails overhung with the bean-laden branches of velvet mesquite and sweet acacia, knows that wildlife doesn't just talk, it absolutely sings. Coyotes yip and bark and howl like a summer cabin full of ten-year-olds. Pallid bats click and chirp as they skate across the twilight. A great-horned owl roosts on an adobe parapet at the neighborhood center, *whooing* and *whooing* the cool night into dawn.

Creating community that includes wildlife—the native species of the places upon which streets and houses and parks are later built—is important for a number of reasons. Sharing our built environment with wild animals, even the likes of coral snakes and Gila monsters, ensures that we avoid an antiseptic life that would be apart from rather than a part of our desert habitat. That would not be life, but lifeless. Defining the desert based only on its inanimate structure—rock, mountain, cactus—creates a flawed definition. Wildlife is as integral to the desert landscape as the giant boulders of Sabino Canyon, the pinnacles of the Santa Ritas, and the Tortalita Mountains' forests of saguaro and ironwood are to the definition of the Sonoran Desert itself. "The last word in ignorance is the man who says of an animal or plant: 'What good is it?'" writes Leopold in *Round River*. "If the land mechanism as a whole is good, then every part is good, whether we understand it or not. If the biota, in the course of aeons, has built something we like but do not understand, then who but a fool would discard seemingly useless parts? To keep every cog and wheel is the first precaution of intelligent tinkering."

Yet we must also acknowledge that humans are likewise a critical cog of the system. Though we more often act as a clog, the legitimate community comprises the landscape natural and built, the living and dying species of plants and animals and humans, and more. That must be what is meant by *sense of place*. If we truly seek a sense of place, not just an acknowledgment of a locale's unique identity, but an understanding and appreciation of the place and its elements—and I wager that we must—then all of the parts are required. It's not only a matter of who was here first—the standard argument—but also how we are to evolve as a human species. How, instead of living through subtraction, we can exist by addition. Not the multiplication of our own species, but the survival of all species.

Perhaps that is why the Civano Community School, the shared-grade neighborhood school that Ann-Elise and Juliet attend, emphasizes community in its fullest context. Here, community is defined as our supportive relationship with and integrative part of the natural whole. Students complete work based on design principles that include self-discovery, empathy and caring, diversity and inclusion, and the natural world. While the modules are at first separate, principle builds upon principle, so that a recent discovery of Gamble's quail eggs in a school garden plot, for example, prompted a lesson on urban wildlife and the students' responsibilities in living amiably with it. The students were delighted at the discovery, and without prompt guarded the plot to allow the eggs to hatch and the chicks, guided by their quail parents, to survive within the setting of the schoolyard.

Yet survival is not enough. The collective species—quail and human alike—must thrive. Humans thrive when aware of and connected to the community, and chance encounters with wildlife represent our most innate connections. More than the adrenaline rush and heightened emotion, the encounter brings us to a heightened consciousness. Stumbling upon a male tarantula that, after an afternoon of rain, stumbles upon you in his incessant search for a mate; or finding the mother hummingbird, star-throated and wispy-winged, feeding her chick on a thin stalk of a hesperaloe; or startling a badger that hisses its way back into the crevice a short walk from the path's turnabout—these encounters are important because they recall a time and place before subdivisions and cities. Perhaps to a world where there are no communities, or only a single community that is the whole world, unwalled.

This is the realm of the unconscious, a connection to our origins ancestral as well as spiritual. It is a deep place—planted like an original seed within each person and the species as a whole. Or it is shallow, on our surface as light and mobile as a water strider, and therefore easily brought forth by the interaction. The result may be called spiritual ascension or religious experience or transcendent function. However we define what we become at that precise moment, the act of becoming and its impetus—the chance encounter—are real. And they are essential, even if they sometimes carry great risk.

Each spring, wind tumbles down the Rincon Mountains, through a valley stitched by the Pantano Wash, and into our neighborhood. It is a good season for flying kites, and on this last week of spring Ann-Elise, Juliet, and I weave a path to a wide park, naming cardinal and pyrrhuloxia, desert hare and tiger swallowtail along the way. The kites my daughters curl on the afternoon's high winds shine like windows against the endless blue dome of the sky. The windows' thin panes are battered then released, the strings tighten then slacken and tighten again. On the second afternoon, our friend Lynne and her daughter Amelia join us. Amelia skips and then stops, jumps and then dives in an attempt at synchronizing herself to the kites. Lynne brought the five-year-old's kite, but the twine is tangled, and our best efforts to straighten the stubborn string are no good. Regardless,

Amelia—who is not much bigger than a kite, perhaps nearly as light—squeals and laughs. It's not long before Juliet joins her, and together they race across the low-grass field while Ann-Elise and I maneuver the kites, without expertise yet with a certain grace.

On the third afternoon we cannot return, but other kites snake through the air. Amelia, delighted, can see them from her front yard, with its low stucco wall and wrought-iron gate that fronts a meandering path not far from the park. She calls to her mom that she's going to see Juliet and Ann-Elise. "They're flying kites!" she yells, beaming. Eyes locked on the colorful tails trailing from what must look like paper diamonds, she swings the gate wide and slides onto the path. In an instant, something is wrong.

Her eyes drop to the ground, to the sharp pain in her sandaled toe, as a young rattlesnake cocks back its diamond-shaped head to strike again. She jumps back and screams, terrified. She runs into the house, still screaming. She launches herself into her mother's unexpecting arms.

Lynne and Gail cannot calm their tiny daughter for minutes. To Amelia, it feels like hours. Once her parents see the two puncture marks on the already swollen toe, they rush into action. Lynne dials 911, and the operator says to wait for the paramedics, who arrive in less time than it took for Amelia to relate what happened. Gail, meanwhile, grabs a flat-ended shovel from the garage and, already in her work boots, moves swiftly to the gate. She finds the snake curled and agitated, its two-bead tail buzzing. In a flash, it is uncurled and headless, its tail still vibrating. She scoops up the limp body and head and places them in a plastic bag. She drops that inside a canvas bag, then inside another for good measure. When the paramedics arrive, they identify the parts as a western diamondback, and know which antivenin to provide.

Still, they rush Amelia to the hospital. Her adrenaline is pump-
ing so that the toxin in her toe, the tissue already dying, does not
yet hurt like it will. She requires eighteen vials of antivenin over
the next two days, and even more on subsequent doctor visits.

Can one explain, let alone defend, the value of chance encounters
with wildlife to a girl pierced by the fangs of a venomous snake?
Or to her parents, or the elderly neighbor whose aluminum
walker scrapes over the gate's exposed threshold? Are there some
wild animals more deserving than others to be in our community, and how should we choose? Wolves have been extirpated
from most of their range because ranchers fear for their sheep
and calves. Grizzlies are but a memory in the Colorado Rockies,
bountied and hunted into nothingness. I crush the black widow
on the front porch and sweep away the web. The stain of her
deflated body lingers.

It is difficult not to want to kill or drive off dangerous wildlife.
Community implies, in its highest form, an amiable relationship among members. But there is little to like about venomous
snakebites, or the agony from a black widow or brown recluse
bite, or the stiletto-quick sting of a scorpion. One wonders why
the poison far exceeds the required dose for the creatures' typical
prey. Evolution has its reason, no doubt, but that's little comfort
when confronted with a venomous conclusion. On the other
hand, there is little to like about the simple ease with which
humans can level a habitat, or pollute the air, or send noxious
and unknown chemical plumes seeping into the aquifer. Tit for
tat? Hardly.

Perhaps one solution, one way to reach the compromise that is
community, is the tandem of boundaries and caution. As a human
species and as a culture, we can set boundaries beyond which we

will not establish neighborhoods: stay out of the swamp, and the cottonmouth and alligator will stay out of the yard because there is no yard to begin with. Similarly, we can use simple caution; keeping, for example, our eyes pointed to our feet in a desert environment where rattlesnakes are so common. Unfortunately, the modern history of the human species provides little hope for either approach. Boundaries have and continue to be exceeded on a regular basis, sometimes for subsistence, sometimes for economic gain. And caution? Even at our most cautious, we cannot foresee all possibilities, nor plan for all contingencies. To a five-year-old, and probably to her parents, a skein of kites shining in flight like multicolored geese is too great a temptation to stop and remember to look down. And then there's protective coloration, which deceive pack rat and human alike.

Yet extirpation cannot be the preferred response, nor can chemical repellants that poison our bodies, even if we don't know it, just as they poison the "pests." The answer could lie in how we construct our communities. Just as alternative building approaches like passive solar orientation and rainwater harvesting are needed to take advantage of sunlight and other renewable energy sources—for a more efficient and sustainable home— wildlife-friendly plans that are also amicable to humans might limit the overlap of humans and dangerous creatures. They could create in some cases corridors not necessarily of chance encounters, but instead of controlled encounters: wild set-asides at the community's edge, raised walkways among riparian areas, cleared brush along building foundations.

Perhaps, finally, there is also a solution through the noble and conscious striving for a coexistence with wild animals. Leopold offers advice here as well: "We shall never achieve harmony with land, any more than we shall achieve absolute justice or liberty for people. In these higher aspirations the important thing is not to achieve, but to strive."

It is afternoon, and I have just returned to my office from a meeting. I check my phone and find two new voicemails. What greets me on the other end is hysteria. Between sobs, Ann-Elise chokes out a few words—"lizard...holding...blood"—but no more. I call my wife, who is not at home but has talked to our older daughter. Ann-Elise thinks she has killed Squeaky.

When I finally arrive at the house, a neighbor and her daughter are also there, trying to console Ann-Elise. As I open the door, she lunges at me. Her thick sandy hair is a mess, eyes red and agonized. She explains, barely more audible than her phone messages, that she was trying to grab the small lizard from its terrarium, but it was running from her. She had to strike fast to catch it. When she brought it out, between the clenched fingers of her hand, she noticed a line of red around its jaw. She opened her hand as usual to let Squeaky climb up her arm, but the lizard didn't move. She prodded it with her finger, gently touching the striped back. Nothing.

Then fear and horror and guilt consumed her, and, hand shaking, she placed the lizard on the basking stone to warm it up, to give it some last incentive to move, to end the frightening charade of death.

Now she takes my hand. She holds it lightly, as if any pressure would break the lizard-length bones of my finger like, she realizes, she has broken the body of the whiptail. She leads me to the terrarium, which rests on the back of the craft table in our dining room, beneath the window that looks onto the porch and the front yard. In the yard, a palo blanco sways in the breeze while an acacia, bright green in the slanting afternoon light, hosts a nest started by cactus wrens, completed last year by curve-billed thrashers, and used this year by ground doves. A Costa's hummingbird visits the scarlet-necked autumn sage before rising to dart gnats. Beneath the enormous blue agave, a lizard scurries over a rock to find a plump cricket, too slow. Now gone.

I place my hand into the glass box and as my fingers approach the stone, I feel its radiance. The few remaining fruit flies cannot fly out, but that doesn't stop them from jumping onto my arm. I brush them off and pick up the lizard, which does not move. I lift my hand from the tank, close the lid, and examine the reptile. Already the eyes are sinking and have no gleam. The jaw is locked in a thin red smile.

"Squeaky is dead," I tell my daughter.

She takes the body from my hand, face full of new tears, and rushes outside to the corner of the backyard, to the small garden plot she and her sister maintain, to the very corner of the plot. She digs a hole with her hand and lays the lizard in it, fills the hole, and tamps the dark soil around the body. She says an indiscernible message or prayer and looks as forlorn as I've ever seen her.

I watch Ann-Elise from the back door and wait for her to come in. When she does I hug her and do not let go for nearly a minute. She does not struggle for escape. I do not want to tell her what she already knows—that love and desire can sometimes be suffocating things. There is no need, either, for the voice on high to speak of responsibility and lessons learned. Instead, I take her by the hand and lead her to the front door, though we do not open it. I am searching for the right words when the parallel between the death of the whiptail and the rattlesnake bite occurs to me: no community is without its perils. We strive for acceptance and inclusion but encounter misunderstandings and mishaps. A girl kills a lizard; another girl is nearly killed by a rattlesnake. Neither action is intended, both arguably avoidable. But in the larger scheme of community, these are the outcomes of risks worth taking because the interaction and belonging of community are intrinsic. We cannot live outside of community, whether harvester ant or human. And community is not true without the sum of all species.

CALENDARS
OF SUN AND MOON

As morning light stipples the concrete floors of our house, Billie and I take down the past year's calendars, those marked and re-marked with twelve months of music lessons and birthday parties, dance recitals and teacher conferences—the events that fill and drain the weeks of the year like water cycling through the soft stone fountain of a Sonoran courtyard. It is *jueves*, Thursday, three days after Christmas and three days before the new year. On walls the colors of desert wildflowers, the calendars advertise glossy rooflines in January and red canyons in August, emperor penguins in April and crested rockhoppers in October.

Every year we are reluctant to toss the old calendars out as we hang the new ones in their place. Perhaps we are afraid of throwing away something of ourselves, the scribbled squares that amount to a diary of the year; or if not a diary, then a medley—the resonant pitch of viola on Wednesday from 3:00 to 3:45 against the pirouettes of ballet on Monday from 4:00 to 5:30. Or the monthly art itself may restrain us. Not every entrancing landscape or black-and-white portrait can be saved, but the photograph of Liv Tyler as the elf princess Arwen—the one with the misty forest background where pale skin is backlit as if in a dream of twilight, the black hair tinged with cobalt to reveal an apex of elfish ear—maybe that one we could keep? Billie sighs and hands me a new calendar.

Outside, the half-moon dips beneath a wintry line of clouds as light rain appears—not falling exactly, but filling the cold Arizona air from within. Inside, our daughters Ann-Elise, nine years old, and Juliet, six, sleep as we ready the van for the day's journey: Tucson to Álamos, Sonora, an eleven-hour drive from the lush Sonoran highlands to the foothills of the Sierra Madre Occidental, to an almost unfathomable mix of cactus, deciduous hardwoods, and tropical evergreens known as Sinaloan thornscrub. Before we leave, we complete the ritual of changing the calendars so when we return in January, the days will be unmarked and we may begin anew, or at least without schedule.

Except for our early departure, the trek to Álamos with seven other neighborhood families is also unscheduled. Billie and our daughters have not been to Mexico, and are anxious. Despite the paperwork of passports and permits, and the challenges of bringing and preparing food for a child with allergies, the lure of the colonial town, once the hub of the Spanish silver-mining empire, is strong. For me, the trip represents passage to a place comfortable with its own slow pace—a town and region that rely upon and celebrate the rhythms of the days and seasons. Years matter, but not as directly as months. Months matter, but only in the context of renewal—a repeating cycle without beginning or end. North of the border, we cannot help but operate on the literal consumption of time, a time linear as opposed to cyclical as it constantly races on: no roundabouts or turnoffs on this desperate straightaway.

On our trip, we'll pass from 2006 into 2007. In cyclical time, the past is infinitely repeatable, dependent only on the length of the cycle—events of the past year (and much before) may repeat, rising and falling like hills on the arcing horizon. On the sleek hood of linear time, however, the prior year and its events are lost, irreversible, the days of 2006 passing like roadside markers as we drive toward 2007 and beyond. "In the one view past is prophecy; in the other it is prologue," says ethnohistorian Nancy M. Farriss. In traveling to Mexico, are we trying to give time the slip by sliding into a new geography, if only briefly? Or is there a larger ritual at work?

In 1957 the carpenter Guillermo Jordan Engberg and three other men painted an enormous hillside version of Nuestra Señora de Guadalupe, Our Lady of Guadalupe—the virgin patron saint of Mexico. She is brilliant, overwhelming at forty feet high along the barren eastern face of Sonora's El Cerro de las Víboras. The large Hill of the Rattlesnakes radiates in a fleshy mix of organ pipe and cardón cactus, mesquite and palo verde beneath a shallow sky tracking us since Magdalena de Kino, where the rain finally broke.

A half-dozen miles south of Hermosillo, our caravan of small SUVs and minivans turns in to the dirt lot at the base of the shrine. The Virgin greets us with coral dress and a teal robe. Her distinctive aura coils in yellow and red behind a pale Indigenous face and tight black hair, ending in robes that fall to the out-stretched arms of a small boy who may represent Jesus but looks more like any of the *niños* selling warm tortillas at intersections and toll booths along Mexico Highway 15. He is clothed in scarlet beneath solemn eyes and combed black hair. The mural begins 150 feet above the base of a white stairway striped in red and green. Square flags—green and white and red, laced with images of Our Lady—flutter along wires held high in the wind, clasped to a thin crucifix at the hill's summit.

On December 9, 1531, the Virgin of Guadalupe appeared before Juan Diego, a converted Aztec, at Tepeyac Hill outside Mexico City. In his native Nahuatl language, she told him to build a temple for her so she might remedy the people's pain and suffering. Diego took the message to Bishop Zumárraga, who refuted it. As Diego passed the hill on his return, the Virgin appeared a second time, with the same request. Again Diego met with the bishop, who demanded proof. Three days later, Diego approached the hill where once again Our Lady appeared. She told him to gather flowers from atop the hill in his winter cloak and deliver them to the bishop. Diego watched as the thorn-branched flowers he had never seen before bloomed in the summer of her breath. Then he gathered the flowers, presenting them to the bishop. As Bishop Zumárraga accepted the flowers he recognized as Spanish Castilian roses, he was convinced—not only by the coral-red petals but also by a vestige of the Virgin's image imprinted on Diego's cloak. The bishop then built a temple at Tepeyac, where the cloak, hermetically sealed, still drapes.

As an Aztec—a Mesoamerican like the Mayans and Olmecs before—Juan Diego held a cyclical sense of time, in which events of the past foretold and even constructed acts of the future. The conquest by Hernán Cortés provides a famous example. Though modern scholars doubt that the monarch Motecuhzoma Xocoyotzin believed Cortés was the predicted "returning god-ruler" Quetzalcoatl, Aztec rulers and priests read the sacred calendar and foresaw massive change before his landing. The arrival of white men on ships like floating cities could only be a recurring event, albeit over an era beyond their lifespans. When

Cortés descended, the Aztecs fought, because battle was inevitable, noble. And because they always fought, even and especially under the dark sky of cataclysm. And though they succumbed, the Aztecs also believed their people would rise once again.

Climbing the steps, my daughters and I find a weird collection of hand-etched plaques, cast-off casts and medical devices, and a slag heap of discarded candles in homage to the saint's healing. The scent of wax is dull yet persistent. Roses and other flowers, mostly plastic, line every crevice, crammed beside handwritten notes pushed farther in with the next or, when the wind picks up, lifted from the granite hillside in awkward flight. The notes disappear over the ridge or collect on the many-armed organ pipe cactus, held until the next rain some weeks or months away. We are held, too, by the hillside mural; not just its immediate vastness, but the shrine's enduring presence for the people of Sonora. Ours is a family devoid of religion, where spirituality most often finds us in a contemplative hike through the desert. My daughters and I are speechless in the image of faith painted across the rock, a conviction as tangible as the fallen petals of a rose we see fluttering like metalmarks between the flags, over the solitary cross, and into the turquoise sky beyond.

The Aztecs, like the Mayans before, observed cyclical time through a pair of largely independent calendars. The *xiuhpohualli* calendar of 365 days accounts for the solar year—charting the seasons, serving as a guide for agricultural and other earthly events. The *tonalpohualli*, or day count, is the sacred calendar of 260 days. In addition to scribing an "ancient future," it assigns distinct days and rituals to the Aztec gods, a critical division that referees the deities' unrelenting attempts to procure power. The *tonalpohualli* provides equilibrium. "Without it the world would soon come to an end," says researcher René Voorburg. "This equilibrium is in constant danger of being disrupted by shifting powers of the gods, of the elemental forces that influence [the people's] lives." The Aztecs lived in a world that at any moment might unravel, save for the *tonalpohualli* and the guidance and rituals of those who could divine it.

Though the *tonalpohualli* defines twenty weeks of thirteen days each, the *xiuhpohualli* includes eighteen months of twenty days, with an additional five days at the end of each year. Every fifty-two years, the two calendars align for a period called the calendar round—a crucial overlap foretelling significant events, cultural and environmental both.

South of Guaymas, I cannot help but think of the calendar round, the provocative yet inevitable rotation, as the December sun slips toward the Sea of Cortés. I wonder too about sacred space. Even now, driving deeper into Mexico, are we not shifting in time and space? Large, dark raptors with white heads and tails and banded white wings trace the thermals. They seem limitless in these dimensions. As I push the van to seventy-five miles an hour on the shoulderless four-lane highway, it is difficult to judge their size. Ann-Elise thinks they are bald eagles, a reflection more of her menagerie back in Tucson—a homemade eagle's nest knotted to the top bunk of her room, walls filled with bald eagle photographs and posters—than actual identification. Billie radios the first vehicle in the convoy, and the crackled response from Jerry, our resident birdwatcher, sounds like "*caca.*" We eye each other. "Caracara," he repeats.

Also known as the Mexican eagle, the crested caracara ranges throughout South and Central America and as far north as California, Florida. My family and I have not seen this raptor before. More than the landscape, which has flattened near the sea and thinned in vegetation, the bird reminds us that we are in a foreign land. At one glance this should not be easy to forget—tabletop shrines to the Virgin are found at every stop, as are vendors of freeze-dried shrimp and tamales smelling of corn and humidity. Yet I can barely read the kilometer indicator on the van's speedometer, so stick with miles per hour. Our music and conversations, the movies the girls watch on the DVD screens mounted to the backs of our headrests, these are in English. The entire cabin is clearly American, from its Anglo-Saxon occupants to the Trader Joe's detritus of wrappers collecting between the girls' seats.

The effect is at once comforting and disturbing. Three hundred miles south of Tucson, our pattern of travel has changed only slightly. Gas is full-serve, and I request *verde* or *rojo*—green for regular unleaded, red for premium. *Por favor* and *muchas gracias* are among the few Spanish phrases I know, but I use these informally in Arizona as well. The ease of traveling into Mexico is a singular goal of Solamente Sonora, Only Sonora, an expedited permitting process designed to increase American tourism, and therefore spending, throughout Mexico's second largest state. It is working. Yet as Americans infiltrate Sonora, I fear not only for the authenticity of my own experience—the perennial ability to lose myself in a wide and wild place—but also for the Mexican and Indigenous cultures and their native landscapes. I am aware of the hypocrisy, the same odd logic of any distinct place worth saving: welcome me, if you please, but shun all others.

Our group of twenty-six neighbors is traveling to Álamos, the traditional, plaza-centered town of ten thousand founded in 1684, precisely because it is not the Americanized entertainment gateway that larger and more accessible tourist destinations like Ensenada and Puerto Peñasco have become. We cherish the *tacos de pescado* in both locations, and enjoy too the Coca-Cola made with pure cane sugar instead of the refined stuff north of the border. But the Costcos and Home Depots, the McDonald's and Burger Kings are better left in America, where their ubiquity fast becomes a riddle of place: What is the difference between Tucson and Tulsa and Tacoma? On any given street corner, look for the saguaro, but look out for tumbleweed.

Deep in Sonora, however, the intersections are defined by cholla and organ pipe, amapas and palo santos, small-leafed trees tangled in gray and green among thorny succulents. Street signs? They provide no clue, nor should they. Here nature's calendar quickens, perhaps following the eighteen months of *xiuhpohualli*, where despite the latitude seasons last only weeks at a time, if the waxing and waning of the flowers are any indication. Just now the barren wood of the palo de muerto, the tree morning glory, rivulets into silver. The two-story tree is leafless, yet white flowers bunch on the thinnest of branches, an indicator clear as named day that we are past the winter solstice. Here, nature keeps its calendar by the seasonal changes of flora and fauna: the migration of songbirds and windstorms, the sparse rainfall above blooming thickets, the keen sentinels whose wingtips flare in the afternoon's topaz light.

Jerry's radio voice clicks and whirrs like an excitable grackle, quoting excerpts from his worn *Birds of Mexico* guide. The broken documentary gives us the sentient details: crested caracaras are primarily terrestrial, and the only member of the falcon family that actually constructs nests. Billie and I turn our heads in opposite directions, beyond the tinted glass, in search of a crazy stick nest perched, maybe, in the crotch of a tall senita cactus or on the crooked shoulder of a cardón. No luck. Their faces have fleshy pink patches separating gray beak from amber eyes, he continues. Long, yellow legs built for sprinting and ripping help the carrion-feeder catch fish, crabs, and lizards—or steal prey from other birds. Though rare north of the border, caracaras are common throughout most of their extensive range. For this, and our first sight of the Sierra Madre Occidental as we turn east onto an uneven ribbon of new highway out of Navajoa—now just forty miles from Álamos—we sing.

In the salon of the Casa Encantada, a ten-room hacienda built in the 1850s along Álamos's busy Avenida Juárez, an eclectic mix of colonial furniture, artwork, and décor greets visitors. On the large ironwood table at the back of the room—beyond the tall, trellised fireplace and to the right of the folding screen hand-stenciled with the profile of a stern European dame—rests an unmarked calendar. And behind the calendar, propped against the wall, is an oil painting of an Indigenous Mayo woman. The artwork is framed in silver, offset by bronze candlestick holders and their leather-colored candles. In the painting, the woman's dark hair is tied back. Her daughter, about three years old, sits on the mother's right knee, wearing a white dress trimmed in a pattern of roses, mint-green leaves, and opaline lace. The girl bites a piece of fruit—golden apple or yellow pear, glowing.

Early morning light slants into the room from the windows along the street, revealing rays of dust, thin and active, that adorn the painting. I move through the light. In her left hand, the mother holds a pair of calla lilies, the yellow stamens light against lush, milky petals. In the soft crook of her arm, a boy perhaps a year old sleeps, his lips curling happily around his mother's nipple, the breast exposed, expectant and compliant. Pearls loop around her neck, against a floral blouse of red and black and green. Her dark but pleasant eyes look to the right and past the viewer. On her coppery face, a slight smile.

The mother's contentment is familiar and welcome. Billie also nursed, though initiation was difficult. When Ann-Elise was born, she tried feebly to breastfeed but could not. Time was against us, for Ann-Elise lost weight, and though we declined formula, that singular, artificial alternative to breastmilk encroached like the spruce's shadow across our Colorado front lawn. Working through frustration and escalating fear, Billie and I devised a plan: she pumped her milk into bottles every two hours; I placed a dropper into the bottle, then into Ann-Elise's delicate mouth. In between, Billie lifted our daughter to her breast. The cadence of the pump made me dream, in those half-lit days of little sleep, of cycles—time slowing yet returning, the constancy in each crucial moment between mother and child, and now father. After a week, after our daughter slimmed and the lactation specialist wearied in our persistence, Ann-Elise finally nursed. Billie then relaxed, and I gave thanks for this simple intimacy.

We have been in Álamos three days, and of the many images— the baroque church La Parroquía de la Purísima Concepción completed in 1804, the view of the densely wooded valley from El Mirador, Plaza de Armas with its white ironwork gazebo—the painting in our hotel's salon may best represent the small city and its history.

The first European to pass through the present site of Álamos was the Spanish conquistador Nuño Beltrán de Guzmán, who in 1533 captured Mayo and Yaqui peoples, named after the major rivers of the region well north of the Aztec and Mayan lands, to sell as slaves. In the many years since, the history of the Indigenous Mayo and other tribes has been predictably agonizing—military and missionary contact and dominance, widespread disease, loss of territory, rebellion, deportation, more slavery. Yet the Mayo today remain the largest Indigenous group in Sonora, with a population of seventy thousand. As in pre-European times, the Mayo continue to ranch, fish, and fabricate. They weave blankets, craft wire baskets, and carve ceremonial masks.

By the 1700s, the Álamos region was prosperous from silver mining, cattle ranching, and agriculture, despite a series of Yaqui and Mayo skirmishes and the expulsion of Jesuits from Mexico in 1767. Only a decade later, Álamos was the richest town in Sonora, with a population over thirty thousand. By 1800, the community shipped more silver than any other mining area in the Spanish dominion. Fifty years later, however, the population plummeted to four thousand, the result of rampant cholera and an exodus of miners to California. By the time the Mexican Revolution began in 1909, most mines had closed and much of the city was looted. However, in the 1950s—with the completion of dams that provided electricity and irrigation (by flooding entire Indigenous villages) and the highway from Nogales to Navajoa—Álamos's resurgence began. The refurbishment of large haciendas built by silver barons changed the city's fortunes. And as with our hotel, most of the funding was provided by Americans, who continue to own many of the inns and restaurants. A growing residential area today known as Gringo Gulch attests to the dedicated population of expatriates.

The community, though, amiably resists many American temptations. Unlike many Sonoran towns, the majority of residents do not speak English. And they don't mind a good chuckle at nonfluent tourists like myself who, when trying to order six *tacos de carne asada* along Plaza Alameda late one evening, awkwardly request *elderly* tacos instead. There are no fast-food restaurants (if you don't count that delightful mix of taco, hot dog, roasted corn, and fruit drink vendors lining the plazas with their silver carts), no hotel chains, no big-box retailers. Álamos, in sum, is idyllic, enduring—but you won't like it, so please don't go.

To account for periodic flooding, Álamos's original streets—a cobbled mix of river rock and brick pavers—lie three feet lower than the adjacent sidewalks and patios, doors and windows. Steps coupled with ramps for horses, still commonplace in the dense town center, provide access to wide walkways inlaid with stone and tile. Walking through Álamos, we notice the narrowness of the streets and their irregular grid pattern. We notice too, here in the *ciudad de puertas*, the amazing array of doors. Arched patios line the two main plazas, and deep in the shadows of the porches, double wooden doors display carved shapes of cottonwood, prickly pear, and native flowers. The doors are stained or painted, hold pocked glass and bronze, unfold from ancient handles and chimes. Lintels provide little shade above the portals, instead accenting the flat-roof colonial architecture, providing sharp resistance to the smooth walls painted in salmon and sage, silver and swan.

Every front is a façade. Behind the elegant face is a deep courtyard, a mystery for those on the street but an oasis for those inside. At Casa Encantada, the bedrooms buffered by a wide, richly furnished porch surround a lush interior space, roofless and planted with tropical species I cannot name but recall from the photographs of an old rainforest calendar. Shining leaves from November, bright white buds in August, flowering vines across February. From the hotel's barred front door, however, we would not know the sacred space within. Wandering from block to block along the haciendas and mansions, my neighbors and I made a habit of peeking between door cracks. Rude? Perhaps, yet we were rewarded with thin views of multilayered fountains, hand-crafted furniture, aged tapestries, and abstract murals. More often, this architectural voyeurism was not necessary, as open front doors announced garnished interiors and mosaics of Moroccan intricacy.

"¡Año nuevo! ¡Feliz año nuevo!" The hoarse shouts of the sons and daughters of Álamos fill the evening, for it is New Year's Eve. Between their calls, old pickup trucks loaded with children limp down the street, resonant bass shaking the walls, horns barking through dimly lit porticos. Firecrackers dance off the quick hands of the boys who ignite them. Stray dogs cower in dark corners, whimpering, or chase the revelers madly, rabid looks in their backlit eyes. Billie and I walk back from Casa de los Tesoros, where we enjoyed a five-course meal as fine as any I can imagine: fresh baby greens, pine nuts, and dates sprinkled with chutney and goat cheese; yellow pepper-and-mushroom soup; steamed prawns stuffed with spinach; herb-crusted salmon and prime rib with ruby center. The challenge following dinner was simply rising from the long, linen-covered table. We finally exited as dancing began in an open courtyard hung with purple balloons the shapes of bunched grapes, green ribbons curving like tendrils toward the floor.

Buttoning my blazer against the cool evening, I take Billie's warm hand. Her fingers twine into mine, a reflex as natural as breathing after thirteen years of marriage. "I could live in Álamos," I say, thinking of exchanging our overloaded calendars for a community wise in its own rhythms.

"I know," she replies, mouth curved in a slight smile, cerulean eyes bright behind thin, purple-framed glasses. "But I could not."

I am not surprised. The desire to relocate to Mexico and, perhaps, any location with a distinct sense of place is mine alone in this union. While I pore over maps, dreaming of adventures and opportunities along craggy coastlines and remote metropolises, Billie prefers to be more sessile, adopting a place and making it her own. Though she may be less receptive to extreme weather conditions and alternative foods, the home she makes is well worth the return. The home we make together with our daughters, though often as hectic as any American family's, is comfortable, inspiring, welcoming. I think of these things as a quick kite tail of fireworks lights the sky, as we continue our stroll back to the hotel.

New Year's Day is *lunes*, Monday, and our final full day in Álamos. Throughout the region, New Year's and other festivals are a distinct mix of Catholic and Mayo rituals, a blending of religious and cultural beliefs giving rise to events rich in color, meaning, and passion. At the remote town of La Aduana, eight rugged miles west of Álamos, a festival is held each November to celebrate the miracle of discovering silver. Legend tells that a group of Mayo men saw a woman, the Lady of Balvanera, on top of a many-armed cactus. They piled rocks to climb in an effort to rescue her, but she disappeared. As the vision faded, a rich vein of silver appeared in place of the rocks. The church Nuestra Señora de la Balvanera was constructed to commemorate the site. Surrounded by leafy fig trees, the modest but stout church is extraordinary because of a massive organ pipe cactus growing from its side, twelve feet off the ground. In certain light, the cactus casts a shadow in the shape of a woman, praying.

The festival begins with a 4:00 a.m. procession from Álamos to La Aduana, followed by a week of pilgrimages across the southern half of Sonora for Catholics and Mayo alike who have made vows to the Lady. Small bands of Mayo identified by distinct

village flags travel many miles to pay homage, later performing
the traditional deer dance among a jubilee of songs, drumming,
and simmering Sonoran dishes.

On the day before our return—before our own pilgrimage
ends—Ann-Elise and I ride in the warm back seat of a neighbor's
car as it crawls along the dirt road to La Aduana. Though never
large, the village now resembles a ghost town, an empty space difficult to envision any other way, despite the festival's annual return.
Only a few old pickups, a handful of quiet residents beneath the
shade of a giant fig at the church's front wall, and gardens of
bougainvillea, agave, and torch cactus betray the image.

We enter the plaza that serves as cul-de-sac. It wraps like a
vacant traffic circle around a dry fountain, white as bleached coral.
To our left, high walls of broken stone and red adobe hold the
ruins of the old assay office, the smelter, a small garrison's outpost
perhaps. Carved into the thick base of the wall, a small room
with open windows and a solitary door hosts a women's artisans
co-op. To our right, a duplex of single-story colonial buildings
painted olive green and white appears empty. But it feels like we
are being watched, and soon a tawny woman in a colorful skirt
and white blouse crosses the road to the co-op, beckoning us to
come in.

After visiting the first shop and buying a few curios, we climb
the stairs left of the church to another boutique. Here I choose
a handmade doll in yellow and green for Juliet while Ann-Elise
purchases a scorpion sculpted from copper wire. In both stores,
our neighbor Deirdre finds three dolls for her Mexican doll collection, her favorite a scarlet *la Diabla* with a long tail, stiff horns,
and sea-blue bandana.

As with the church in Álamos, I do not enter Nuestra Señora
de la Balvanera. There is no religious or other significance in

either abstinence. Rather, I opt to walk around and apply my spirit to the outside, where the ceiling is wide and my camera takes finer photographs. At La Aduana, Ann-Elise and I find the thick and healthy cactus growing from the western wall of the church. Thin ribbons of red, green, pink, and gold are tied to many of the arms—a feat requiring an extendable ladder or a courageous vicar willing to teeter on the concrete sill of a nearby window. The cactus's shadows are tight against the rough-stoned wall, which ends in parapets set against cloudless sky and daylit moon, near full. On the opposite corner, a single bell tower with four large arches rises against the overgrown hills. A pair of large bronze bells is open to the elements yet silent this afternoon, like my daughter and I who once again are delighted, humbled. We watch a magpie jay swoop into the canopy, its long sapphire tail gleaming in the sunlight, then walk back to the waiting car.

Yesterday, after the trip to La Aduana, the girls and I drove the well-graded dirt road east from Álamos toward El Fuerte, Sinaloa. After half an hour viewing ranches carved from thick stands of leafless deciduous trees intertwined with vines, brambles, and cactus, we turned back. Pulling over a shallow hill, I pressed hard on the brakes to stop ten yards short of a large bird, a crested caracara. The raptor stood motionless in the center of the dirt strip, even as the dust from our approach floated over, and even as I grabbed my camera and put my slow fingers to the van's door handle. I halted there, looking into the bird's jeweled eye, taking in its black cap, sharp gray beak, muscular neck and legs. Then I pushed the door. At that the caracara leapt into the air, unfolded banded wings, and pushed itself out and over the riotous trees.

The distant image of the bird's eye is with me this morning as our convoy, tightly packed, departs Álamos. The sky is black, stars hidden by the sharp corners of the buildings we soon leave behind on the highway to Navajoa. Out of the city, the dark road crests against the indecipherable silhouettes of the forest when, suddenly, like the giant yellow eye of a mythical bird of prey, the moon reveals itself on the horizon. Its radiance veils the stars and paints the road before us. For the next forty minutes I drive in a hypnotized state, watching the road yet inhabiting the wide moon. The caravan thins but my mind is on that satellite, how the branches of roadside trees hold its eerie light, how thick chords of clouds dissipate in its aura, how the calendar seems to stop entirely in this great, glowing presence.

Only after the massive eye slides behind the deep lid of the horizon do I recover. The moon, it appears, held us all in a trance, as Billie and the girls too shake off the lunar spell. We speed up to catch the convoy in the soft twilight, then brake hard before a police truck in a turnout. Too late. Red and blue lights flash as the truck spins around behind us. I pull over and wait. The lights approach, stop, and then a young Sonoran officer greets me in Spanish.

"Buenos días," I say as I hand him my Arizona driver's license. He replies with a long question, mentioning Álamos I'm sure, to which I say, "No hablo español." He leans in a bit and sees the girls with their headphones on, watching a movie, the interior of the van flickering blue. Billie smiles. His flashlight finds my license and he reads my name aloud. "Sí," I say.

For a long moment he is silent. In the darkness his warm features and brown eyes radiate so that, despite the stories of Mexican authorities I've heard or think I've heard north of the border, I am not nervous. He hands me my license as if in agree-ment, nods, and concludes, "Buenos días." We remain motionless as the officer walks back to the truck, turns off the lights, and lurches onto the road ahead of us.

Billie pats my leg and we merge back onto the highway, miles behind our neighbors, ten or more hours from home. In the rearview mirror I see Ann-Elise and Juliet give me a thumb's up, grins on their lit faces. We find our right speed, then drive into the morning, soaring through Sonora as if on the day's lofty thermals.

SATELLITE

The sun scorches the asphalt as my daughter and I drive west on the two-lane highway from Tucson to San Pedro, Arizona. It burns the road's reflection into the back of my brain, a straight steel blade that severs the horizon, and after an hour I must turn onto a side road to give my eyes a rest. Ann-Elise tumbles out and heads for a jumble of boulders. I watch her scale the rocks, my eyes adjusting to the verdure beyond the pavement. The desert here is rich in ocotillo, cholla, and globe mallow, the deep orange buds just opening. The charcoal limbs of mesquite arc against a thicket of palo verde. Above and beneath it all flare the brittlebush, each silver-green shrub adorned by a halo of yellow flowers, like daisies or quarter-sized sunflowers, saffron-centered. On the near hill and far mountain, thousands of brittlebush purge the scene to yellow. As my body lets the vibrations of driving slide away and tunes into the calls of curved-bill thrashers and the pale scent of the wildflowers, I am also purged. Nothing brings as much clarity as the unobstructed desert in bloom.

Today, however, we seek a different kind of clarity. Ann-Elise and I are headed to Kitt Peak National Observatory, deep within the Tohono O'odham Nation, for the nightly observing program. Planets and stars and nebulae are on the agenda. This is our third attempt—the first two canceled by poor weather—and even though a "cloudy evening program" is expected, and the full moon will shine bright, we have waited months for the opportunity. So a few rivulets of clouds like those high above us won't, we insist, interfere.

Though I haven't said it aloud, I seek clarity on another matter as well. Over the last year, both Ann-Elise and her younger sister, Juliet, have grown seemingly beyond their years, something I especially notice in ten-year-old Ann-Elise. She shares the mood swings typical of a girl not far from puberty, certainly, but also the sensitivities that remind me of my own childhood bouts of depression. Already Ann-Elise presses the uncharted edges of our relationship: one moment burrowing into me as I read her to sleep, the next flailing in a tantrum, a tiny supernova of angst that is the culmination of stress from schoolwork and friends, expectations at home, and extracurricular activities like drama and viola. What my wife and I want is to guide her into the world prepared and ambitious, self-confident and compassionate. What we want, too, is to shield her from the darkness. Is it possible to do both?

I sling the camera strap over my shoulder and scuttle down the hill to join my daughter. After snapping a few photos of her reluctant poses, I pick my way past clumps of grass and move farther from the road. Kneeling to frame a wide-angle shot, my foot slips and I yelp. A fist-size nub of cholla has embedded itself in my shin, the barbs digging deeper with each movement. Ann-Elise races over, a look of real panic in her indigo eyes. "Dad!

What's the matter? What is it?!" She scans the ground for a scaly culprit, though she has not yet seen a rattlesnake in the wild, and I'm not sure she would know what to do if she found one.

"I'm fine," I say, detaching the cactus joint and removing the spines one by one. Brushes with cholla, though painful, are a regular occurrence for me this spring as I move through a desert thick with wildflowers that mask the prickly gremlins.

But Ann-Elise is not convinced. "Dad, really, are you hurt? Do I need to get the first-aid kit? Do you need a doctor?" Her insistence, as if she were the parent, would be comical except for the strained look on her face. The blood on my leg and her tense stance urge me not to joke as I walk toward her after extracting the thorns. Instead, I hold her hand as we walk back to the car.

"Sugarbug," I say, "I promise you: I am not hurt." Yet her concern remains palpable as we rejoin Highway 86, shuffle through a Border Patrol checkpoint, and begin the climb to Kitt Peak. At the turnoff, however, we find the narrow road to the observatory closed to entering traffic, a sign noting no visitors are allowed past 4:00 p.m. It is now 4:45.

I swerve gently to avoid the gate and press the throttle when suddenly Ann-Elise shouts: "We can't go in. It's closed!" Even after I explain that the sign doesn't apply to us—that we were scheduled to be at the summit by 5:25—her uncomfortable shifting in the back seat signals that she is unconvinced once again. So it goes for the twelve slow miles up the mountainside. We stop a handful of times at pullouts beneath granite cliffs—agaves clinging to fractured rock, scrub oak along lichen-brightened ledges—but Ann-Elise refuses to leave the car. We park too close to the edge, or are running behind schedule, or really shouldn't have been taking photographs of the observatories that gleam like quartz altars atop the mountain. Her resistance becomes an awkward ritual—I suggest and she declines, back and forth until we reach a stalemate and silence ensues. "Ann-Elise," I finally say as we pull into the visitor center parking lot, wide views of the distant valleys on either side, "I'm excited you're with me." And though I am, her expression is unfathomable as we step into the cool air.

The rituals of my boyhood years in Tucson—those I recall, for the finer points of my memory are irregular at best—centered around the desert: wandering the arroyo near our home, exploring the adobe ruins at Fort Lowell Park, shuttling once a month or more to the grounds of the Arizona–Sonora Desert Museum. Though I didn't understand it at the time, my divorced mother suffered from bipolar disorder, the seasons affecting a chemical migration of sorts in her brain. During the spring and fall, she seemed to move at an amazing pace, accomplishing tasks and planning broad and ambitious schemes: setting up her own real estate agency, continuing the detailed work of researching thoroughbred racehorse pedigrees, coordinating a complex matrix of local events. During the winter and summer, however, she became so depressed that she rarely left her bed. My sister and I moved more slowly during those months, too, floating in a solution of insecurity and concern, compounded when I also felt myself slipping into unexplained sadness for days on end.

To offset my depression and help keep me active, my mother enrolled me in Cub Scouts, her distance resulting in a kind of surrogate parenting by the troop leaders during scout events. One spring when I was ten, the den master drove a half-dozen of us to the Boy Scout jamboree in the Santa Catalina Mountains north of Tucson. I remember being overwhelmed in my navy Cub Scout uniform with the yellow kerchief, creased sleeves like fins over my gangly arms. With a shock of blond hair, thick-framed eyeglasses, and sneakers instead of hiking boots, I didn't know if I was more out of my element because of the bigger boys swarming around us or because I'd never been in the rugged mountains of the Southwest. At one level my neck craned to look into the faces of all these khaki-clad brutes who hooted and hollered; at a much higher level, I felt like I was losing myself to the steep slopes and towering pines. Either way, I stuck close to my pack.

After the evening bonfires and skits, but before sinking into our sleeping bags, a troop of older Boy Scouts rounded us up. Now was the time, they informed us, for snipe hunting—a jamboree tradition, a ritual in which the older boys directed the neophytes in catching the elusive snipe, an animal they never described yet assured us was there. I was no expert on southern Arizona animals, but I had been to the Desert Museum enough to know that whatever snipe was, it wasn't common. A sudden energy came over the pack, me included, and with our popcorn (the bait) and twenty-five-gallon garbage bags (the traps), we set off across a thin pasture. We were instructed to hold the mouth of the bag open with one hand and with the other shake the back of the bag. That was the job for half of us. The others were responsible for walking through the field at arm's length, yelling a particular *whoop* to scare all the witless snipe into the bags. I imagined them as rabbits: poor nocturnal critters flushed by a ludicrous pack of Cub Scouts howling across the night. After a half-hour or so, noticing the Boy Scouts cackling like some other kind of wild animal at the pasture's edge, I became suspicious. I crept over to a tall boy stoking a campfire. "There really aren't any snipes, are there?" I said. He just looked at me and smiled. It was all the confirmation I needed.

While the snipe hunting ritual may seem malicious, to me it was a harmless initiation. Once in on the joke, I felt more comfortable among the Scouts. It also provided confirmation of my own ability to decipher the real from the artificial. At home, life was often surreal: my mother's depression and my father's absence reflecting a life different from most of my friends. Moving between home and school, my days seemed gauzy, undefined. Only the trips to the Desert Museum, explorations of the nearby wash, and escapes such as the jamboree freed me from the inertness. They filled in for the tangible experiences, such as a tour of Kitt Peak, that I rarely shared with my parents.

Ann-Elise is not concerned that our journey will be a snipe hunt—the stars and planets are definitely up there, after all. What troubles her instead, I think, is a matter of placement. How does she place herself in a public setting with her father at hand? How, perhaps more importantly, will her father behave with others around? She and I both know it is part of my nature to act every bit as much like a kid as she does, often more so. Yet we are nearing the stage of her adolescence when embarrassing her can have serious consequences—in her own mind, and in our relationship. Gone are the days when I tickle or wrestle or sing aloud in my terrible Scottish accent as a means to draw her closer to me in public. With Juliet, such moves might cause her to blush, but at seven years old she will still come dancing into the arms of her goofy dad. For Ann-Elise, anything is still game at home, when friends or strangers are not around, but the public eye is a different focus altogether. I might as well ask her to shake an empty garbage bag and holler for imaginary creatures.

Walking toward the visitor center, I place my arm around her. For a moment she leans into me, but just as quickly she slips from under my arm. That is hint enough and I let her run ahead. Ten minutes shy of program start, we have time to explore, and she jogs across the patio until settling in front of a large display. A table-sized slab of stone is marked by pictographs dating back eight hundred years, to the Hohokam ancestors of the Tohono O'odham. The images are simple: lizards, deer, boxes clustered in what the interpretive sign speculates is a village, and a large sun. A desert community. The rock was discovered near the mountain's base during Kitt Peak road construction, which began in 1958. The two-hundred-acre site was selected after a three-year survey of more than 150 mountain ranges across the United States. Today, Kitt Peak hosts a collection of more than two dozen optical and radio observatories atop the sacred mountain the Tohono O'odham call Ioligam, for the manzanita plant, and is perpetually leased as long as the site is used for scientific research.

As the other nightly observing program participants make their way into the visitor center, I beckon Ann-Elise over to an old building with a small metal dome. It looks like a residence, and the sign by the handrail reads "Employees Only." I slip past the warning and onto a wooden deck that extends behind the building. I am after a photo of the large observatory sometimes visible from the Tucson skyline: the Mayall 4m telescope. The eighteen-story building with its white dome was visible most of the drive up, and in the quickly approaching sunset shines like a star in its own right. But as Ann-Elise stops I realize this is another test. She is tempted by the view yet reluctant to join me in an area marked off-limits. I realize, too, that I am a bad influence. A moment later, though, she decides to join me and is rewarded less by solidarity with her father than by a small patch of snow she hadn't noticed before—a desert rarity more tangible, for now, than star clusters and ringed planets. Perhaps my little rule-breaking teaches her that crossing the line is acceptable every now and then.

After check-in, we grab our box dinners and settle on a bench to watch a video about the formation of the moon. Though fascinating, it serves only as filler before the formal program begins—time enough for us to eat. Relying on preprepared meals is a tricky business for Ann-Elise because she suffers from severe food allergies. Wheat, egg, and dairy products are off-limits. Fish and nuts could send her into anaphylactic shock. From the box containing a turkey sandwich, chips, cookies, a granola bar, and bottled water, she can only consume the chips and water. That's not surprising, so my jacket pockets are filled with other goodies—wheat-free pretzels, fruit roll-ups, rice crackers. Plus, she ate a full meal before we left home. Though these constraints have been second nature most of her life, Ann-Elise is aware of the difference and glances around to make sure no one gawks at her for dismissing the sandwich and Oreos, which she offers to save for her sister. She doesn't make excuses nor try to hide the allergies—she is not ashamed. Neither am I, but as her father I am concerned both for her health and, less tangibly, her vulnerability. The temptation is to overprotect when what she needs instead is direction: the ability to make the right choices because she appreciates what she can have and knows the risks of the wrong choice. Still, she is annoyed as I continue to ask her how she is doing. This is my bad habit, like saying "Be careful" over and over. To the parent, that means "I love you." To the child: "I don't think you can take care of yourself."

After the box dinner our guide leads us on a short walk to the sunset overlook, adjacent to the Southeastern Association for Research in Astronomy observatory, a silver-domed building not much larger than a shed, housing a o.9m telescope. We cram into the observatory to ogle the optical scope, which we learn is operated remotely from universities based in the southern United States. Though most observatories on Kitt Peak are public, certain telescopes, like SARA, are funded and used primarily by consortia of universities and research organizations. Once in the observatory, I step back against the wall, conscious of my height. Ann-Elise moves to the center of the room, garnering the best view, though out of my line of sight. I admit it makes me uncomfortable—not that she will disappear but that we won't fully share this experience together. She drifts around me like a satellite in orbit, each pass more distant, and I am unsure when I should exert a more fatherly gravitational pull, or if I should at all. I decide to let her range and then move off myself, slipping out the door to photograph the red sun against the dome, the geometric silhouettes of the other observatories in the coming night.

Telescope size is based on the amount of light that can be gathered through internal mirrors. The larger the mirrors, the more light captured and the deeper into space the telescopes can peer—whether in the visible or infrared spectrum. Eyepieces on optical telescopes are then used to clarify the image, and like lenses on cameras may provide narrow or broad focus. In viewing single stars or planets, a narrow focus is ideal. For observing wide galaxies and star clusters, a broad lens provides a more comprehensive view. Even in the larger telescopes, though, stars appear about the same size. An exception is Kitt Peak's McMath-Pierce solar telescope, an enormous white building shaped like the number seven tipped onto its front. Its design is so eccentric that it won an architectural award upon completion in 1962, a rare feat for an observatory. The solar telescope can produce a thirty-inch image of the sun through the use of mirrors along a five-hundred-foot corridor (three hundred feet of which is underground) that forms the back of the seven. Along with the two radio telescopes, it is the only observatory on the mountain that can be used during the day.

Outside SARA, we watch the sun slip behind the Comobabi Mountains twenty miles west. The valley before us shimmers like an inland sea, and the guide urges us to keep an eye out for the green flash more commonly seen over open water, though rare nonetheless. It is an optical phenomenon occurring with sunrise or sunset, when a green spot or ray shoots up from the sun as the first or last of its light pierces the horizon. The flash occurs when the sun's red light is obstructed by the Earth, blue light is lost to broader sky, and green light refracts along a layer of atmosphere suddenly visible to the human eye. Once the sun dips beneath the peaks, the guide asks if anyone saw it, but no one says yes. It is possible, he says, that some may while others may not. Walking back to the visitor center, the sky mostly clear and the first stars revealed, Ann-Elise tells me she thinks she saw the green flash. Holding it like a secret, like a hard-won jewel, her quick green image is just the thing she needs to find her place among her father and thirty-some strangers on a ridge of odd-shaped astronomical buildings. With her newfound sense of accomplishment, a trust in seeing what others may not, she twines her fingers into mine and we walk down the hill, the low moon like a candle's flame over the mountains to the east.

By the time the nightly observing participants divide into three groups and are trained in the practice of reading star charts, the moon is high. We follow our guide onto the patio, the red beam of his flashlight sweeping the ground and pointing out the pillars and benches we might otherwise bump. The telescopes are unaffected by red light, but white light—headlights, streetlamps, the harsh lighting of billboards—works as a fog the scopes find difficult to cut through. With the vast number of observatories across southern Arizona, a higher proportion than anywhere else in the world, strict light pollution ordinances keep Tucson and the surrounding counties mostly dark. Though Tucson sprawls ever closer, the observatories at Kitt Peak are impacted far more by the unregulated light of Phoenix, the larger metropolis a hundred miles north.

With binoculars in hand, Ann-Elise and I point our eyes up, working to find the North Star, Polaris. Finding the Big Dipper in the constellation of Ursa Major is easier as we face north, looking up and slightly to the east, and then follow the two outer stars of the ladle west to Polaris, slight but surrounded by no other visible stars. Despite popular belief, it is not the brightest star in the night sky. To the west, we find Cassiopeia, a wide M, the middle serving as an arrow that points to Polaris and confirms our naming. Once Ann-Elise has Polaris in her sights, she sets off without me again, keeping within the boundaries of the patio but finding her own place to gauge the night. Our guide points out the vibrant star Regulus, the constellation Bootes (an ice cream cone, he jokes), the sky's brightest star Sirius in Canis Major to the south, and the unmistakable Orion. Just beyond Orion in the Taurus constellation is a fuzzy cluster of stars: Pleiades, the Seven Sisters. At this Ann-Elise finds me, and I help her locate the open cluster, as well as the faint Orion Nebula in the hilt of Orion's sword, just visible with our seven-power binoculars. It is not insignificant that Ann-Elise comes to me instead of the guide, a dynamic man who would be as successful at stand-up comedy as he is at leading stargazers. As the darkness encroaches, her distance lessens and I welcome the bond.

Though I have seen more and brighter stars in other locations, I could name little of what I had been viewing. Atop Kitt Peak, I am as excited as a ten-year-old, practically bouncing as I scan the sky and then reference the star chart before peering skyward again. In my enthusiasm I turn quickly to the east and am blinded by the full visage of the dazzling moon. I lower the binoculars and turn away, warning Ann-Elise not to make the same mistake while letting my eyes readjust to the darker half of the sky.

When finally our telescope session arrives, a voltage of excitement passes through the group. By 10 p.m., the night air at the 6,900-foot summit is brisk; Ann-Elise and I huddle close. Our guide leads us to the Levine 0.4m telescope, a forty-year-old observatory refurbished six years back. The telescope is small compared to the massive scope next door—the 3.5m WIYN telescope. Though our instrument contains only a sixteen-inch mirror, it is still anchored directly to the mountain. As we enter, the telescope remains motionless even as the lead-colored building trembles from our footsteps. Once we sit in the folding chairs around the dim circle of the observatory—a rope of red lights outlining the room's circumference—the guide hands the two-button control box to Ann-Elise, informing her that she is the dome driver for our first object. He punches coordinates into the telescope's keypad, backlit in dim orange, and it swivels slowly up and to the west. On his command, Ann-Elise pushes the left button, moving the dome clockwise, away from the line of the scope. She nimbly adjusts by pressing the right button, and the dome grinds counterclockwise until the guide tells her to stop, praising her quick response. I squeeze her knee and she shares a wide smile.

We are the last two in our group of twelve to view Castor, an elusive binary star system in the constellation Gemini. It is elusive, our guide informs us, not because it is difficult to view with the right telescope, but because there are not two blue stars as it appears but rather three, and in fact each of what appear to be three single stars is a binary itself, so that Castor is a related set of six stars fifty light years apart, held together by a central gravitational pull. Binary stars comprise an estimated 75 percent of the hundred billion stars in the Milky Way. Only a quarter of the galaxy's stars are solitary, like our sun. And just as a large planet or set of planets impacts a sun's gravitational center, binary stars tug at each other so that their orbits may shift.

That is an easy metaphor for Ann-Elise and me. Even though she just flashed a smile, when I ask her moments later how she is doing, she grimaces and withdraws from her overprotective father once again. But the metaphor stops there, for like all children she must eventually move beyond a shared core. Maybe, then, the question isn't whether I should hold up or hold back— as if I'm the only party, capable of full control. Maybe the question instead is how we define our proximity: what parameters we consciously and unconsciously set, what instruments we use to hone our focus, what benign forces fix our placement. It is easy to think of ourselves as binary stars, a common orbit for our constant motion. But we are just as often like solitary stars on independent paths. And there are also other forces at work.

Over the next half-hour we are treated to an array of objects— to start, M41 in Canis Major, an open star cluster 2,300 light years away first described by Aristotle in 325 BCE as a "cloudy spot"—as well as the guide's entertaining discussion of all things astronomical. From choosing the right eyepiece to the collapse of stars, our guide's sharp stories pace the visual wonders. After M41 we view the Eskimo Nebula, NGC 2392, a glowing cloud of dust resembling an Inuit face in a fur-lined parka ejected by a dying star some 3,000 light years away.

With time running short, the guide advises us that we may only see three more objects. He programs the coordinates and rotates the dome. We peer in the eyepiece to see Saturn and its brilliant rings. If we hold still enough and focus closely, some of the moons are also visible. Then the dome shifts again and the telescope reveals the Great Orion Nebula, a teal, pterodactyl-shaped "stellar nursery" thirty light years wide with enough material to create ten thousand stars the size of our sun. It's the same nebula I earlier helped Ann-Elise spot with binoculars. As a nursery nebula, it not only gives birth to stars but also sends them deeper into space, where they form clusters and constellations—spinning off from the parent nebula, finding their own places in space and time. That's the true metaphor, of course: the guided arc of our children as they grow up and more distant.

Each time Ann-Elise stands to look into the telescope and its eyepiece, she takes off her glasses and hands them to me. When she returns I hand them back, and by the time we view the amber sphere and rings of Saturn, our moves become a dance of the slow give-and-take—the tug and release at the core of every strong relationship. I look up to see a strip of stars that is the sky, the moonlight a thick strap spilling into the dome. Echoes bounce oddly in the space. When the couple twenty feet across from us whispers to each other, they could be talking directly into our ears, though I can hardly hear the man three chairs down. Despite the technology of the telescope and the soft voice of Enya singing from a stereo in the background, the space feels timeless. Up here, the discoveries of William Herschel and Galileo and Aristotle are as fresh for us this evening as they were hundreds or thousands of years ago. And though the spaces between the stars are nearly unfathomable, at least to me, an unfathomable number of stars are within our view.

Finally, our guide programs the telescope to focus on the moon, though he notes it is the worst time for viewing because its reflection is so bright. There is little depth, but he zooms in on the satellite's edge, where a thin line of darkness can still be observed. This shadow line is the horizon at which the light meets the dark. Because the moon spins at the same rate that it orbits the Earth, the same side always faces us and the shadow line tracks back and forth as it waxes and wanes. I needn't put my eye to the telescope to realize the strength of the night's moonlight. The guide holds his hand six inches from the eyepiece and the moon's brilliance lights his palm. But drawn by curiosity and the urge to take this risk before my daughter, I place my eye against it anyway, and before I can focus on the wide orb I am half-blinded, an intensity far beyond the binocular view. I return to my chair dazzled if not dizzy, holding onto Ann-Elise to ensure the Earth itself doesn't slip away.

Exhausted but elated by the night's events, we move through the gift shop at the program's end. After everyone checks out, the visitors exit the observatory together, headlights off to keep the mountain dark. Our guide leads the line of two dozen cars down the first mile of the winding mountain road. My car closes out the convoy as Ann-Elise falls asleep, her pillow nestled against the door and a blanket tucked under her chin. Beyond red taillights, I can just make out the pavement in the moonlight. I imagine the challenge of driving down the road under a new moon and am thankful at last for the extra glare. As we pass the turnout where the guide flashes his orange parking lights, I switch on my headlights and watch the other cars pull ahead, one by one or, sometimes, in accelerating pairs.

STOPOVER

In the muted flatlands of Nebraska's Platte River valley, the horizon stretches in bands—pewter river, ochre cornfields, graphite tree line, tungsten sky. It is mid-March 2012 in the cool, wet center of the Central Flyway, the migratory bird route that stretches from Costa Rica to Canada's Northwest Territories. Bound generally by the Rocky Mountains on the west and Mississippi River and Gulf of Mexico on the east, the Central Flyway hosts more than 50 percent of North America's migratory waterfowl. And where it narrows along an eighty-mile stretch of the Platte River—its wide, shallow channels like slow-poured mercury beneath an overcast sky—it serves as a key stopover site for the world's largest gathering of Sandhill cranes.

My eleven-year-old daughter Juliet and I have driven 1,200 miles to view these tall, talkative birds. It's a distance that seems significant to Juliet and me, folded as we were into our silver sedan for two straight days. But for the cranes, whose migration may take them from central Mexico to eastern Siberia and back, that would represent but one leg of an annual journey that has taken place in one form or another, and in one geography or another, for at least nine million years.

"The Platte River is new to cranes in the longevity experienced as a species," says Allison Adelle Hedge Coke, the poet who invited my daughter and me to Nebraska to view the cranes. "Existing fourteen thousand years, maybe less, the Platte allows the perfect stopover for the annual grand council of cranes on the narrows of the hourglass flyway that was once the pathway of the Inland Sea."

The pathway Juliet and I took east out of our Sonoran Desert home this spring was much less sea and much more basin and range. We'd had a dry winter; wildflowers were sparse along the route that turned north onto Interstate 25 out of Hatch, New Mexico. Brown and yellow-brown mountains and mesas funneled us north, as did the wide ribbon of highway edging the Rio Grande. But rust turned to gold and then finally green as we passed the Bosque del Apache National Wildlife Refuge where, two years earlier, the Sandhill cranes changed my spirit, if not my life.

I'm not certain how I convinced Billie to join our daughters and me to view cranes over New Year's in 2010. Like me, she appreciates a good panorama, but she's never been one to pull on a pair of hiking boots to explore places more deeply. So on my camping and hiking journeys with Juliet and Ann-Elise, she often stayed at home. Perhaps, then, it was the promise of the (admittedly low-budget) hotel room in Socorro instead of a tent, or the fact that we'd be gone over a holiday. More likely, she joined us simply because she could spend time with us—and I wouldn't force her out onto a nature trail. Not a long one, anyway.

In the middle of winter, central New Mexico's Bosque del Apache is a landscape of contrasts: placid blue ponds next to the brown braid of the Rio Grande; amber bulrush and cattails against ashen, leafless cottonwoods; the low, cinnamon-colored Chupadera and San Pascual Mountains against a pale turquoise sky. In a word: sublime. Yet what appears as a natural wetlands caused by seasonal flooding from the Rio Grande is in fact man-made. The 5,700-acre refuge was established not just in recognition of the outrageous diversity of waterfowl and other migrating birds that overwinter there, but also because of changes settlers made to subdue the river, beginning with the arrival of Spanish colonists in the sixteenth century.

"A river that overflowed and dug new routes every season was seen as a problem—especially if your house got flooded or your crops washed away," says literature by the U.S. Fish and Wildlife Service, which manages the refuge. "So, people started building dams and irrigation ditches to manage the flow of the river and divert water for crops, livestock, and homes. Taming the Rio Grande was great for people—but not great for wildlife. The once-grand river shrank to a shallow stream."

Flooding was not only constrained but ultimately eliminated, and with it native plants such as chufa and millet. Not long after, migratory birds along with year-round native species began to disappear. With its designation as a federal refuge in 1939, how-ever, the area now just a short distance from I-25 could be man-aged for wildlife and native plants, beginning with work by the Civilian Conservation Corps to restore the floodplains. Today, water is moved seasonally from the river through the refuge's fields, wetlands, and ponds via a series of gates and ditches before it is returned to the river.

We planned our visit to the Bosque del Apache to be quick: drive the backroads surrounding the wetlands looking for wild-life once we arrived, settle onto a viewing deck for the evening, find a late dinner twenty miles up the road in Socorro, and then return to the refuge before sunrise the next morning, before the cranes would head out for the day. And before we'd make the six-hour drive back to Tucson.

What we hadn't expected when we arrived in the amber light of the afternoon was that there weren't any cranes. "Where are they?" Juliet asked as we walked a path beside one of the refuge's marshes. Stepping onto an observation deck, we saw coots, mallards, and other ducks, and in a cottonwood to our left, a bald eagle, but no Sandhill cranes. Ravens worked the branches below the eagle, their croaks carrying across the reed-edged water. But where we had expected to find a gathering of cranes, there were none.

And then, as the winter sun sank behind us, we heard them— the otherworldly chortled bugles of the Sandhill cranes, flying in from farmers' fields up and down the Rio Grande. In twos and threes and then in groups of a dozen, three dozen, a hundred, the cranes arrived, their thin legs trailing from the vases of their bodies as their long necks led them forward. They landed almost acrobatically before concentrating along the far shore.

My daughters *oohed* and *aahhed* as we pulled coats and scarves tighter, as the temperature dropped. My wife tucked into me, whether for warmth or joy did not matter—she had not seen cranes in the wild before—and, joined by other families and a host of long-lensed photographers, we watched the scarlet-capped cranes ruffle their gray feathers and hold congress in the shallow water as the sky grew dark. In a nearby pond a thousand snow geese turned the blue surface white, and in this wetland and the next, the birds' raucous calls were a crazy delight, the chilled air filled with the strange, flocked symphony that resonated as deeply in the human onlookers as in the water and land beyond.

The next morning, Billie and I nuzzled the girls awake in the darkness, ate a quick breakfast, and loaded into the minivan. The hotel parking lot was a frenzy of people doing the same, all with the singular goal of driving to the Bosque del Apache to view the cranes and geese before the birds flew off for the fields.

Our headlights lit the two-lane road as we made our way south, through the crossroads of the village of San Antonio, and into the refuge. We found a parking space not far from the observation deck of the previous evening and, as quietly as possible, shuffled onto the deck, squeezing between two photographers. The eastern horizon was a shifting watercolor—plum to red, orange to yellow above low, purple mountains. As the sky lightened, the silhouettes of the cranes became more pronounced: hundreds of birds, dark legs straight, thick bodies hunched, heads nestled into the down of their backs. A single black duck trailed across the water, and then another. Unlike the previous evening, the surface was not smooth but instead rippled by the breeze, cutting in its chill. Finally, the sun crested the eastern mountains and, as if on cue, we all sighed in anticipation of the warming day, our faces glowing in the new light.

Then, all at once, a thousand or—who could know in this cacophonous scene?—ten thousand snow geese erupted from the far edge of the pond, an enormous, luminous flock of white birds reflected in the water and rising. To call it breathtaking is to settle for cliché, and yet that multitudinous release took our breath away. It likewise triggered the cranes, who themselves became more vocal, more active.

Yet even in all this avian glory, the girls had had enough. Amazing, yes, but terribly cold for these desert dwellers. So we loaded into the minivan and headed north out of the refuge toward San Antonio, where we would turn west onto the freeway.

Driving now in the morning light, however, we saw what we could not on the drive south—lining the west side of the road, only yards away, hundreds of Sandhill cranes had settled in ice-edged ditches and marshes, closer than we'd ever been or could have imagined we'd ever be.

I pulled over. My wife and daughters understood.

Leaving the girls in the warmth of the minivan, I stepped quietly into a scattering of photographers and, like many of them, kneeled. The closest cranes were some forty feet away. Though a few of the Sandhills remained hunched from their nighttime sleep, most now moved around, cracking the ice at the top of the water, stretching their dusky wings, raising their slender necks and pale heads, foreheads bright red in the golden light. Behind them, just on the other side of the interstate, the soft peaks of the Chupadera Mountains drank in the light, becoming vermillion-tinged, the sage a kind of green-gray fire against the copper hills.

The cold breeze was constant but seemed to be rebuffed in the glow of the birds, who stood three or more feet higher than the surface of the water. Like those around me, I snapped photo after photo. But then I lowered the camera and rose, closing my eyes so that the gurgling calls and snicks of the birds flowed over and through me. When I opened my eyes, many of the cranes were queueing to take off—not an airstrip, exactly, but a loose line of Sandhills near the middle of the watery plain where the birds flapped and stretched. I watched them launch, one at a time or in twos and threes. Were the hills to the west responsible for this breeze, or was it brought on by the birds as they took flight, a short run and leap into the pearly sky, water streaming behind them like a whip of light?

"Non-being is the greatest joy," says Lao Tzu. In this moment, finally, I knew such joy: I was not myself, not a being, but I was present—a presence, a movement, energy, a part of something so much larger and more basic than myself, than my body or soul had known before. I was not flying with the birds, was not the birds, and yet I was the air around the birds, the smallest particles of the air passing through them, the water beneath them and the ice crystals atop the water, the lift in their wings and the hollow bones of their wings, the weaving of gray and charcoal and cream feathers and also the single feather that floats down to the surface of the pond, sinks to the bottom, decomposes, renews. I was renewed. Reborn.

My expectations are high as Juliet and I drive into Kearney, where we are staying with Allison and three other writers. The gathering of Sandhills along the Platte River in March is legendary even though, from Interstate 80, the cranes remain hidden. Yet the Sandhills represent only part of my expectations on this trek. This is the first extended road trip Juliet and I have taken by ourselves, and she is a different kind of traveler than her older sister. Where Ann-Elise is an outgoing and inquisitive explorer, Juliet—with her long, sandy hair, light skin, and braces—is shy, preferring to spend her time drawing instead of hiking. And while Ann-Elise can be quick to show her temper, Juliet can just as quickly withdraw. One is never fully prepared for parenthood, of course, but before Juliet was born, what preconceptions I had that our daughters would be similar, wanting and liking the same things—let alone those pursuits I most enjoy—were dispelled early on in my journey of fatherhood.

Yet Juliet, at eleven, reminds me of myself at that age. Like her, I spent hours at a time drawing. I would sketch a map of an imagined country in a long-ago time and then draw a walled city and fantasize about its industry, the armory, the royalty and soldiers who protected their home, the monsters in the dark woods beyond. (Thanks, *Dungeons & Dragons*.) Not long after my mother, sister, and I moved to Tucson from Kentucky, however, I was drawn less to the landscapes I created and more to the strange desert landscape itself, trading my hours inside for long walks in the arroyo outside, trading imagined monsters for the very real scorpions, rattlesnakes, and raptors of our neighborhood. As we raised our daughters in Tucson, I continued to explore arroyos both near and far, my daughters joining me as often as I could convince them. But Juliet has not shown that same love for the desert, or bright skies and warm days, even though she has lived in Tucson her entire life. So here in central Nebraska, in our travels to a new landscape, is a chance for my younger daughter and me to form a stronger bond—and not too soon, I know, since she is nearly twelve, nearly a teenager, and I've learned by now what a seismic shift that can be. But let's not get ahead of ourselves. Let's not yet consider the worries-to-be of any father whose daughter is becoming a young woman.

When we arrive at the house, down a long gravel driveway a mile or two north of the interstate, the sky is gray and the clouds low. Juliet perks up in this weather; I hope the grayness won't last. Allison, whose hair flaps like a banner in the wind as soon as she steps outside, greets Juliet and me with a smile and a hug. It is the first time I've met the educator, activist, and writer whose work I've long admired, though I can't help but feel we have known each other for much longer. She is that friendly, that passionate about culture and place. We step inside to meet the fellow writers: Lee Ann Roripaugh, a poet and editor of *South Dakota Review* whom I know from editorial correspondence but had not yet met in person; Kimberly Blaeser, a White Earth Nation, Anishinaabe poet, photographer, and scholar who a few years after our visit would become the Wisconsin poet laureate; and Renee Sans Souci, an Omaha Nation poet, educator, and activist. That is a lot of new adults all at once for Juliet. She holds her own, but it becomes clear she wants to escape to check out the room where we are staying and then investigate the large yard.

Although the land all around us is flat, it has two enduring qualities that our native desert does not: tall trees and abundant water. After unloading, Juliet and I head outside to find a few of those impressive trees plus a small pond edged in cattails and grass. Though there aren't any cranes, a handful of ducks makes small wakes across the choppy surface—mostly mallards that stick to the water and large Muscovies that hustle to the shore once they spy us. The mottled birds aren't shy about expecting handouts, though they eventually waddle off, disappointed, when we ignore them. Their comical jockeying is anything but disappointing to Juliet, who laughs out loud, which makes me laugh out loud, which makes the birds reconsider and try their luck again. On their return, I coax my daughter into feeding one a handful of grass, which she agrees to reluctantly, snatching her hand back as soon as a drake approaches, the leaves floating to the ground. Realizing the jig is up, he scolds us before hustling off, trailed by the other Muscovies and our own laughter, rising to join the wind tittering among the trees.

We settle then onto the grass and watch the ducks tip their heads into the water, their stubby tails waggling for a few seconds before they surface again, pink beaks dripping. This evening, Juliet and I will attend a reading on campus with the poets and then chuckle as a couple of our housemates get high in their room after we settle in for the night, their laughter a wind chime resonating through the house. The next day, we'll rise early to see the cranes we'd come for. But just now, here among the grass and the water, the wind and the waterfowl, we have found the connection I am seeking. I am in no rush to move on.

On the drive from Tucson to Nebraska, Juliet and I saw a bumper sticker that read, "It's not the destination, it's the journey. — Gandalf." Though Gandalf (or the quote's actual author, Ralph Waldo Emerson) never had to battle a hydroplaning Honda Accord at seventy miles an hour as Juliet and I did on a particularly drenched stretch of eastern Colorado highway, I think he's right—at least, considering my expectations for this particular journey. Yet sometimes it is the destination itself, as driving 1,200 miles to view Sandhill cranes in central Nebraska or even 400 miles to central New Mexico is no small endeavor. Fortunately, southern Arizona hosts its own overwintering grounds for Sandhill cranes: Whitewater Draw.

Located in Sulphur Springs Valley, a hundred miles southeast of Tucson and just north of the Mexico border, this high desert landscape of ranches, grain fields, and seasonal wetlands has long been a destination on the cranes' annual migration. The number of cranes that overwinter at Whitewater Draw vary from a few thousand to thirty thousand or more. The Arizona Game and Fish Department reports that since the 1950s, the number of cranes has increased considerably, likely due to the rise in nearby corn farming. Though any negative impacts of a warming, drying habitat due to climate change may take years to gauge at Whitewater Draw and nearby Willcox, where the cranes can number up to twenty-five thousand in the winter, the birds' increasing population in southern Arizona over the last several decades is a conservation success story. Accordingly, this state-designated wildlife area has become the mecca for my own annual crane pilgrimage. It's a holy trek indeed when one of my daughters joins me.

One February in 2009, Juliet and I made the two-hour drive to Whitewater Draw to celebrate my birthday. I admit that my daughter may not have been riding along to see cranes or walk the wide paths but instead to gift her presence to me for my special day. In either case, I was happy to have the company of this shy, sweet, and sassy eight-year-old to inaugurate the last year of my thirties. Indeed, her only real complaint on the drive came when I mentioned the "Crane Cam" website, where we could watch the cranes in real time.

"Why didn't we just look at the cranes from home?" she asked. Probably I started into a lecture about the ills of swapping technology for real life, about the need to get out into the real world—the *natural* world—because otherwise we substitute a pixelated version of a limited nature as presented to us by who knows who, for an actual, chaotic nature we are submersed in, or at least witness to, firsthand. Probably she then threw a handful of Chex cereal at me, or had by then fallen fast asleep. I've learned a bit about slipping into dad-lecture mode since then.

The entrance to Whitewater Draw is a slow and dusty two-mile drive down a dirt road, which is itself a turnoff from another slow and dusty, unevenly paved road. From there it's a quarter-mile walk on a gravel path to the wide trail that runs adjacent to a couple small ponds before heading west across the caramel-colored water of the playa, which can dry up completely in the summer. Often I'll see dozens of red-winged blackbirds around the permanent ponds. But one gray afternoon on a previous visit, the reeds and willows were thrumming with hundreds of boisterous yellow-headed blackbirds, the first time I'd seen these birds in the wild. The blackbirds—striking in their

saffron hoods—flew two or three feet into the air, one by one or
in groups of three or four, before diving back, over and over, into
the seemingly cheering crowd. I was unprepared for this brilliance, let alone this behavior, and though I had come to visit the
cranes, I stayed to converse with the blackbirds that reminded
me, in coloration anyway, of the hooded orioles that sometimes
visited our feeder back at home in Tucson. Unlike the blackbirds,
which live in the valley year-round, the orioles migrate to central
Mexico and farther south for the winter.

Before making it to the blackbirds and their ponds, Juliet led
us on a detour to an old hay barn, sans sides, near the parking
lot. There a sign suggested we look up for roosting great-horned
owls. And so we did, finding a silhouette of the bird pair on a
rafter beneath the metal roof. Though the urge to hoot like an
owl is no doubt universal, Juliet and I both resisted, if just barely.

Once back on the path, it wasn't long before we spotted hundreds of Sandhill cranes, their gray feathers soaking in the late
afternoon sun, the cirrus clouds feathering the pale blue sky
above them. The cranes socialized far from the path, which had
been constructed several feet above the wetlands to account for
varying water levels and provide the best vantage. On this visit
the water was as high as I'd ever seen it so that—we later discovered—the farthest end of the trail was submerged. Rounding
the first bend, I was disappointed to find neither red-winged nor
yellow-headed blackbirds, though a number of small ducks swam
the pond to our left, and a group of birders pointed out a red
tailed hawk perched in a nearby cottonwood.

Unfortunately, I forgot to bring binoculars, and Juliet wasn't
interested in looking through the telephoto lens on my camera.
But soon she spotted the observation deck, which hosts a pair
of silver scopes with steps that allow a child to enjoy the view.

After walking the perimeter of the deck to admire (I hoped) the expanse of playa backed by low desert mountains, she stepped up to the scope and, with my assistance, focused on the closest Sandhills—her first time really seeing the majestic birds.

She looked, concentrated, looked harder, and said, somewhat plaintively, "They don't move much, do they?" This particular group did not, except to swing a crimson-dabbed head or stretch the occasional wing. We'd need to stay for another hour, I reckoned, before the cranes grazing in nearby fields would fly in. I wasn't sure I could eke that kind of patience out of Juliet, though the weather wasn't particularly cold and the wind gusted only now and then.

"About the time the sun sets, we should see them fly in," I said. "That will be awesome." Whenever I use that word, *awesome*, I think of Scott Russell Sanders's book *A Private History of Awe*, and how he laments the use of the word as a kind of default "cool" or "right on" or "neat" or other generational slang. Awesome, stemming from *awe*, should only be used when we are truly confronted by something that is awe-inspiring, he writes—meaning connected to spirit, the sacred, holiness. But *awesome* is absolutely the right word for Sandhills as they fly in to roost, the crosslike silhouette of each bird overhead multiplied by a hundred or a thousand to form a vast, thatched aerial quilt; the flying birds a flowing, living horizon in parallel with the fixed horizon of the high desert valley as they approach the water's surface; the large feathers at the tips of their wings outstretched in a kind of angelic embrace as the birds finally touch down. And it's not just a visual awe, for the cranes call out as they arrive, not a song exactly but still somehow lyrical—a chortling croak, a prehistoric yawp that harkens back to the age of flying reptiles and is as convincing an argument as any that the Sandhill crane is among the oldest surviving bird species.

"Okay," Juliet said, taking my hand as she marched off the platform and back onto the path. From there we walked west, following the raised path beside a pond, past more ducks and now some red-winged blackbirds and, over there, a great blue heron—and finally to its slowly sinking end, where we found ourselves close to several small gatherings of cranes, perhaps only thirty yards away. We waited for a trio of humans to leave before settling near the waterline to watch the cranes as the water brightened in the reflection of the setting sun and those awesome, sweeping clouds.

More and more, then, the cranes flew in. But it was less the site of their circling and somewhat clunky landings than it was the sound of their calls that made us rise and look back to the east, where the birds now painted the dimming sky in broken skeins before arriving, finally, wonderfully, en masse. Juliet and I watched and listened and had no choice but to immerse ourselves in the cranes' return, which, in the end, lasted longer than she could. We had been out for hours and though it was not much later than six o'clock, it would be another hour before dinner at a truck-stop diner along Interstate 10 and an hour from there back to Tucson. Too tired to trek back on her own, she asked if I would carry her to our car. I obliged, in love with this little person who might not become the naturalist I hoped she'd be, after all, but who still happily joined me on my birthday adventure. A few minutes later she was out, head on my shoulder, her slight, warm breath on my ear, wave upon wave of cranes serenading us from above.

When Billie and I moved from Denver to Tucson in 2000, we agreed that she and our daughters could spend each summer in Oregon, staying with her mother, Annie, in Eugene. It would be their own seasonal migration to avoid our Sonoran Desert summer heat. If we hadn't already signed that pact by the time the moving truck delivered our furniture that first May—the afternoon soaring to 108 degrees—she just might have emblazoned the contract into my skin that very day. Unfortunately, Billie would have to wait until the following summer for the annual passage to begin, as Juliet wasn't born until July. I'm not entirely convinced that my lovely bride, seven months pregnant when we arrived, has yet forgiven me for moving our family to the desert during summertime. Given our initiation by fire—or nearly so—I'm not so sure she should.

Though local media discusses immigration often, given our location just sixty miles north of the Mexico border, I hadn't thought much about migration, outside of my wildlife biology classes in college, until Billie and the girls began their regular summer visits to Oregon. After marrying my American father in her homeland of Sweden, my mother immigrated to the United States. That was a few years after she had made her own journeys to England, Italy, and Rhodesia (now Zimbabwe). But her lifestyle in the United States once she divorced my father after only ten years of marriage—when I was two—was more like a slow nomadism than any kind of regular return home to Sweden. She moved my sister and me every four years, driven by a mix of wanderlust and bipolar depression. We lived in Tucson when I was young, and that introduction to and immersion in the desert in my formative years is ultimately what drew me back to southern Arizona as an adult, even though Billie and I debated moving to Portland, Oregon, instead (and have since dreamed of following the seasons annually from Tucson to Denver to Portland and back). Once we relocated our young family to Tucson, however, the urge to escape the desert heat—to migrate annually to the Pacific Northwest—was, admittedly, immediate.

The practice of migrating peoples is as old as human history, journalist and immigrant Sonia Shah tells us in her book *The Next Great Migration*. And it's not just the movement of people caused by changing weather patterns, environmental catastrophe, or war, though certainly environmental and geopolitical factors play a role, particularly in modern history. Rather, writes Shah, "In the broad view of human history, we're all migrants in every place we live, outside parts of Africa.…Scientific findings have made it clear that migration is not an exception to the rule. We've been moving all along. And there's no singular factor that explains why."

On our last day along the Platte River, I consider migration, both for our family—Billie, Juliet, and Ann-Elise will be making the round trip to Oregon again in just three months—and for the Sandhill cranes, who arrive in central Nebraska exhausted, their body weight down 15 to 20 percent. The cranes migrate south in the fall because of extreme winter weather conditions in their breeding grounds of Siberia, Alaska, and Canada, and then back north in the spring to reach their isolated breeding grounds that offer food and shelter in the wide, shallow waters and nearby plains. One could argue our impetus to migrate between Arizona and Oregon was similarly environmental—escaping the searing heat. But that, as with most human migration, tells only part of the story. Neither Billie nor I have parents near Tucson, and Billie is particularly close to her mother. Like my mother, Billie's mother divorced when her youngest child was just two and then raised her children on her own. She likewise relocated every few years, until she finally settled in Eugene, where she lives now. It is important for Billie to spend time with her mother and for our daughters to know their grandmother. Even though Annie lives a thousand miles away, she is their closest grandparent. Indeed, while the annual visit to Eugene is a convenient way to escape the desert during much of the summer, I'm certain that Billie would have struck a similar deal if we had moved somewhere else—or not moved at all.

So, environment and family both play a role. But is something still deeper driving us, something revealed by my trip with Juliet along the migratory path of the cranes, by playing witness to their timeless gathering before the birds' journey continues once again?

Juliet and I awake to a cool, dark morning, the songbirds outside just beginning their dawn confessionals as we dress. Although we won't have to be quiet until we near the viewing blind along the Platte River, few words pass between us as we eat breakfast with Allison and the others before sunrise, though whether the silence is from sleepiness or anticipation or grace, I can't tell. Allison is a Sandhill elder and our guide both ecological and cultural to the birds we are to view in our short time in central Nebraska. So we take her lead in our preparations accordingly—setting cameras and cell phones to silent mode, bundling up against the damp chill, accepting her request to keep a respectful distance from the cranes if we find ourselves among them. There are no special instructions or reiterations for Juliet, as the only child among us—yet another kindness Allison extends.

A light rain begins as we drive through the darkness from the house north of the river, then east on I-80, across a low bridge spanning the Platte River, and to the Iain Nicolson Audubon Center. Sited along a wide bend on the south side of the Platte, the center is located a few miles east of Kearney and just north of a stretch of cornfields at the 2,900-acre Lillian Annette Rowe Sanctuary. Purchased by the National Audubon Society in 1974 at roughly one-sixth of its current size, the sanctuary includes five miles of river channel, riverside wildlife habitat, agricultural fields, restored prairies, and facilities to support cranes and other wildlife. After parking, we follow Allison into the warmth of the straw-bale center and, with another dozen visitors, listen to the Rowe Sanctuary guide, who provides similar instructions: silence, distance. What need not be said: gratitude. He surveys us as he speaks and, eyeing Juliet, repeats his policy that we remain quiet once out on the trail and in the blind. Juliet nods, leaning into me. From there we walk as a group through the center's back door to a trail that skirts fields on our right and leafless cottonwoods and perhaps eastern red cedars on our left. Beyond the trees lies the expanse of the Platte, its sandbars and sedge textured between shallow braids of river. Out on that sustaining river, though we can't yet see them due to the waning darkness, thousands of Sandhill cranes ruffle and rustle and call. Still, we keep quiet as instructed, following the silhouette of our guide, the only human noise the low chant of our feet on the trail, the swish of a rain slicker, the distant rumble of an occasional truck on the interstate north of the river.

When I was about Juliet's age, I went duck hunting with my older brother in the swamps of central Florida. Until this visit to the Rowe Sanctuary, that was my only experience with blinds, and along the edge of that southern cypress swamp, the blind's camouflaged cover was no bigger than a two-person tent, and really more like a permeable tarp thrown over a clothesline. At the sanctuary, however, the tall, rectangular blind is the size of an RV and just as sturdy. It is easily large enough to fit two dozen people. We file in and take our places, the interior dark but dry, windows placed at intervals so that someone as tall as my six-and-a-half-foot frame or as short as Juliet, or shorter still, can look out without struggling.

In so looking out, however, another kind of struggle might ensue—one of containing a loud gasp or of forgetting to breathe entirely, for the scene before us is, as Scott Russell Sanders would no doubt agree, awesome. As far as we can see in any direction, Sandhill cranes fill the shallow river, thousands if not a hundred thousand of them. Though Juliet and I are not as close to these cranes as we had been at the Bosque del Apache or Whitewater Draw, the power and beauty here is less about proximity than about the sheer number of cranes spread across the river and its dark sandbars. And unlike the congregations we have seen in the Southwest, these stopover cranes are more social both in their closeness to each other and in their movements. In pairs that mate for life, the birds face each other, raising and holding back their wings that span up to seven feet before stretching their bodies into a jumping, not entirely fluid dance. They lift their necks and heads and beaks to the gray sky before swooping their heads down, beaks sometimes dipping into water or sand—or when among the fields, picking up a corn cob or twig—before pulling back up quickly, tossing any beaked prize above their head, and then hopping away only to bow once again. And again. These could be dances between mated pairs or dances between cranes seeking mates. In either case, the breeding itself will occur once they reach their summer grounds to the north. Still, crane dancing on the Platte in spring is commonplace and one reason the region has become known as "the greatest singles bar for cranes"—at least according to the Nebraska Game and Parks Commission, which perhaps shouldn't come up with marketing slogans for crane viewing, after all.

As the sky continues to lighten, the birds come into greater focus from our hidden view that looks northwest across the river. I admit I nearly forget my daughter in the uncounted time that follows, as I raise my camera and snap photo after photo of the multitudinous cranes, their dances, their flights in the morning's blue light, the sheer abundance of it all.

The cranes, which number up to a million in the central Platte Valley from mid-February through mid-April, come from three distinct subspecies: greater, Canadian, and lesser. From our distance they are impossible to tell apart; the difference in the Canadian and greater birds relates to how far back the red patch on their head extends, while the lesser Sandhill crane is some two pounds lighter than the greater and has a shorter bill. But at least one white crane stands apart from all three subspecies, and when it is spotted, gleaming among its gray compatriots, there is no keeping the viewers quiet, for this is an endangered whooping crane, the tallest and among the rarest birds in North America. In the early 1940s the whooping crane population fell to as few as sixteen birds thanks to habitat loss and overhunting for meat and feathers. Their salvation as a species remains slow—the birds today number perhaps six hundred worldwide—and that the population growth is happening at all is thanks to captive breeding programs that in some cases place whooping crane eggs in active Sandhill crane nests. If we were in a boat, I would fear capsizing as everyone rushes to the windows on the north side of the blind to scope the majestic bird with its red cap, black cheeks, tan bill, and thin black legs among a body as white and elegant as porcelain.

I watch and take photographs and praise our luck and as quietly as possible swap my camera's lens and refocus and watch some more and take more photographs and give silent thanks again until I realize Juliet is no longer standing next to me. I turn to find her sitting cross-legged, pink coat zipped and hood pulled tightly. She is facing away from the windows and nibbling Chex

Mix pulled piece by piece from a bag in her pocket. Allison and I
exchange glances, and with that we turn from the windows, gather
ourselves, and step out of the blind before quietly walking back to
the visitor center, the light rain blunting the morning light.

At the parking lot Juliet and I load into our car and drive
west, cranking the heat and defogger before following the red
Jeep carrying Allison. The road turns through several fields of
corn stubble before we find its end just south of the river, where
a bank of cottonwoods stands like ghostly sentinels, blocking
our view of the Platte but creating a striated and strangely
peaceful scene nearly black and white in its composition if not
for the cornstalks, themselves muted to tarnished gold in the
mist. And then they appear likes ghosts themselves—pairs or
trios of Sandhill cranes stepping between the rows of cornstalk
stubble, close enough to greet in a low voice if we so choose.
We keep quiet, remaining in the car as I snap more photos
and Juliet admires the birds between handfuls of Chex Mix
and mouthfuls of questions: What do they eat? Where do they
sleep? Which is the baby? What was the white crane? What's
for lunch? Can we maybe get Dairy Queen on the way home?
I answer as best as I can, referring to both a field guide and
local map I'd brought along. For their part, the cranes ignore
us, searching among the stalks for corn and other delights like
snails, earthworms, and insects, filling the stores they'll need to
continue their migration north.

And with that, Juliet and I are ready to fill our own stores for
our two-day drive south, where we'll cover only slightly more
ground in a day than the cranes, who can fly up to five hundred
miles between dawn and dusk on their migration. We wave our
goodbyes and mouth our thanks to Allison, Lee, Kimberly, and
Renee. We wave our goodbyes and whisper our thanks to the

Sandhill cranes, too, which disappear in our rearview mirror much as they had appeared, the mist closing in around them.

As we drive toward the interstate, I once again consider the long and regular journeys humans and animals take—for environment, for family, for survival. Viewing the cranes from the Rowe Sanctuary blind, it is easy to think of the birds as a kind of single organism, moving in unison as they appear to do when flying or even wading en masse along the river's edge. Upon closer view—foraging in the cornfields of central Nebraska or in a roadside ditch south of San Antonio, New Mexico, for example—we see the birds for what they are, of course: individuals, no one bird exactly like the other. So it is with migration, says Shah: "Movements that were once dismissed as robotically controlled by genes appear to be the result of dynamic interactions between individuals, each responding to subtle cues in the environment and from one another." Yet the birds also get what scientists call "migratory restlessness," she writes. "As the time to leave approaches, a restlessness sets in....It's hormonal."

But hormones and physiology more broadly aren't driving Billie and the girls in our own familial summer migrations, just as that impetus alone is not what keeps the cranes flying on. What, then, could it be? As we get up to speed on the interstate, leaving the rain behind, the Rockies not yet a scribble on the western horizon, I think of Ralph Waldo Emerson again and another of his widely known quotes: "Experience is the only teacher."

And that's it, isn't it? Whether human or animal, migration is a journey—an educational process, an experience—that teaches us how to move through the world, the routes to take, how to find the right altitude, the stops to make, the places to avoid, the promise of coolness or warmth, food and shelter, family, love. More than the simple sum of environmental, family, and physiological factors, the experience of the journey—rich with the instruction of our parents and more broadly the community with which we move—determines our success not only on the current voyage but on all future journeys to come, until and even after we pass on our knowledge to our children in turn.

"Sure, Dad, whatever," says Juliet, pulling me out of my soliloquy. "But what about Dairy Queen?" I'm not precisely sure what that cool treat will teach us, but it's a stopover I am happy to make down the road a bit. And so we do.

SONGBIRD

I hadn't meant to kill the bird. He was a robin, as best I could tell at fifty miles per hour—the road loping through the Vermont countryside, green on green except for the occasional field of dandelions, a congregation of black-and-white cows beside the baptistery of a watering trough. The bird arced out of the roadside brush and into the passenger side of the windshield, thinking perhaps the glint was a sudden stream, dragonflies and water striders ready for the taking. On impact, the beak dropped and neck must have snapped before he bounced and landed light but lifeless on the pavement behind me. I could hear the initial impact even with the buds of the iPod planted in my ears, the chords of the Rolling Stones' "Bitch" rolling with the small hills. I may have invoked the song's refrain—*Love, it's a bitch, alright*— as I watched the pear-sized life pass. It's not so much that love is a bitch, I thought, as that sudden collisions are a bitch. I'd been warned to watch for moose, and have certainly pinged birds before, but something about this encounter resounded, as if the robin instead pierced the curved glass, a dart nested in the pane of my deeper self.

I paused the iPod and removed the earbuds—this was 2008, after all, before the proliferation of iPhones and AirPods and Apple CarPlay. The sound of the engine filled the cavity of the rental car. Still, as I slowed to forty I could just make out the calls of other birds in the birches and maples, the whirr of a riding mower on a lawn, the whine of the car's small tires. At the time, Billie had owned an iPod for about a month, raving about it daily, telling me at every opportunity how much I'd like one, her own foreshadowing of just how ubiquitous listening to music and podcasts on small handheld devices or smartwatches would become. I'm not interested, I insisted. But with a trip from Tucson to New England coming up, I began to see the value. No more searching through radio stations as I drove the rental car. The chance to have our full music library digitized and at my fingertips. And an easy ability to watch films on the sleek, black device as well. I gave in, and it was only a matter of days before my new iPod held more than 1,900 songs and a handful of movies; not exactly today's seemingly unlimited cloud-based libraries, but a worthy media catalog nonetheless.

I accepted the digital music player with a mixture of anticipation and regret. As with my adoption of any new technology, I knew it would change my habits and relationship with the wider world. Though I designed websites and worked on computers all day, I was wary of new gadgets. It's not that I was old-fashioned; instead, there was something about losing a connection to the visceral world, an unwillingness to substitute the virtual for the actual.

I didn't blame the bird's death on the iPod. But over the few days I had the player on that June trip, I felt its ability to lure me away from the natural—and perhaps just as essential, the unnatural—sounds around me. I wasn't shocked, then, to learn that the iPod was often called the isolation-Pod. Today, isolation and loneliness associated with what the iPod has evolved into—the smartphone—have only increased, resulting in significant psychological and societal changes that we are only now beginning to comprehend.

According to research by Kristi Baerg MacDonald and Julie Aitken Schermer, "Communication and relationships have been dramatically altered among emerging adults thanks to the rapid adoption of the smartphone in just over a decade." Young adults, in particular, are at greater risk of loneliness and report being more stressed out about their loneliness. "Correlations indicated loneliness was positively associated with screen time, social media app use, neuroticism, social recognition, communication anxiety, and nomophobia," MacDonald and Schermer write. (Nomophobia, according to the National Institutes of Health, is a psychological condition when people have a fear of being detached from their mobile phone connectivity; literally "no mobile phone phobia.") The researchers' conclusion: "More time spent on one's smartphone and on social media apps is related to increased loneliness."

For Billie, after a day of teaching second graders, isolation was a reward: her escape into synthesized rhythms and soothing vocals, if only for the brief periods before dinner or after our daughters were in bed. My escape was also from monotony—the drone of engines on the airliner, in the car. But back at home or moving around town, I preferred the honeyed song of the lesser goldfinch, the raucous cry of a cactus wren, even the regular echo of a fighter jet arcing above the local air base. Fifteen years later, I still do—all evidence to the contrary, considering my

Spotify catalog is now three times the size of my original iPod library. Clearly, though, sound is every bit as much a part of place as image.

So, passing through New Hampshire's White Mountains on my way to Vermont, I was surprised, in those early days of portable digital music players, to encounter a teenage boy with iPod earbuds nestled in his ears, volume up, music tinny but nonetheless audible. In a hooded red sweatshirt and baggy jeans, he walked along the trail that edges the Flume Brook at Franconia Notch State Park. The Flume is a thin gorge nearly three football fields long, lined with dark walls of granite and basalt, overgrown in ferns, moss, and the dangling branches of alder. At the ravine's head is Avalanche Falls, four stories high and thirty feet wide. The wild rush of the brook is as visceral in sound as in sight, yet without both the experience must have been diminished for the boy.

Or perhaps that's only my antiquated view, for isn't it possible the teenager's experience was actually heightened by his music? The melody didn't sound like Wagner's "Ride of the Valkyries" or even the Rolling Stones' "Gimme Shelter," which would have been appropriate given the waterfall's overspray, but his on-demand soundtrack played on, and he appeared as engaged as any of us. Yet at what point does synthetic sound replace natural sound and thus authentic experience? At what point do we lose our intrinsic connection to the physical places around us because we've become absorbed in the virtual places that technology makes so easy to access?

After I arrived in Vermont, friend and jazz clarinetist David Rothenberg, author of best-selling books on bird, insect, and whale song, said, "Why not try walking through a wild forest listening to a recording made in Times Square?" My immediate reaction was to do the opposite: load up the iPod with forest recordings for trips to the city. The last place I had seen David was New York, and I well remember the cacophony of sirens and subway trains, vehicles and voices.

Without an accessible urban recording, however, my options were limited to the songs already on my player: I skipped "Gimme Shelter" for another topical Stones song, "Street Fighting Man." Placing the smooth, wired buds into my ears, I reached the edge of a tattered trail near Craftsbury, Vermont, where I was staying. Guitar riffs announced the song, but right away I realized that I had to slide up the volume to hide the swishing of my feet through the high grass and pine needles that covered the cross-country ski lane. The trail dropped into a forest of hawthorn, birch, and pine. Ferns and intricate wildflowers of blue and white drifted into the path or edged the filtered shadows of the trees. I raised the volume once again to cover the cries of crows so that I could no longer hear even the internal cadence of my own breathing.

Almost immediately—as Mick Jagger crooned and a sitar bent in the background—I felt disconnected from the trail and broader landscape. My eyes cropped the shapes of the verdant maple leaves against speckled limbs and the gray granite against darker trail. But I saw few birds. A humid breeze washed my face and hands, mosquitoes took residence on the back of my neck, and the scent of the pines was light yet persistent. But I saw no wildlife. And soon my head swayed back and forth in a rhythmic, almost unconscious scan far from normal. By the time the song ended and "Sympathy for the Devil" began, my walk felt more cinematic than anything else—not so much surreal as half-real, a vital sense not so much cut off as held captive. I could neither deny that the experience was compelling nor endorse its isolation.

The path reached a wide clearing and then a road, but I kept going, music blaring, northern Vermont's pastures and soft, forested hills on every horizon. The nature of the acoustic environment of the landscape—the soundscape—made little difference in my walk, except when I passed the swift but narrow Black River, where the trill of red-winged blackbirds forced me to wind the volume to its maximum, to the same level the iPod needed to overpower the jet engines just outside my seat on the commercial flight from Tucson. I hadn't realized the sheer amplitude of the natural world, always assuming the mechanizations of humans were louder by default. I was tempted to pause the player to listen to the fen but instead stepped off the road onto a faint trail beside the marsh's edge and headed for a hill a half-mile distant. Along the way I saw dozens of birds—warblers and blackbirds, finches and mallards—plus the outline of a turtle just below the water's dark surface. The breeze picked up and I found myself slapping the back of my neck less, the forest's tiny fiends left behind. Knee-deep in wildflowers and grass, I trudged to the base of the hill, choosing my steps through the water-logged pasture carefully, my shoes and pants already soaked. And I was delighted, for even though I wasn't exposed to natural sounds, there was a certain cadence to the digital songs that rolled into my ears, immersing me completely. Though I was still certain the boy at the Flume missed the full natural experience, I realized he hadn't missed experience altogether. I conceded that his exposure was rich, even if not truly authentic.

Or wasn't it? At the base of the hill, I stopped once I recognized there wasn't a trail after all. I turned south and looked across the fen as the wind built behind me. Suddenly the grass undulated in vast uneven ripples—like the parabolic waves of sound itself—and I became unstable, disoriented. I knew this experience was an illusion both optical and aural, yet the entire sheet of green and yellow-green grasses rolled row after row into the dark braid of the Black River even as my feet dug hard into the hillside. The misty green horizon represented the forest I came through, but it didn't move. Only the saturated meadow between us receded, shifting with the wind and dropping into the river like a wide, thatched conveyor belt. "You Can't Always Get What You Want" filled my head when I realized that I could no longer deny that the boy's experience was any less authentic than my own.

"But if you try sometimes," the song's chorus continued as I recentered myself, "you get what you need." What I needed to ask, then, wasn't whether synthetic sounds in nature lead to a less authentic personal experience, for I now knew that individual experience can be authentic regardless of acoustic source. Instead, I wondered if the loss of natural sounds leads to a disconnection from place altogether. That is, do we become numb to landscapes when they lose their natural sounds?

The answer may lie in how human-caused noise is perceived. For example, National Park Service managers have concluded, based on scientific research and visitor surveys, that park quality is generally inseparable from "natural peace and the sounds of nature." So, an effort has been under way for more than two decades to better manage their soundscapes, which are threatened by flyovers, automobile traffic, and snowmobiles. One of the first parks studied was Sequoia–Kings Canyon National Park in California, where researchers set up equipment to establish sonic benchmarks—what the Acoustic Ecology Institute calls a "voiceprint of habitat." The researchers' goal was to monitor the soundscape as an indicator of overall ecosystem health: the more natural the sounds, the healthier the park ecosystem and the more connected visitors feel.

The ecosystem of my family back in Tucson was our stout bungalow plus the city and Sonoran Desert beyond. Our soundscape was mostly a wonderful mix: not only local birds but also neighbors on front porches, vehicles on streets, and the wind among acacia and mesquite. Lizards scampered beneath sage and prickly pear while bees nuzzled vibrant flowers. Inside, it was not uncommon for the soundscape to be composed of music—Ann-Elise practicing viola, Juliet on piano, a song or composition on the stereo.

That year, however, technology silenced our house even as my wife and daughters heard more music. In January 2008 my daughters' school was selected from among more than three thousand others by talk show host Ellen DeGeneres as the greenest grade school in America. Civano Community School was known not only for its progressive expeditionary-learning model but also for its focus on community and environment. Solar photovoltaic panels provided power, a school garden maintained by students supplemented lunches, and recycling was old hat. With the award, each child received a green iPod Shuffle and solar charger. It didn't take long for Ann-Elise, then in fifth grade, and Juliet, in second, to load their matchbox-sized players with their favorite songs.

"Finally!" my older daughter said as she eased the iPod out of its case. She was one of the few remaining students in her class who didn't already have one, just as she was one of the last students in her class to receive her own smartphone when she was in high school. Though we defined the amount of time they could listen to their iPods, the effect was immediate, and silencing. More often than not, I found the girls walking around the house, iPods on, oblivious to my call. They hadn't become zombies, because they danced or skipped or hopped to the beat, but they certainly became isolated—and were happier for it, just like the millions if not billions of children and adults today who listen to music through wireless earbuds as they move from class to class or task to task in the wider world. But were they healthier, and was our family?

My wife was already a chronic headphone wearer, connected to a portable CD player, before I gave her the iPod for Mother's Day in 2008. After school she often worked late into the evening grading student work and creating lesson plans. For these repetitive tasks, and for exercising and housework, she listened to music. Upgrading to the iPod was a logical evolution, both in technology and practice: it was smaller, used less power, and contained more music than the CD player. Yet once Billie programmed her iPod, listening increased and our home became quieter still. That wasn't necessarily bad when I was working at my desk, but it could be downright eerie otherwise.

In addition to isolation, loneliness, and anxiety, there may be other dangers, too. Beyond the real possibility of hearing loss— listen no more than five minutes at full volume or four and a half hours at 70 percent volume per day, researchers have determined—the broader risk is disconnection from landscape and community altogether. Video game developers, computer manufacturers, and the corporations behind them may well want us to substitute virtual for actual reality (and with today's threats to environment and people worldwide, who isn't tempted every now and then?). After all, the less engaged we are the more complacent we become, and complacency breeds a willingness to purchase whatever product is placed before us, to acquiesce to whatever those in power tell us. But it seems to me that being a part of the community's full landscape requires informed and active participation. And active participation is not possible with earplugs (Zoom town halls and civic activism webinars notwithstanding). Instead, face-to-face communication, sustained discourse, and keen listening must prevail.

Back on the edge of the Vermont marsh, without a trail to guide me further in my research, I removed the earbuds. The wider world rushed back, and with it the fen's own sporadic music. Between the blackbirds, finches, and surprising bass notes of hundreds of frogs I hadn't heard or seen earlier, it was a symphony indeed. I trudged back to the road, my shoes squelching in the lovely muck, and sat on a stone beside the bridge. The Black River's current carried leaves and twigs beneath me, but the river also had its own lyric, not quite lapping at the edges but still resonating off the brambly shore and among the reeds.

I sat for a long time savoring the sounds—both natural and artificial, for trucks on a nearby highway held the frequency of waves on a beach—before walking up the road toward the trees. The wind shifted and a clique of birches gossiped, bright green leaves rattling, before I made my way into the forest where the higher pines had their own shushing talk. As the trail shifted from gravel to mud to hard-packed earth, the tempo of my footsteps changed accordingly, here a thud, there a scrape. Behind me a bird called, almost laughing in its nasal song, and I turned just in time to glimpse a nuthatch. Walking uphill through the forest, I saw that with the music playing, I lost not only my sense of hearing but also my sense of time and distance. Clearly, I wasn't tuned into the landscape in many ways.

My full appreciation for hearing the sounds around me, however, wasn't set by the blackbirds or frogs or trees, nor the bubbling of small brooks on either side of the trail. Rather, it came all at once, as I approached the edge of the forest, when a single crow's sudden and rapid cawing made me jump. I couldn't say who was more startled as the black sentinel circled high before flying off. But it left me silent, ears fine-tuned before I took another step.

A few minutes later I was deep in thought on sound and landscape when a distinct chipping rang from a pear tree in a pasture ahead. The call was from a robin, with flashy auburn breast and charcoal back. His yellow beak moved rapidly with the song, but his bright black eye focused on me—the kind of gaze I use on my daughters when they're up to no good. His scrutiny had the same effect: we were both leery. I approached slowly, aware of my reputation with robins in these parts. I was sorry for killing the other robin but argued, in my head anyway, that there was little I could do to avoid the collision. At this he looked away and began singing loudly. He called more and more rapidly until I discerned two songs, though I could not see the other robin. Their intensity rose so that the calls could have been mistaken for an electronic synthesizer, keys dancing wildly, frequency and amplitude high. I half expected the ground to begin undulating once again. But the path held and I walked on, into the abounding ballad of the afternoon.

THE BELLS OF SAN BORJA

The Sonoran Desert stirs with an aromatic mosaic of wildflowers this spring: yellow senna, orange globe mallow, crimson fairy duster, violet nightshade. At the Misión San Francisco Borja de Adac of Baja California, a pair of simple bells also stirs the air, ringing across a thin valley and echoing into the volcanic hills beyond. Six hundred miles north, our sprawling urban homescape of Tucson chimes with its own bells—a multitude of tiny chalices and painted beads on strings swaying from mesquite and palo verde, desert willow and sweet acacia. What history brings us this resonance? What beauty? What agony, too?

Though I returned home late from San Borja, I wake early this morning in 2005 to my daughters' yearning faces, their mouths curved in anticipation of a promise made months ago. After a quick breakfast, Ann-Elise—eight years old and a budding naturalist—presses into her roller skates, dons a silver-starred helmet, and ushers her younger sister and me onto the back porch. There I yawn, stretch, yawn again, and craft a tale to persuade them that a couple hours more sleep would do us good in our worthy pursuit. As usual, they don't give in.

Juliet—at five, already a sensitive artist—unfolds her snowflake quilt, climbs into the plastic wagon, and points north toward the pedestrian path that slopes down to the shallow arroyo on the neighborhood's edge. The trail leads past a series of low bluffs lined with creosote, its rich smell the unequivocal scent of the desert. North it is, and I grunt with the first pull of the wagon, grunt as much to hide a quick laugh as I look over my shoulder to find the girls, glinting helmet to canvas hat, planning our route in animated detail.

Ann-Elise takes the lead, but after a block, after we reach the edge of the neighborhood and begin our descent, she instead takes my hand. She needs the balance, and so do I. After a week in Baja— no contact with family, no daughters to share the uncountable constellations so bright I swore I'd never seen true stars before—I find traveling is fulfilling but the return home more so.

As usual, she is the first to spot wildlife: a covey of quail bobbing in formation beneath the mitt-sized pads of purple cactus. The Santa Rita prickly pear is flowering, its waxy yellow buds fully open, the bees' delight evident yards away. "What kind of quail?" I quiz her. "Gambel's," she says quickly, and precisely. On the first leg of our journey she tallies others: a cardinal balancing atop a leaning ocotillo arm, the thorns no deterrent, the scarlet flowers only a slight challenge to his brilliance; mourning doves, pink feet against dusty body, blue-ringed eyes watching intently; and a curve-billed thrasher, a beetle in its glossy beak.

Past the bluffs and beyond the neighborhood paseo, we merge onto the Pantano Wash walkway that meanders like the waterless riverbed itself, from southeast to northwest, toward the city's center. The smooth railing helps guide Ann-Elise and, as we rise out of the basin, gives me leverage as I tug the wagon. Juliet is calling out directions from the map she made the day before. I'd prefer not to convince her that we need to stay on the paved path. Why shouldn't she have the better directions, urging us to bypass the sidewalk and head straight for the thick stand of saguaros on the distant rise? Neither of us sees the bells we're after in that direction, though who can tell, really, among the acrobatics of raucous house finches, the bickering of comical cactus wrens?

Ann-Elise pushes on, and though we live on the outskirts of Tucson, there is some hope that we'll find one of the chimes. Between her keen eye and Juliet's navigation, they make a formidable team. I'm needed only for my brute strength and length of reach.

Slowly the bluffs give way to more level landscape, where block walls replace fences of mesquite and ocotillo. At the top of the next rise there is movement, something larger than a bird, and suddenly Ann-Elise is skating hard, nearly sprinting. She's no roadrunner, but a lizard flees from her wheels just in time. As she reaches the crest I see another family, a young boy moving animatedly, his excitement betrayed not so much by his dancing as the glint of the object he holds—a colorful string of beads, the almost imperceptible jingle floating down as we clamor upward.

These are Ben's Bells—a project Jeannette Maré-Packard and her husband, Dean, initiated less than a year after the death of their son Ben, just shy of his third birthday. Ben died that morning of croup, after he turned blue, when his airway swelled shut, even as his mother performed rescue breathing and CPR. In the long, slow, and undoubtedly painful aftermath, his parents turned their grief into action by converting their backyard pottery studio into a place where, joined by friends, they created bells. Strung together by thin straps of leather or string, containing hand-painted ceramic beads of their own crafting—cylinders and balls and stars—the bells resemble the multicolored tails of kites, flowing from the single copper device with its subtle chime. The purpose? To reciprocate the kindness of strangers the family received after Ben's death, to "find a way to pass on that kindness and to help others in the process," says Jeannette.

On the first anniversary of Ben's death, in March 2003, the Packards and friends and family—including their older son Matthew, who more than anyone else gave them hope in this difficult time—first distributed the bells throughout the Tucson valley, placing them in random locations: along the branches of yellow-flowering acacias at the Rillito River park, for instance, or in the parking lot of midtown's Tucson Medical Center. And each included a paper note with a simple message: "Take this bell home, hang it up, pass on the kindness."

I first learned about Ben's Bells when I escorted Ann-Elise and Juliet to the Packards' studio, then located in an Italianate court-yard of white-barked sycamores just west of the University of Arizona. Here, volunteers gathered to help create the bells—by forming clay into acorn-sized beads, painting the flat glaze that gleams after the kiln, and assembling the bells.

The studio was nearly as bright inside as the beads are outside, and throughout the converted home, photos of little Ben deco-rated the walls, his white-blond hair and toothy grin, the vibrant blue eyes: the constant reminder that these bells are his work, that in their creation—by the time the bells are assembled, at least ten people have worked on each set—a whole community is remembering not only this child, but the kindness of every child.

On that mild winter day, my daughters and their friends took their instructions and set to work on painting beads, the small brushes touching the paint's tense surface before sweeping onto the hard, off-white clay. For some it was simply arts and crafts, but for others in our group, the older girls who had seen the photos and knew the story and in one case knew Ben before he died, this was an important and uplifting project. Glazing the beads in red and yellow and green, there was a visceral connectedness— not to the individual who would find the bell when distributed several months later, but rather to the spirit of community and the spirit of grieving.

I quickly filled my camera with images of the hanging bells and yet-to-be-fired beads, the girls with their golden hair pulled back, the sun on their concentrating faces, the adults whose eyes grew watery because we have children and in our nightmares our children are also taken from us, maybe painlessly and maybe not. This is a compassion and fear that only parents can know, but by sharing in the making of these bells, all can begin to understand.

Months later, my daughters are delighted to finally see a Ben's Bell "in the wild." They are not so happy to realize that it is the only bell we see on our entire search—one they had missed by minutes. On the return walk, as the sun trails us like a burning kite, Juliet talks about the beauty of the bells, down to each particular bead. Recalling colors and textures in her uncanny, photogenic way—not only from this particular bell but from her work at the studio in January—her premise may be that beauty is something to be found as well as created, something that can be generated even from intense sadness. Beauty can be the visual and aural brilliance in a brightly colored bird and its even brighter song, for example, or the sublime suddenness of a small, unexpected discovery—a split geode on the trail's edge, a small bell glittering in a tree.

If the adage is correct and beauty is what we make of it, then
the discovery of beauty is simply a matter of refocusing to find
even the smallest bit in any object—to first agree that there can
be beauty in some capacity in anything and everything, and then
to identify beauty in an object through a sort of systematic scanning, closing in through passes of greater and greater detail. This
is the logic of statisticians: finding beauty is simply a matter of
assigning probabilities to any given object, in any given location.
There is an increasing probability of identifying it if we divide
the object—whether animal, vegetable, or mineral—into smaller
parts, much as sections of an ancient site are divided and sifted
one by one at an archaeological dig. A particularly large rock in
and of itself may not be beautiful, for instance, but a closer look
reveals a rich mix of lichen, striations of quartz, and patterns of
other minerals that are indeed beautiful. Or perhaps not, and we
move to the next.

But can beauty really be so clearly divided, so systematically
defined?

In traveling to the mission at San Borja, I seek beauty, surely, but
I am still uncertain of the context. Like Ben's Bells, I wonder if
beauty there can also come from pain—in this case, from the
enslavement of Native peoples, their forced conversion, their
unpaid labor to create such a massive building in the center of an
otherwise unstructured desert arcadia where the high clouds of
the central Baja sky weave blue on white on blue.

There is, at least, a rugged allure in seeking the mission. The
dirt road trailing south off Mexico's Highway 3 remains long and
unkept. It regularly washes out in the floods of summer storms.
Its ruts are littered with the jagged shapes of basalt and fractured
limestone, pitted with cholla and yucca. It rises and falls and then

turns back upon itself as if confounded, as if it well knows where it wants to go, but not how to get there. That is a beauty to get lost in.

And suddenly the mission, perched among an improbable mountainside oasis of Mexican blue palms, towering cardón cactus, and subtropical mesquite. Inaugurated in 1762 by the Jesuits, the stone mission stands next to the ruins of the original structure built in 1639, wedged between the cold springs of surrounding peaks and hot springs just yards away. Yet it was abandoned in 1818, maintained today only because an eighth-generation family continues to care for the structure on their property, sharing both its complicated history and classic beauty.

I arrive with two friends the week before Easter, when the guest book is open to visitors who made their own long journeys. Like us, they drove the transpeninsular, two-lane highway that only takes us within two dozen miles of the mission. From there, a poorly marked dirt road continues through the rugged terrain. The trail to the mission has never been much of a road to begin with, no matter who travels it. Chiseled from the Vizcaino Desert in the 1750s, it was a kind of penance for missionaries then and for visitors today—a good challenge in any vehicle, worth every banged axle and bruised knee.

Though rich in topography, the Vizcaino landscape is bizarre at any height. Forests of wiry boojum, or *cirio* as locals call the succulent, mix with *cardón*, the bluer kin of saguaro. Over centuries, the tallest boojum—and the tallest known plant is only thirty miles from the mission—grow to more than ninety feet. Generally, these cousins of ocotillo, which taper from thick bases like enormous overturned carrots, grow straight up. But in times of extreme heat or near frost they bend, collapse, and the next season begin their upward growth again so that arched and looping boojum also grow among the straight specimens. It is a desert of Seussian proportions. The sentinel cardón rise to sixty feet. The new growth, which we see on every cactus, is more blue than green, lined with rows of gray spines that fold into the leathery skin as the plant matures. Beneath these massive natives grow Mexican tree ocotillos, their trunks two feet thick, branching at torso height into a dozen arms tipped with bell-shaped vermilion flowers that lure bees in daytime and bats at night. Ground-dwelling yucca with black trunks and sage-bladed leaves, thick-spined agave, dozens of species of cholla—some with hollow, light-filled spines four inches long—and numerous other thorny plants fill out the invitingly treacherous desert floor, which itself is an uneven mix of sand and volcanic tuft.

The mission at San Borja is not a "white dove of the desert" like the widely visited Misión de San Xavier del Bac just south of Tucson. It is long and flat, not terribly large as missions go, tan-gray from the surrounding hillsides, mostly undecorated except for the main entrance. Here, massive double doors are planked in dark mesquite beneath an arch fanned like the hard rays of the sun, each ray a wooden slat. The door's architrave—its carved stone border—is comprised of simple scrolls etched a half-inch deep and ending in roses, except at the keystone, which is blank. On both sides of the door, two ornate columns, each with seven identical flares, rise to a layered stone shelf that breaks and arches slightly below the bell tower's window. Carvings above and beneath the shelf symbolize the Jesuit order: a branch with four seven-petal flowers laid over a cross, and a circle with a flowered cross. The tower has been rebuilt so that the remnants of a larger arch are barely visible before the flat and crudely stacked stones end at the roofline and a simple white cross.

Within the block walls laid without mortar, pressed into place by brute strength and fastened by granite shards, there is a side portico with a spiral staircase. The light is warm and dusty, welcoming in an otherwise echoing space of high curved ceilings, though it slips to darkness quickly in the short space of the portico's entrance. I have an image both on my camera and in my mind's eye of that stone staircase—viewing it through the light and uneven floor of the chapel, through the darkness of the wall so thick it becomes a short corridor—and of the steps, spiraling like the cross-section of a nautilus.

As I bend through the entrance, my feet fill the depressions in the steps worn smooth from two and a half centuries of use. I am guided up the tight spiral by the walls, rather than handrails—guided more so by the press of curiosity to climb, even while my brain's logical half, the half that insists upon the paradox that I am tall but scared of heights, wants to keep me down. The top portico opens onto a narrow loft, without a wall or other barrier from the floor twenty feet below. It overlooks the chapel with its few tall windows, the afternoon light bringing focus to the opposite walls, the wooden benches, the simple pulpit.

Dizzyingly close to the edge, I turn back to face the front entrance of the mission and see two bells, one much larger than the other, hanging from a wooden pole bracketed into the walls. Beyond, a wrought-iron awning separates this bell tower from the mission's wide front yard. The larger bell is bronze, oxidized at the seams, with a pattern of line-drawn fish around simple crosses. Stamped into its side, facing the chapel, is an image I cannot quite make out—the Virgin of Guadalupe with her shining aura, or Jesus himself? The white rope tied to the bell's tongue looks new, implying it is replaced periodically, worn like the surrounding stone from years of use. Strong enough to ring but not strong enough to last. The smaller bell to its left is copper, with a turquoise-colored flatness that resonates against the gray blocks and the sunlight ringing through the window. Its clapper rope is new, too, though already dyed blue from the copper bell, a promise that even in the arid lands of central Baja, the essence of the weathered bell persists.

I attempt to convince our guide to let me ring the bells, but he tells me they chime only on days when mass is held. And what right do I—a tourist who is not even Catholic—have to make such a request? More than the fact that ringing the bells is something to do, there is something in their wholeness, in the stillness of the space around them, even in their binding to the smooth wooden stake, that makes me want to reach out and create percussion, some resonance, to authenticate this experience in aural as well as visual ways. I want to give further personal meaning to their beauty: to create, if not a song, then at least a chorus that floats above and beyond this building, this valley, these mountains, the nearby sea—taking with it the pain of our past, the dark loneliness within, if only for those few sweet seconds of reverberation.

The French novelist Marcel Proust writes that the real voyage of discovery consists not in seeking new landscapes but in having new eyes. Maybe beauty is the same: everything is brilliant if we look at it not in greater detail but from a different perspective altogether. And sometimes that viewpoint is not by choice, as for the Packards and Ben's Bells, in which tragedy leads quite unexpectedly to loveliness, even as the loss itself is always present.

After dinner and bedtime stories, as Ann-Elise and Juliet brush their teeth, I think of the bells of San Borja, how they must have sounded as they rang at mass this morning—undoubtedly deeper than the hundred or more new bells around Tucson that chimed in the day's wind. The stories of those who found their own Ben's

Bells are pouring into news stations and posting to the organiza-
tion's website. Without exception, the discovery of a bell strung
with colorful beads in an ordinary place like a school parking lot
or a community garden is a significant finding for the recipient.
"What a moving and unexpected delight to find a Ben's Bell,"
says one person who shared her story of discovering a bell the
previous year. "I am a preschool teacher and brought the bell in
to share with my class of four- and five-year-olds. It created an
opportunity to talk about loss and sorrow and how to channel
one's feelings creatively; as well as talking about kindness and
how often the best gifts are not objects but rather what we give
from our hearts."

As I turn out the lights in my daughters' bedrooms, first Juliet
and then Ann-Elise, the wind chimes on our porch plink in
the breeze. I open the back door and step into the cool night.
Moths flutter beneath the porch light as the air itself flitters
with jasmine and desert bird-of-paradise. Beyond the tight
square of our backyard, the orange lights of Tucson wash into
darkness. To the east, a yellow moon hangs above the Rincon
Mountains. The wind is blowing in from those mountains this
evening, singing down the ridges, through shallow box canyons,
across the wash, into our yard. From here it continues west along
many paths, including the route my daughters and I took this
morning, perhaps nudging the Ben's Bells yet to be found. If I
listen closely, I may be able to hear them. If I close my eyes and
trust that the world still holds beauty, even in death, I may also
be able to hear the bells of San Borja. They ring and ring across
the fragrant night.

MY WILDFLOWER BROMANCE

Finding that I'm not at home, my friend Scott Calhoun—neighbor, landscape designer, and author of *Yard Full of Sun: The Story of a Gardener's Obsession That Got a Little Out of Hand*—dashes over to our activity center and waits almost diligently for my neighborhood board meeting to end.

As we convene, he rushes up to me with a sparkle (or perhaps mad gleam) in his eye: "What are you doing tomorrow and the next couple days?" It's a loaded question, I know.

"Working," I reply honestly. It is, after all, only two days until a big project is due.

He dismisses my priority and tells me we've got an emergency. After all the late winter rains, native flowers are blooming on both sides of the U.S.–Mexico border like they haven't in a decade or more. Reports have it, he says excitedly, that the flowers are nothing short of amazing at Sonora's Pinacate Biosphere Reserve, officially Reserva de la Biosfera El Pinacate y Gran Desierto de

Altar. He looks me in the eye and says without a hint of sarcasm, "This is a wildflower emergency. Are you in?"

No doubt many in the meeting behind me are similarly enthusiastic about the forthcoming baseball season, grilled, pepper-smothered footlongs and frothy beers balancing on armrests along the first base line, the crisp *pop* of the baseball ringing across the infield. Not Scott. And not me, for that matter. Spring training's got nothing on a good home stand of spring wildflowers.

"Hell yes, hermano. I'm in."

MONDAY, 2:44 P.M.

Our trip is confirmed, but we cannot leave until Tuesday because I'm taking care of my daughters while Billie attends class. Since Scott has to be back on Wednesday midday to meet with a client, and my project is due the following day, that leaves us roughly thirty hours to cover some six hundred miles, two languages, two national parks, three columnar cacti species each growing more than twenty feet tall, dozens of wildflower species of every imaginable color and maximum density (we hope), and one seafood restaurant in Puerto Peñasco, on the northern tip of the Sea of Cortés, to enjoy fresh sea ray tacos and cold Negra Modelo.

TUESDAY, 10:20 A.M.

We've just finished loading my Honda Accord, a malachite-green, four-door sedan logging 150,000 miles. What information on Pinacate there is—and there's not much—generally advises a *quatro por quatro*, but she's all I've got.

The snack collection we've assembled mirrors the hurried nature of our departure: turkey jerky, Fig Newtons, Swedish Fish candy, granola bars, husked almonds, and plenty of water. With all the gear we've packed—tent and lantern, sleeping bags and camera bags, tripods and wildflower guides, boxy coolers and wide-brimmed hats—you'd think we were driving the lonely road down Baja California rather than dipping into Sonora on one of Mexico's better roads.

11:11 A.M.

Less than an hour west of Tucson, as we're coasting down State Highway 86 before reaching Kitt Peak and the Baboquivari Mountains, a small hill rises from the cholla, saguaro, and mesquite dotting the landscape. My mind must be playing a trick on me because suddenly it's autumn and a massive stand of aspens is aflame. Because I lived in Colorado for years before moving to Tucson, it's the only metaphor for this vibrant yellow landscape I can find. Where, then, are the blue spruce and ponderosa pine? The chill in the air and the dusting of snow beneath turquoise sky?

As we approach, the illusion passes to the ecstatic realization that the hill, about a half-mile south of the highway, is blanketed in Mexican gold poppies and bright yellow bladderpod. Already we've seen wildly pink penstemon, orange globe mallow, waxy desert chicory, and owl's clover nearly glowing in its fuchsia blush—but nothing like this.

Not far from where a few other cars have stopped—drivers hunching over glossy hoods to stabilize their cameras—we slide into an opening on the road's shoulder, don our hats and camera bags, and set off for a hike. Despite the cactus, this is clearly rangeland, and we evade the barbed wire as we cross into the field. Immediately we are in a different world, and while the sun is higher than we would like, our first real stop for wildflower photos, still so close to Tucson, is an unexpected delight, and a great success.

1:19 P.M.

Through the Tohono O'odham Nation and into the town of Why, Arizona, we spot more but far smaller patches of poppies, and also Goodding's verbena, and pink, purple, and white globe mallow, a distinct and noteworthy difference from the more common orange blooms around Tucson. Turning south toward Mexico on Highway 85, we enter Organ Pipe Cactus National Monument and stop for some advice. At the visitor center, a park ranger tells us about her trip to Pinacate only last week, saying we won't be disappointed in the blooms, though in a passenger vehicle our range will be limited.

Don't underestimate the trusty Accord, I think, though I realize the last thing we want to do is get stuck in one of Mexico's largest deserts, especially when there's already a travel advisory for Sonora. (In fairness, the advisory is based on problems encountered along the New Mexico–Mexico border, leagues east of here.)

"You have two options," the ranger tells us. "Take Mexico 2 west out of Sonoyta and enter Pinacate from the north, where there are dunes and large volcanic outcroppings. But that's a rough road with a wash that's probably too risky to try without four-wheel drive." Alas.

"Or take Highway 8 south and enter the park from its south side, where the visitor center is located." After some discussion we agree this is the best plan, in part because we intend to camp in the park tonight and still need to register.

3:12 P.M.

There are times, and this is one of them, when we shouldn't give ourselves as much credit as may be due. Take Scott, for example.

He recently published a book, rich with text and photographs. That could, in theory, make him a professional photographer. And as his accomplice of sorts, that might make me a professional photographer, too. The problem, as we learned from a Pinacate Biosphere Reserve administrator—a serious, uniformed woman with a keen eye for protocol—is that to officially take photographs in a national park or biological preserve, there's a process that goes something like this:

1. You request permission, in writing, a month or more before your visit.

2. You await an affirmative response.

3. You provide a gift of thanks once you arrive.

For two tourists who have suddenly become professional photographers, this doesn't bode well. With the interpretive help of an actual professional photographer visiting from Mexico City, however, we are able to strike a deal: we may continue into the reserve to take photos and then return this evening to get the director's verbal blessing that will allow additional photography in the morning.

(At this point it's worth noting that Scott speaks Spanish fairly well. Your otherwise trustworthy narrator does not.)

4:04 P.M.

With the sun well past its zenith, any deal is a good deal, so with camping permit in hand I guide the manual transmission Accord slowly over the sand road and into the heart of Reserva de la Biosfera El Pinacate y Gran Desierto de Altar with the goal of making it to El Elegante Crater, a massive, near perfectly round volcanic crater formed some 150,000 to five million years ago by rising magma colliding with groundwater. The pressure from that prehistoric meeting resulted in an explosion with the power of an atomic blast, creating a series of bowls blown from the desert terrain, some a mile wide and a thousand feet deep.

Elegante is one such maar crater, and we fear the photographs will not adequately show the massiveness of the crater and its caldera, which at the bottom is ringed by poppies and also seems, along the dark red volcanic cliff edges, to create its own wind. Perhaps its own weather altogether.

Hiking along the edge, Scott and I are nearly speechless from the stark, geologic beauty of the crater and the surrounding landscape, with its wild collection of senita and saguaro cactus, stunted elephant tree, palo verde, ironwood, blooming ocotillo, and glowing teddy bear cholla. Though the flowers here are fewer—mostly the amber, daisylike brittlebush and some ground-dwelling, tiny purple beauties—the vastness of the scene is worth the trip alone.

And then I meet the Arizona blister beetle, which is not the legendary namesake of the park—the Pinacate beetle—that we hoped to see. Kneeling for a closer look, I call Scott over and while we don't mean to impose—apparently it is blister beetle mating season and their orgy is spread before us like the Moulin Rouge in miniature—we stick around a bit to watch the interesting black-and-orange insects. And since most are mating end-to-end or in more traditional hump-backed manners, there seems little concern with getting our own skin blistered, which is otherwise a legitimate risk of these cantharidin-carrying critters.

6:11 P.M.

As the shadows grow and the landscape begins to absorb the last light, taking on that golden desert glow we've waited for all day, we drive back toward the biological reserve station. Along the way, we take liberal stops to photograph the smooth green senita growing from the ashen soil between ironwoods. We photograph the rare Ajo lily. We photograph cholla and saguaro and ocotillo. As the light leaves, the yellow and on rarer occasion white evening primrose begin to open, giving us hope that tomorrow our wildflower expectations will not only be met but perhaps even exceeded.

TUESDAY, 4 A.M.

After hearing the wild pack of dogs and that singularly damned cricket all night—as short as the night was—I may have preferred to camp at Pinacate rather than falling into this budget hotel room just north of Puerto Peñasco. Still, my fellow wildflower chaser and I insisted on a seafood dinner last night, and we need to be on the road early this morning.

We're heading north on 8, into and through Sonoyta, and then west on 2, toward Mexicali. Between the administrator and the Mexico City photographer, we learned yesterday that kilometer markers 72 and 79 are the best (and perhaps only) places to stop along Highway 2, places where we can walk or drive a short distance into the park to make our photos.

Last night the Pinacate director never made it back to the park. The only gifts we could have offered, we realize, are the Sonoyta oranges at fifteen pounds for two dollars I unceremoniously backed up traffic to purchase on the Mexico side of the Sonoyta port of entry and the cold Dos Equis in the cooler. It turns out, however, that we needed that beautiful pairing for breakfast, so it's a good thing we didn't give them away.

5:26 A.M.

We've just turned south onto the cobbled dirt road off Highway 2, kilometer marker 72. Right away we know this is where we need to be. Primrose, sunflowers, sand verbena, and a number of others we cannot yet identify explode upon the sand dunes, for now lit only by the sweep of our headlights. While the inertia of magma and groundwater created the rare maar craters south of here, the inertia of millions of energy-clad seeds and a marvelously wet winter created this spectacular floral event—and we have to believe this is *the* peak day for blooms, as it was yesterday for the Mexican gold poppies and bladderpod along Arizona 86.

Words cannot convey what we hope and trust our photographs will, but here's some of what we see, set against sharp purple mountains in the background and shallow dunes in the fore: clumping violet sand verbena, pale cerulean lupine with airy geometrical leaves, western peppergrass atop the cheddar-colored dunes, large white evening primrose, a sea of dark-centered yellow sunflowers . . .

Scott and I make our own diverging paths as the sun begins to rise, being as careful as we can not to step on the plants—an impossibility, I quickly realize. By the time we return an hour and a half later we are, as poet A. R. Ammons reports, "At dawn returning, wet / to the hips with meetings."

The heavy dew on the plants covers our shoes and long pants. We are drenched, and drunk from the encounter. After burning through seventy-two old-school slides and more than a hundred digital shots, it's time for breakfast—the aforementioned, surprisingly fulfilling collection of oranges, granola bars, and cervezas.

9:08 A.M.

Back at Organ Pipe—after a requisite visit to a Sonoyta mercado and three carne asada tacos each—we have another decision to make: head home, arriving by lunchtime, or take the twenty-two-mile Ajo Mountain Drive into the rolling hills and small, sculpted mountains of Organ Pipe National Monument. After consultation with the ranger we met yesterday, we decide on the drive.

Once again, we are not disappointed. Beginning with a sprawling display of deep yellow flowering brittlebush against the burnt red scarps, we've discovered a psychedelic collection of flowers among organ pipe cacti and their driftwoodlike skeletons, saguaro, palo verde, and ever-present cholla. Here we see more Mexican gold poppies, globe mallow, penstemon, lupine, Esteve's pincushion, desert chicory, a wonderful light blue lily called covena, deep blue larkspur, chia, chuparosa, anemone, and desert marigold.

We are also happy to brake for a dirt-road traffic jam caused by a rattlesnake crossing, watching as the four-foot beauty settles beneath a roadside creosote, the airy, wax-leafed shrub famous for its rich desert aroma after rain.

3:22 P.M.

Pulling into our southeast Tucson neighborhood, we're hit by how much ground we've just covered. And we're exhausted in the best kind of way.

In addition to the photographs and the sheer adventure of it all, I've quickly developed a new relationship with many of the desert plants I had been taking for granted, like brittlebush and globe mallow. We see these common desert shrubs planted as single entities or perhaps grouped in twos or threes in yards and medians. But to see them in uncountable numbers along a jagged hillside, or rising out of a sandy wash, or even in haphazard rows along the side of the highway gives me a new appreciation.

So to them, and to my compadre Scott, and the Organ Pipe ranger, and the Arizona blister beetle, and the towering cacti, and the massive caldera, and the desert ironwood, and the late winter rains, and the resulting fields and hills and canyons of a raging floral fire, and to you, my dear readers, I give my thanks for this rare wildflower emergency.

THE BITER ON TAP

The walk to Yellowstone Valley Brewing Company from the Billings Sheraton is not easy. Those intimate with Montana's largest city may be quick to note the distance is barely a mile, a straight shot down First Avenue. But on this late winter afternoon in the mid-1990s, only the fiery discharges of the Conoco oil refinery lit the six full blocks. As I stepped from chipped sidewalk to icy street, freight cars reverberated on the Montana Rail Link, down past Division Street and into the shadow of the mesa to the north. Now and then, engine brakes echoed from Interstate 90 where it curves around the flat, gray scythe of the Yellowstone River. And the wind—cutting, ambitious—attacked my uncovered flesh and drove the snow at unnatural angles before me.

But the weather could not drive me back, for my goal was golden—or rather dark amber, with a rich and milky head, a spicy aroma of malt tinged with just-turned earth, a subtly glowing effervescence. I was after beer, handcrafted ales with names like Black Widow Oatmeal Stout and Renegade Red Extra Special

Bitter, and women and men both have labored through worse conditions than these for such a lofty pursuit. "Many battles have been fought and won by soldiers nourished on beer," said Frederick the Great, the Prussian philosopher-king known as one of Europe's most adept military leaders (yet also a staunch advocate of music, the arts, and religious tolerance). This was not even a skirmish.

At the time I made the trek to Billings for my work with the U.S. Department of Energy some thirty years ago, analysts alleged that the craft brewing movement was near its end. Though I logged microbrewery visits across the West like a birder tallies songbirds, brewing was an enterprise that wouldn't amount to much more than an unremarkable population of homebrewers overshadowed by ten national breweries, they said. That would leave only the leviathans to define our domestic beer options—Anheuser-Busch, Coors, and Miller Brewing Company—plus a few limited-distribution breweries like Lone Star in San Antonio and Samuel Adams in Boston. Today, however, there are more than 9,700 small breweries in the United States alone—regional craft breweries, microbreweries, taprooms, and brewpubs—a number that has nearly doubled in the last eight years. Clearly, the craft brewing movement did catch on, and the Brewers Association reports that craft beer industry production has grown more or less consistently, excepting 2020 thanks to the pandemic, over the last forty years. The result: 23.4 million barrels of handcrafted American beer produced in 2023, at a retail value of $28.9 billion.

Craft brewing is more than a retail phenomenon, however. It is woven throughout American culture—from local cuisine to regional music festivals, from environmental management to the fetishes of crazed collectors. Collectors, I learned on that blustery day in Billings, such as me.

By the time I reached Yellowstone Valley Brewing Company under a starless sky, only a few minutes before closing, I was ready for any beer the brewmaster and his rosy-cheeked staff could offer. Unfortunately, in my research I had not distinguished between microbrewery and brewpub. Only the latter serves beer brewed on premises, often with a food menu. Yellowstone Valley, located in a corrugated metal depot in the decaying Billings warehouse district, then brewed solely for distribution. And the sampling taps? Closed for the night.

Though not a religious man, I may well have prayed to Saint Arnold, the Belgian bishop canonized as the patron saint of beer for his eleventh-century brewing. Reprieve was granted, at least partly, when I asked the young bearded man about pint glasses. He stopped hauling kegs—the silver barrels gleaming in the tungsten light of the loading dock—then stepped into a tight doorway and out of sight. Moments later he returned with what he assured me was their last glass, a translucent stein in flawless condition for my expanding collection. In wickedly thin lettering that tapered to a point, the words *Black Widow* arced across one side, behind an image of a black widow spider, with its infamous red hourglass. Beneath those words: *Oatmeal Stout*, and finally the name of the brewery. I paid the generous man three dollars and turned to leave. Then, on a glossy poster hung beside the exit, I caught the beer's ingredient list:

Hops: Magnum, E. Kent Golding (British)

Malt: Pale, Caramel, Chocolate, Dextrin, Wheat, Roasted
    Barley, Flaked Oats, Spider

The walk back in the darkening night, the refinery flares at my back and the wind as reckless as ever, was inspired. Is spider truly an ingredient of the beer? That remains a mystery—a secret recipe, no doubt—but I enjoyed the Biter, as it's referred to locally, once I found my way back to the warm hotel bar.

Discovering breweries and collecting pint glasses entail a certain amount of adventure. Yet a passion for craft beer flows from a deeper tap and relies on a mixture rich in personal experience and local community. Handcrafted beer represents the industry, knowledge, and creativity of a distinct locale, a product that both results in and stems from a community's sense of place. Why drink widely manufactured lagers when there are thousands of handmade beers as distinct as the breweries from which they are poured? Why not share this noble truth with friends and neighbors who also seek a certain linkage to place?

I have visited perhaps 175 microbreweries and brewpubs, collecting more than three hundred glasses over the last thirty-five years. Without exception each glass tells a story, often hosting the brewery's award-winning lager or experimental ale before finding its place among the others on my shelf. In only a few rare circumstances, the glass had to be liberated—for its own good, of course. Why the now-defunct Bitter End Bistro & Brewery off Austin's hip Sixth Street didn't sell its elegantly curved glass is beyond me. But holding onto the vessel after downing the luxuriant Bat City Lager—a coppery ale without a hint of additives—seemed the only alternative. I hoped the tip made amends for my small crime, and check that sin into the same lonely chamber as the Belgian monastery full of brewing monks surely might, the building fronted by a sign that reads, "The good Lord has changed water into wine, so how can drinking beer be a sin?"

The prize of my menagerie is the pint glass from Fish Tale Wild Salmon Pale Ale, sold at the former Fish Brewing Company in Olympia, Washington. In addition to the salmon-tailed logo, five black-headed salmon swim the circumference of the glass, *Wild Salmon* scripted at its base. Fish Brewing was both microbrewery and brewpub, and when I had the good fortune of regularly traveling from Denver to Olympia for many years in the 1990s, my coworkers at the Washington State Energy Office initially suggested we dine there. Our conversation centered on resource efficiency—how a small town in California helped pay for the redevelopment of its downtown from streetlight savings, for example, and how electric utilities in South Dakota used geothermal energy for inexpensive heat. And how a handful of government employees could guide our respective energies to our own line of local lagers.

Yet I learned that beer by itself is not always enough. After that first Fish Brewing visit, I insisted on returning regularly. The menu provided no small amount of argument for frequenting the downtown pub, featuring grilled oysters, smoked wild salmon, and a thick seafood stew simmering with sea scallops, bay shrimp, and clams. Between the distinct, hoppy aroma of the brewing, the low sizzling of the brewery's organic house-made fries, and the spare calls of gulls off Budd Inlet, it is difficult to imagine a more enticing brewpub dining experience.

But for me there is one: Walnut Brewery. Boulder's first brewpub opened in the historic City Electric Building in 1990. Here, among the oak-paneled interior and against the backdrop of the iconic Flatirons, I first fell for handcrafted beer. When I moved to suburban Denver in summer 1991 straight out of college, I quickly made friends with other recent graduates, but our beer pursuits defaulted to the local bar, and the sanctioned beer was

Miller Lite. On one occasion we drove to Boulder and parked just outside the Pearl Street Mall, a downtown pedestrian mall adorned with ash, spruce, and open-air plazas where residents, tourists, and street performers gather in numbers. Local restaurants, art galleries, and bookstores line the four-block stretch. We passed through the crowd, around the sunken play area where boulders rise in islands from the sand, and onto Walnut Street. The brewpub's brick façade greeted us with wide, spherical lights that offset the slow stain of dusk.

We entered through glass doors to the mellow horns and brushing drums of a jazz quartet playing above us, on an outcrop of black metal stage cabled to the wall like the sliced bottom half of a first-generation elevator. The band's notes wafted down. The dusty but pleasant aroma of fresh barley and yeast wafted over. Laughter and talking and pouring and the tinkling of cutlery combined in harmony until I found myself in a whirl of pleasures that quite nearly pulled the soul from my body. I traveled then among the ether, for seconds or perhaps days. The tingling in my hands and feet did not subside until my return, until our kind server delivered the beer: Buffalo Gold. It was a full pint, with a resonant caramel base and thick, foamy head that quivered slightly at the edge of the glass but did not run over, nor falter in its slow retreat into the smooth body of the ale.

American mass-produced beer, with its meek undercurrent and frail, sudsy head, this was not. Bringing the Gold to my nose, it was light of scent—neither plain nor bitter, but passively spicy and grain-filled, an image of sun-tinged wheat fields a hundred miles to the east. Sipping now, it is clichéd to call it "liquid gold," and yet Buffalo Gold was to my palate the fair equivalent. All I had to compare it to was blown away. The Stroh's and skunky Mooseheads I snuck in high school, the Michelobs and Millers of my later college years—these all dwindled in the radiance of Walnut Brewery's craft-brewed ale. I closed my eyes and swallowed, letting the crisp finish, a hint of citrus at the cusp, take me. When again I opened my eyes, the world looked no different, yet it would never be the same again.

And then the food arrived: meatloaf of sirloin, pork, and sun-dried tomatoes in a brown ale mushroom sauce; top sirloin seared to nutty brown outside, tender pink inside, alongside garlic-buttered green beans; and blue corn enchiladas under a fine drizzle of sour cream, sided by red ale rice and shining black beans in a delicately spicy sauce. All fine choices, no doubt; but none as divine as the alder-smoked salmon fish and chips now resting before me. Dionysus surely approved from his ever-flowing tap atop Mount Olympus. Battered in brown ale, the salmon nestled among seasoned fries, brewery slaw, and remoulade sauce. I moved between the Gold, with its whispers of refreshment, and the fish and chips, with their bold affection for my tongue, in a haze of bliss (and possibly drool). Ordering another pint at meal's end as a sort of final evening praise, did I realize then that this would be the first of my craft brew symphony's many movements over the coming years?

There is no creation myth for beer, nor a single individual credited with crafting the first brew, even though Plato said, "He was a great man who invented beer." If anything, he was a *she*. Before modern times, women were primarily responsible for both cooking and brewing, often serving as religious brewmasters. In the Cerro Baúl colony that predated the Inca of southern Peru, for example, a brewery incorporating giant ceramic vats has been excavated. A series of intricate shawl pins found onsite leads to a singular conclusion: "The brewers were not only women, but elite women," says Donna Nash, adjunct curator at Chicago's renowned Field Museum. Likewise, in early Babylon, priestesses brewed beer under authority of the goddesses Siris and Nimkasi. "God bless the woman who gave birth to the brewer," says a Bohemian proverb. Indeed.

Ancient tablets suggest that beer was brewed at least seven thousand years ago in what is now Iran. Other references date back five thousand years—to China with its *kui* and to Egypt, where beer was an essential part of the diet of nobility and peasants alike. Beer was crafted from lightly baked barley stew, and it is widely held that it predated and, yes, gave rise to bread. Under the Egyptian pharaohs, beer served as drink, daily nourishment, and medicine. Nearly 20 percent of the prescriptions identified in a medical document dating to 1600 BCE contain the Egyptian hieroglyph for beer. It was a noble gift in ancient times as well—a requirement for one hoping to marry a princess, and the tithing to the gods, to the tune of thirty thousand gallons a year, by Pharaoh Ramesses II.

Though not prescribed today, beer serves as elixir nonetheless, especially for the idea of community. In the neighborhood of Civano where Billie and I raised our daughters, craft-brewed beers were as much a part of holiday celebrations as good food. When the girls were younger and we caroled, most of the fathers stood in back, small coolers in hand, and shared the latest batch of winter lager. The brews may have improved our singing or chased away the shyness, but there's more to it than that. Following trick-or-treating, we gathered most often in the front room of my house, where we compared costumes and sorted our children's caches as we drank pumpkin ale. At dinner parties and neighborhood potlucks, backyard movie nights and front porch gatherings, we shared handcrafted beer because lagers and ales support experiences as authentic as the places in which they are brewed.

Indeed, anthropologist and brewing historian Alan Eames credits beer with the creation of urban-rural society. "Beer was the driving force that led nomadic mankind into village life," he says. "It was this appetite for beermaking material that led to crop cultivation, permanent settlement, and agriculture." Regardless of its origins, beer moved from Egypt and the Middle East into Europe. The Egyptians taught the Greeks to brew, and they in turn passed the craft onto Romans, who introduced brewing to the Celtic and Teutonic tribes of Britain and central Europe. By the time Columbus sailed to America, brewing was a vast industry, undertaken largely by monasteries serving as inns across Europe. Columbus brought ale to the New World, where he found that the Indigenous peoples of Central America also brewed a concoction of "maize, resembling English beer." And it is well known—at least in the world of beer lovers—that the *Mayflower* made port at Plymouth Rock in Massachusetts instead of continuing on to Virginia in December 1620 primarily because of low beer rations aboard the ship.

By the late 1800s, brewing that once was as mysterious as alchemy became a reasonable enterprise for the average person. In 1920 thousands of local breweries across the United States crafted European-style lagers and ales. Yet they were laid low during the thirteen-year Prohibition. By the time that abolition of alcohol was repealed in December 1933, most breweries were gone, supplanted by speakeasies and shadowed distilleries concocting much stronger drinks. The craft brewing industry did not revive for more than fifty years, while megabreweries flourished at the expense of local ingenuity and economy.

Since 1979, when homebrewing was finally legalized in the
United States, the hobby has grown considerably—and unprepared kitchens are only now recovering thanks to the advent of
on-premise homebrew stores like Boulder's Beer Store. That's
where I first tried it, in spring 1998, with master homebrewer
Bruce Kirschner. A lean long-distance runner with barley-brown
eyes, cropped gray hair, and a Roman nose, Bruce had already
worked with me for a half-dozen years at Western Area Power
Administration in Golden, the home of juggernaut Coors. He
was my mentor in project management and facilitation, and he
excelled at both, weaving agreements among seemingly disparate
federal agencies, tribes, and municipalities on large hydroelectric
projects as easily, it seemed, as he crafted homebrew with names
like Bison Cream Ale, Wildfire Red, and Dr. Love's Magic
Porter. Whether binding agreement or brown ale, the results
were smooth and lasting.

Every now and then Bruce brought me a dark, unlabeled
bomber bottle full of his latest batch. I'd thank him kindly and
return the refillable bottle soon after. When his wife learned
about the new brew store in Boulder, she packed up his worn
brewing kit and reclaimed the kitchen. Bruce tried the Beer
Store on his own and, finding it up to his standards, recruited me
and two other similarly zealous coworkers.

Bruce walked us through the process slowly, which in most
general terms begins with making wort, a sweetened liquid
resulting from the combination of hops and the liquor of crushed
grains or barley malt extract. Brewing continues with fermenta-
tion—in which yeast turns the sugar in wort into alcohol and
carbon dioxide—and concludes with filtering, conditioning, and
packaging. At the Beer Store, that means mixing ingredients at
one of six low countertops, brewing at an adjacent kettle for a

couple hours, and then returning weeks later to bottle the beer. We agreed on two batches with an estimated yield of a keg each, or just over ten cases of the twenty-two-ounce bottles. It's no pharaoh's gift but would suffice. Then we settled on Uncle Pleasant's 90 Cents, billed as "a light red amber and the flavor is smooooooth," and Bumblin' Wheat Ale, an "ale-based wheat, lightly hopped, single-filtered for a slightly cloudy appearance, with an abundant honey flavor."

As our kettles came free, the store was as energetic as a beehive on a midsummer day. We opened the recipe book that offered more than a hundred brews, noted the ingredients, and got to work. Bruce floated between the chest-high kettles, mentoring us on proper stirring technique, how best to add grains, when to let the potions set. Once I saw him standing back against metal shelves stacked with drawers of ingredients, admiring his crew, a satisfied look on his face. But it was soon my turn to add the ingredients, so he came forward and guided me like the trained moderator that he was. By the time we finished, the hour was late and a snowstorm approached. Though I didn't linger that evening, the anticipation of bottling our brew kept me on track the next two weeks.

We returned on another cool evening, boxes clinking with the empty bottles Bruce provided. Tapping our refrigerated half-kegs near the back of the store, we formed an awkward assembly line at a bottling station unpacking, tipping, pouring, and capping. After the first few bottles we had an undeniable rhythm—a dance in honor of bringing chemistry to craft and craft to consumable—a motion we maintained until leaving the four remaining bottles uncapped.

We gave cheers and thanks, then clinked the chestnut-colored bottles and took a sip. Once again I was transported to an

ethereal place—a fragrant hollow of wildflowers, the rich scent
of pollen and the slow bees happy in their burden. But one of
the bees turned on me, zipping around my head and then down
my throat, where its honey-tipped stinger lingered. It wasn't the
finish I hoped for—but its brashness slid behind me, lurching
me back to the store and these friends with whom I first brewed.

The Beer Judge Certification Program—certifying some 6,600
active members who have judged more than two million different beers in nearly thirteen thousand sanctioned competitions
worldwide—provides style guidelines for beer, mead, and cider.
While I am an enthusiast, I have not sat the three-hour exam.
There are other, less official ways to participate in competitions
and festivals. These festivals, Billie and I discovered when we
volunteered at the Boulder Fall Festival in 1993 and 1994, are not
unlike Renaissance fairs, and as in those ages, bartering prevails.

Whether by choice or blind luck, we worked the first shift of
the beer tent each year. The crowds were thinner from 10 a.m. to
1 p.m., and we quickly learned the unwritten code: serve paying
customers first, serve yourself in-kind second—but always serve.
By the time the sweet smell of bratwurst and grilled onions teased
the air and children dragged parents through the rattling carnival
rides, all this drinking built up a vigorous hunger. Coincidentally,
the amiable folks over at the Old Chicago pizza tent found their
palates dry after baking all those pies. It was natural, then, for the
sharing to begin—pizza for pitchers of beer, pitchers for pizza, a
fair trade by most any standard.

The festival was the ideal location on those crisp late-
September mornings to taste not only old favorites like Buffalo
Gold but new brews like Tabernash Weiss, a German wheat
brewed at Tabernash Brewery in Longmont, just up the road

from Boulder. I recall those weekends largely because of the Weiss, which with one exception—a rare unfiltered rye served to me on a glorious day in Austin—is the best beer I've ever had. But it didn't start that way. Directly following the fresh Gold, the cloudy Weiss tasted muddled, with an intriguing though unsettling bubblegum aftertaste. Yet the more I drank this Bavarian brew—at the festival and then almost religiously thereafter—the more fascinated I became. What I mistook for bubble gum I now deciphered as clove, banana, and nutmeg. The cask-conditioned, top-fermenting ale was unfiltered, the yeast remaining in suspension. Pour it into a glass from the simple brown bottle but stop just before reaching the last ounce or two. Swirl to suspend the yeast, then pour the remaining beer. Now hold the clear glass to the light and Tabernash Weiss drinks it in like honey, thick as coastal fog yet radiant as morning's first light.

This tale, however, has an unhappy ending. Though the Weiss consistently received judges' highest ratings, taking a gold medal at the Great American Beer Festival, Tabernash Brewery merged with Left Hand Brewing Company in 1998, and Weiss production was phased out.

After moving in 2000 from Denver, with its dozens of microbreweries and brewpubs, to Tucson, with a mere four at the time, I made several trips back to the Front Range to retrieve the Weiss. In 2002, however, the bad news greeted me like a series of insults—at every liquor store between Denver and Boulder, and we checked half a dozen, there was no Tabernash, no Weiss. Finally, I visited Left Hand Brewing Company itself and remained seated to take the news of the beer's demise. Though I did find one last six-pack at a small neighborhood store, it could only carry me and my friends through a single night, the evening precious, fleeting.

· · · ·

Queen Elizabeth I noted that "a meal of bread, cheese, and beer constitutes the perfect food." In modern-day America the consumption of beer is not without its detractors, and guys with formidable "beer bellies" don't help the cause.

A weeklong road trip I took with two buddies to Baja California Norte may or may not bear witness. Every afternoon and into evening we drank Tecate, the ubiquitous lager brewed since 1944 in the mountain town of the same name forty miles east of San Diego. A slice of lime added, perhaps, to its vitamin C content. Yet on our return, Billie eyed my midriff plaintively and ordered me on the scale. Much to my surprise—given our daily hikes—I gained twelve pounds, more than 5 percent of my body weight, and was at my heaviest ever. Billie eyed my pint glass collection warily and wondered aloud whether sparkling water boasts such a following. The challenge is in determining whether my new heftiness was a result of the beer or the rich fish tacos we delighted in at almost every meal. Three deep-fried filets of dorado surrounded by corn tortillas and cabbage, topped with spiced carrots, salsa, and guacamole—though the ingredients differed slightly at each roadside taco stand, none disappointed, at least until I stepped on that scale. Since I cannot return to Baja without drinking Tecate nor without eating tacos de pescado, the mystery remains.

Health has long been a concern for brewers and drinkers alike. During the thirteenth century, children were more often baptized in beer than water. Given the polluted nature of nearby water sources, beer was the safer bet—something Saint Arnold of Soissons knew and preached. Consumer protection was also at the forefront of the Bavarian Purity Law of 1516, which allowed only three ingredients in beer: water, barley, and hops. (Yeast was then unknown.) The Foster's Group reports that at one English school in the late 1600s, students were given an allowance of two beers a day in lieu of the unpalatable water.

For the brewers of Fat Tire Amber Ale—with its toasted malt and moderate hop flavors clothed in a seductive auburn hue— community health and longevity are both brewmaster's passion and corporate goal. New Belgium Brewing Company, founded near downtown Fort Collins, Colorado, was the first microbrew- ery to acquire all its energy from renewable resources—wind off the slopes of Colorado and Wyoming and methane released from onsite water treatment. Employee-owned, New Belgium employs a director of social and environmental impact whose oversight reads like a 350.org narrative: greenhouse gas emission reduction, healthy watersheds, green building, and waste reduc- tion, all under the umbrella of social equity. It's no surprise that Fat Tire became America's first certified carbon-neutral beer in 2020. I once toured the remarkable New Belgium facility, though it is difficult to say whether I found the energy-recovery systems or admirable selection of beers in the tasting room more enticing.

Back in Tucson, with its azure sky and cactus-lined ridges, New Belgium's specialty brews remind me that, even in my own locality, a onetime scarcity of breweries does not equate to a lack of quality or community concern. Supporting local breweries like New Belgium in Colorado or Yellowstone Valley in Montana means boosting the local economy and spirit. It means creating communal joy.

About a decade after we moved to Tucson, I learned that Nimbus Brewing Company, then Arizona's largest microbrew- ery, also sought to build community—by creating a mixed-use brewpub, with condos and apartments above, in Tucson's redevel- oping downtown. Nimbus has long been poured at many Tucson restaurants, its intricately decorated bottles packed into nearly every store's cooler.

One quiet evening some twenty years ago now, I found my way to the brewery's original taproom, located in a dark corner of an industrial park. There was a raucous crowd emphatically dancing to Kiss's classic "Rock and Roll All Nite" as I entered. I sampled the Dirty Güera, a southwestern-style blond ale brilliantly laced with honey from the historic mining town of Bisbee, forty-five miles to the southeast. The beer was crisp, light-bodied, with a noticeable sweetness.

As the 1970s rock anthem pulsed through the speakers, though, I was taken even further back, to a January evening in Denver, to a Kiss concert itself—yet another of the band's reunions in full regalia. I am not ashamed to admit it was a wildly entertaining show. The hard rock riffs and melodramatic ballads I grew up listening to offset the band's infamous pyrotechnics and, in a wholly adequate plastic cup gracing my right hand, a Fat Tire Amber Ale. In one divine stroke of good fortune, two distinct cultures came whirling together, and among the thousands of black-clad and face-painted fans—their leather and chains and tattoos like an orgy of mosaic tilework against the arena's hard plastic seats—I was the sole beneficiary. All the young-lust lyrics, each heavy metal chord, and Paul Stanley's crooning—oh yes, he still had it—mixed into the gorgeous, glowing red of the hand-crafted ale as it sung down my eager throat. Can there possibly be another evening so perfect?

The answer is yes. As long as craft-brewed lagers and ales flow from their jeweled taps, as long as autumn festivals unite local beer with local cuisine against a backdrop of artisans, and as long as beer batter and beer bread, beer marmalade and beer bratwurst steam from gleaming kitchens—as long as these inalienable rights remain, there will be uncountable perfect evenings to come.

Let the wind ride in all its passion across the Billings basin. Let alien refinery flames erupt into the night. Yellowstone Valley Brewing Company announces the opening of its Brewhouse Garage Pub. The Biter is on tap, and a new pint glass calls across the miles for my covetous collection.

THE DAYS OF THE DEAD

Draped in black plastic, I lie in darkness. This is not a metaphor. Instead, it's a snapshot of my last half-week in the tight confines of our two-car garage, a hammer and nails, spray paint, staple gun, and duct tape my only company. Tomorrow night marks our neighborhood Halloween party, and the haunted garage, an annual tradition since before we moved to Tucson, is the big draw. The haunting isn't ready quite yet, but with the assistance of ten-year-old Ann-Elise and seven-year-old Juliet, and three days off work, we're nearly there. Good thing, because the pressure to outshine the previous year's production (haunted pirate ship, that one, and magical haunted castle the year before) is real.

Outside, the autumn wildflowers of the backyard hold the morning sunlight, though it's difficult to feel the turning season when the temperature still hovers near ninety. But Tucson is not Denver, where this tradition began, and I accept the warmth knowing that October evenings are already below freezing farther north. Here in the Old Pueblo, we hope for a different kind of chill as neighbors steal through the scary scenes, faces painted in fear or delight. Nearly as rewarding is the act of creating the spooky space, designing the rooms, and placing the wide range of gaudy and cherished decorations alike.

This year the theme is straightforward: haunted house. But we hope the outcome is far from common. Visitors enter beneath a veil of black light that reveals a scaffolding of dime-store cobwebs and lanky rubber spiders. Kitschy stuff, to be sure, but that's the fun. So, too, is the homemade doorway painted in the remaining moss-green paint used most recently on our living room walls. That *Beetlejuice*-inspired portal leans like an exaggerated Gothic buttress, framed by torches hanging in crooked sconces, their cloth flames an argument of crimson and orange. Beyond the gateway, the graveyard is edged by a rickety picket fence while an overhead strobe throws quick shadows—an easy substitute for lightning if I ignore the paced *tik tik tik* of the lamp. That won't be an issue once *Spooky Sounds of Halloween* is playing on the CD player, its wails, moans, and chain-rattling always a big hit. The cemetery grows from a tangle of branches. Fitted with Styrofoam headstones, it is also laced with plastic insects and reptiles that glow aquamarine in the black light. In the adjacent portico, hanging skulls and jack-o-lanterns also glow, and beneath them dried artichoke blooms from our community garden, now painted neon green and orange, are sure to contain some evil pollen that wafts like harbor fog (except there's not enough ventilation to run the fog machine, alas). Next up: a homemade shelf backlit by amber lights. A cauldron bubbles, its aroma subtle, disturbing—the right concoction for this over-the-top ambience. On the cupboard, an eclectic mix of bottles are misshapen, full of leaves and once-living things (the flagon of tarragon vinegar that spoiled two years back, for instance). A half-open wooden sailor's locker, passed down from my wife's father, reveals an arm and leg poised for escape, an unnatural red light leaking from the iron latch. Above the chest, the skeletons of past victims hang with dark glee—or fake blood at least. Beyond the dungeon's exit sits a school desk, an heirloom Singer sewing table, topped by a green-eyed raven that croaks Poe's famous refrain as I pass. A life-size skeleton says nothing, however, as it waits in school robes for the day's lessons. My daughters will scratch those onto the chalkboard soon enough.

From there we turn the corner to…emptiness. Is this the final absence of good, the void from which no one returns? No, it's simply the last room unfinished, much to my chagrin. But walking through the phantom sights lands an idea, and twenty minutes later I concoct a shelf from a garbage can lid, fasten it to the ceiling, and mount a computer projector on top. A white sheet that served as the sail from last year's pirate ship becomes the tattered screen. After half an hour on a clip-art website, I have assembled the Halloween scenes: miscreants and minotaurs, scorpions and skulls. That completes the final room, plus a table spun in black cloth, a globe at its center that channels blue current when touched.

Three long days and nights to craft all this? Have I gone mad? Time well spent, my daughters suggest in not so many words as they race through the rooms of the garage with their widest smiles once they're back home from school. Now that I've finished spray-painting ghouls and scowls and creepy eyes on the glossy black walls and stepped outside to breathe the fresh air, I can think clearly enough again to agree: it was time well spent—though I probably have gone a little mad.

As a boy, I looked forward to Halloween as much as the next kid. I think back on the plastic masks, the pillowcases heavy with the night's sugary haul. As I grew into high school and then college, however, the delight waned so that only the occasional "trick or liquor" raid on a neighbor's apartment kept me intrigued. How, then, do I explain this infatuation—for this haunted garage marks our fourteenth year? We've owned houses for that long as well, but I began crafting costumes and overdecorated porches at my friends' homes even before. Whatever the reason, Halloween has become a family affair. By midsummer, Ann-Elise and Juliet are planning decorations. Their input is vital, a growing excitement Billie and I tap. Halloween is the defining ritualistic holiday for our clan—a growing tradition I find easy to hold, build on, and return to: what we might call *heritage* had we the traditions of our parents to compare.

My mother is Swedish, the only child of a Swedish air force officer and attaché to the United States. She had two cousins who, like her, immigrated to America: Marianne lived in Kansas City, Gunilla on a small ranch in Sonoita, thirty miles southeast of our Tucson home. My mother used to say that if she were born a male, she would be the Swedish equivalent of a count and would have inherited the palace at Ållonö, south of Stockholm on the edge of the sea, where she grew up. Her mother was Countess Gunilla Hamilton, countess by marriage, but the line of royalty, handed down to males, stopped there.

My father is American, of Scottish heritage generations back. Buntin, my last name and the last name of my daughters, derives from Bunting, a small and often colorful songbird. In Scotland, there are snow buntings, corn buntings, Ortolan buntings, rustic buntings, and reed buntings. Given the elegance and freedom of birds, it is an honorable name. Compare it to "bean picker," which is the meaning of my mother's maiden name, Bancroft.

The American indigo bunting is a delightful species of bird

with a lyrical call and sapphire feathers. Ranging through much of the United States during the summer to Central America and the West Indies in winter, it migrates at night, using stars for guidance. The songbird is also the namesake of one of my earliest published poems. I wanted to name our first child Indigo—Indigo Buntin—in honor of the bird and, in some admittedly selfish way, to give my poem more life, linking daughter with poem. My idea was then to paint the lines of the short poem around our daughter's nursery. Billie didn't go for it. She didn't mind the poetry lining the room, but she disliked the name Indigo, thinking it too clever. She was afraid that I'd shorten it to Indy. Though I love our first daughter's name—Ann-Elise—I still think about what could have been. So instead I've named my blue car Indigo. I call her Indy, for short.

I traveled to my mother's Swedish home only once when I was young. My older brothers and sister visited during the summers, and they learned to speak some of the language. Yet the stories our mother told of Sweden are few, even as she painted a northern fairyland. She never told us Swedish legends, though she was told those myths by Nana, her favorite grandmother. She spoke of Nana often, and in time asked our children to call her Nana. Nana Diana, my mother, did not pass the stories on to her grandchildren before she too passed from this world.

For my mother, telling stories of her heritage—of *our* heritage—was difficult not because she could not remember them, but because in remembering them she suffered. She longed for those times, which could not be replicated in America. When I was a child, her Christmastime story made me long for a place I could only imagine, for open sleigh rides in Scandinavian evenings I would never know. Though my sister scorned our mother's unwillingness to share, my strongest feeling is loss. In America, in a country that prides itself on an eclectic mix of many heritages, my heritage was lost in a single generation. All I can relate are the two or three stories I recall from my youth, and what I find in books of Swedish lore. As with any collection of tales, some have more relevance than others, and to these I find an affiliation, but an affiliation of nation rather than family. The essential *telling* of the stories is gone.

When I returned home the other evening, before preparing the heavy work of the haunted garage, I found my daughters on our front porch. They were excited, photographing a spider that had woven a beetle beneath the dim light. The creature's huge abdomen and delicate legs fascinated us as the spider spun the prey around and around. As I tucked Ann-Elise into her bed later that evening, she asked what I thought of the arachnid. If it was deadly, like a black widow, she knew I wouldn't like it within easy reach. But this was an orb weaver. So I told her what my mother long ago told me: in Sweden, spiders are good luck. Ann-Elise knew that meant we wouldn't disturb it. She knew too that the threads of heritage—those practices and legends handed down from the past—are important to me, just as they are to her. In her spare time, and now for a larger school project, she has assembled a report and expanding scrapbook on Sweden. "I'll have to add that spiders are good luck," she said as she closed her eyes before I slipped out of the room.

We spin our own myths every day—in the rituals of bedtime conversations, in our observations of the world around us, in the ways we celebrate holidays like Halloween. Like America itself, however, these myths are still new, fluid, often unanchored to a deeper place. What we seek is that anchorage—the heritage that helps define who and perhaps some of *why* we are.

· · · ·

Two thousand years ago, the Celtic peoples marked the end of summer and the autumn harvest as the new year—what is today November 1. It was the beginning of winter: the long, dark season of death. But it was also cause for celebration and spiritual encounter. On October 31, Druids held the festival of Samhain (pronounced *sow-in*). They constructed enormous bonfires to sacrifice crops and animals to their gods. As these sacred bonfires raged into the evening, Celts extinguished their smaller family fires. They believed that on this evening, "the boundary between the worlds of the living and the dead became blurred," according to History.com. Ghosts returned to the Earth, and in their return they undertook mischievous acts, including damaging crops. But their presence made Druidic predictions of the future all the easier, and for "a people entirely dependent on the volatile natural world, these prophecies were an important source of comfort and direction." During Samhain, the Celts dressed in the skins and heads of animals, not to scare off the ghosts but rather to be recognized as fellow spirits and so ignored. The ceremony ended and the new year began when Celtic families relit the family hearths from the flames of the bonfires, rekindling light and heat for the coming winter.

Samhain morphed as the Romans and then the Catholic Church increased their hold over traditional Celtic lands. Over a span of four hundred years, the Romans combined the Druidic rites with the autumnal festival of Feralia—the late-October day dedicated to remembering the dead—and with a day to honor Pomona, the Roman goddess of fruit and trees. As Christianity moved north, the church created its own sanctioned day to replace the persistent Celtic festival, as a means to absorb (if they couldn't completely dismantle) lingering pagan beliefs. In the seventh century, Pope Boniface IV designated November 1 as All Saints' Day—called *Alholowmesse* in Middle English. The night before All-hallowmass, or All-hallows, became All Hallows' Eve, and eventually Halloween. In 1000 CE, November 2 became All Souls' Day, a day to honor the dead, celebrated similarly to Samhain: costumes, parades, bonfires. The combination of All Hallows' Eve, All Saints' Day, and All Souls' Day was known for centuries as Hallowmas.

In preindustrial England and my father's ancestral Scotland, All Souls' Day festivals included parades during which the poor begged for food. Families along the route passed out "soul cakes," pastries provided in return for the beggars' promises of praying for the family's dead relatives. The church encouraged the dispersal of soul cakes as a replacement for the food and wine traditionally left for roaming spirits. Eventually, this "going-a-souling" became a pastime of children, who moved from house to house in search of food, ale, and money—the forerunner to modern-day trick-or-treating.

European immigrants brought their Halloween customs to America, but the rural nature of the colonies and strict Protestant belief systems of New England limited the celebration's spread. In the southern colonies, autumn festivals called "play parties" were held to celebrate the harvest, and these included the sharing of ghost stories, fortune-telling, dancing, and singing. Fall festivals were common by the middle of the nineteenth century, though Halloween as a custom was still not widespread. Following the 1846 potato famine, millions of Irish Catholics immigrated to America, helping to popularize the holiday. By the late 1800s, though, "there was a move in America to mold Halloween into a holiday more about community and neighborly get-togethers, than about ghosts, pranks, and witchcraft," reports History.com. In doing so, "Halloween lost most of its superstitious and religious overtones."

Anoka, Minnesota, held America's first official observation of Halloween in 1921 with a pumpkin bowl, costumed square dance, and parades. New York City and Los Angeles held citywide celebrations just a few years later. By the 1950s, Halloween shifted from adult-focused dances and other social events to activities for the young. Trick-or-treating revived, and celebrations moved from town squares and civic centers into homes and classrooms (though given its lingering religious contexts, the elementary school where my wife teaches has replaced "Halloween" with "Fall Festival"). Today, Halloween is as commercial as any American holiday: more than $12.2 billion is spent annually on festivities, making it second only to Christmas in consumer spending.

Color me guilty. Though I don't subscribe to the many All Hallows' Eve superstitions—black cats and flying witches and ringing bells to keep evil spirits away—I contribute heartily, and happily, to the crazy consumerism that Halloween has become. Is the cause of my spending just good fun, or is there something richer at work? If Halloween has become the important annual ritual for our family, what does it mean for heritage—the northern European heritage of our ancestors, and the American heritage we bestow upon our children?

Death, and the fear of death, are the prevailing elements in Halloween—and in many myths. The Celts welcomed the dead during a wild night of fire and festival, even as they feared these unknown spirits. For the Swedish and for the northern lands of my mother, the festivals more often praise the light and the living: Saint Lucia Day, a mid-December celebration of the young bearer of light; Walpurgis Night, a Viking festival honoring the return of spring; and Midsummer's Eve, a fertility rite held on the summer solstice in which the Maypole was a phallic symbol for the impregnation of Mother Nature in hopes of an abundant autumn harvest. Yet many Swedish legends focus on death, too, and since my mother died, they have the most resonance, the deepest link perhaps, to my Scandinavian heritage. In some of these tales, death, rather than a long-awaited vacation or a carefree retirement, is a reward for the hard work of life. One in particular begins on a farm at the edge of a forest—a landscape, I can imagine, not far from the girlhood home of my mother. It goes something like this:

A farmer, looking for his runaway horse, climbs deep into the forest along a thin trail. As he crosses a ravine he hears a sudden hissing and looks down to find a large snake trapped between crevice and boulder.

"If you set me free, I'll see that you get your just reward," says the snake. The man, agreeing to help, presses his staff into the crevice, beneath the rock, and with much work pries it up. The snake pulls himself out and then says, "Thank you. Now come over here so I may give you your just reward."

"What is my just reward?" the man asks.

"Death," replies the snake, and cocks back as if to strike.

"I'm not so sure I'm ready for that," says the farmer, stepping back. "Let's ask the first creature we see what my just reward should be."

Before long a bear lumbers into view. "Bear," asks the farmer, "what is my just reward?"

"Death," replies the bear, rumbling past without another word.

"See," says the snake, "now it is time."

The farmer suggests that they ask one more creature, and

then the decision will be final. The snake agrees reluctantly, and shortly they meet a fox, who replies, "Death is your just reward, of course."

"Excellent!" hisses the snake. His eyes glint and tongue flickers. "It is time for my bite to kill you."

When the fox hears this, he holds up a paw and says, "Wait a moment, please. This must be closely considered. First, tell me what has happened." The man quickly explains how the snake was stuck and then freed. "Let's go back and see exactly how it was," says the fox.

The snake leads them back along the trail to the crevice. When they arrive the fox directs the man to lift the rock again with his staff, telling the snake to slide back as he was when stuck. Once the snake is in place, the fox tells the man to lower the rock a bit, which he does.

"Is this how you were caught before?" asks the fox.

"No," hisses the snake. "It was tighter." So the fox tells the farmer to lower the boulder even more.

"Was it tighter than this?" asks the fox.

"Yes."

The fox points for the man to lower the boulder all the way. "Now are you stuck as you were before, snake?" says the fox.

The snake strains and then wheezes, "I am stuck worse than before!"

"Good," says the fox, "then you two are even."

Without a deliberate passage of tradition, how are we to define our just rewards, and so ourselves? With two daughters vying for constant attention, the concepts of evenness and rewards are liquid at best. I am not aware of related Swedish myths that lend wisdom or guidance, and yet I am sure that parables for sharing and sisterhood exist there as well as in other cultures. Lacking an oral heritage, then, we look to the written legends. More often, we create our own.

As the Halloween season nears, and light stretches like a web across the wide valley of our desert home, I recall a landscape nearly as arid and just as ripe with hauntings. In Denver, where my family and I lived before moving to Tucson in 2000, we owned a clapboard bungalow built in 1903. Located on a corner of maple-lined streets, much of the home had been restored before we purchased it in 1998. We moved in just in time to celebrate Ann-Elise's first birthday. The oak floors had been refinished, the kitchen updated with new appliances and glass-fronted cabinets. In the 1960s, the attic had been converted to an apartment with a separate rear entrance. Our plan was to make this a master suite. The day we moved in, I took a sledgehammer to the wall between the pantry and the back stairwell. Weeks later, the doorway complete, we refurbished the upstairs bathroom and recarpeted the rest of the unit. It was a strange set of rooms, and oddest of all was a small door, three feet high, that led from the sitting area to an unfinished crawl space running the length of the room. The door had a handle on the sitting room side only.

Our garage, located on an alley, was both too small and too unstable to host the haunted garage we initiated several years earlier. Instead, I decorated the large, sloping front porch with black, green, and violet lights, spiders and floppy bats hanging by the dozens, and life-size skeletons perched in wicker chairs near the door. It was chilly the evening of our first Halloween, so Billie stayed home to hand out candy as I strolled the nearby blocks, watching my footing on the uneven sidewalks, Ann-Elise swaddled in the plush purple of her favorite Teletubby. When we returned, Billie described the creative costumes of our neighbors, the howls and laughter emanating from the back alley, and noises that appeared to come from upstairs: the branches of a silver maple drumming our roof in the wind, we guessed.

It was not uncommon to hear noises in that old house, and the single-pane windows did little to keep the clamor of the avenues from coming in. One evening, we were jolted awake by a gunshot that echoed through the rooms as if the gun wielder was just outside. Petrified, our first thought was of Ann-Elise, who slept between us. Billie tucked our daughter into her bosom and we crawled into the sitting room, where we finished the night in fits of sleep. Another night, I awoke from the reverberation of a large *crack*, as if the main joist of the roof had split. I lunged out of bed and, with flashlight in hand, patrolled the upstairs, the rear stairwell, and throughout the main floor, finding nothing. After a half-hour, apprehensive nonetheless, I returned to bed. The next morning I saw white dust on the kitchen floor and looked up to find a bulge fractured by a three-foot-long crevice. Old houses are full of surprises, and we wondered what treasure—or tribulation—the fissure would bring.

Though unpredictable, the odd sounds an old house invariably makes were not completely unexpected. Other sounds were—like the scraping Billie heard one night as she slept on the loveseat upstairs. She hurtled into the bedroom, face colorless, insisting the noise was not rats or squirrels as I had just proposed, half-asleep with Ann-Elise on my chest. (Often, the only way to get Ann-Elise to sleep at a reasonable hour was for me to hum to her, pressed against me, in our bedroom upstairs. I usually fell asleep in that position, too.) Or the evening I was out in the yard with our dog Khloe, Ann-Elise already asleep in our bed. Billie had just stepped out of the upstairs shower when she heard that familiar humming from our bedroom. Thinking I was in the room, she entered to find Ann-Elise alone, the room abruptly silent.

Despite our passion for Halloween, we had no rituals to ward off real spirits, and Billie in her mothering sense is certain the bungalow was haunted. Her theory is that a child once lived in the apartment and, as punishment, was locked into the dark space between the walls. Cruel discipline, indeed. Perhaps it was this ghost of a young girl or boy, and not the two frail nails hammered into a single piece of wood, that let the cooking chimney slip and crack the kitchen ceiling? No treasure—just old bricks, sooty and shattered.

These stories are now a part of our Halloween tradition, not told widely but told with meaning and suspense. They create a link between our Tucson home, the only residence our younger daughter Juliet has known, and the Denver home where Ann-Elise spent eighteen months. That bungalow represents a transitory time in our lives; we were never fully comfortable, despite the endless hours it absorbed, and began looking for another home, in the end another city, less than a year after moving in. It also represents the deeper passage every family must make, the difficult decisions about what defines home, what history brings with it, and what part the family will play that might, one day, be looked upon as heritage. Our part, it seems now as then, was to fix the place and move on. And release the apparition within? In the end, I cannot attest to the delivery of a spirit other than our own. Perhaps that was our just reward.

In the desert, on a dark evening following Halloween, there is a tradition dating only to the 1990s, though its origins go back perhaps thousands of years. The All Souls Procession, held on the streets near downtown Tucson, brings together ten thousand people who march and dance and strut through a two-mile route that ends with a fiery finale—the burning of an urn brimming with the written blessings and prayers for loved ones since departed. Throughout the procession, people wear masks of all colors, don costumes of skeletons and angels and devils, play instruments lavishly decorated, lift photographs and artwork and other reminders of those who have died. It is a wild reminiscence, perhaps, of Samhain, but here the spirits are not feared and unknown. Instead, they are welcome. They are family members and friends no longer on the Earth, at least in physical form, but who are missed, remembered still. The annual event has become one of Tucson's defining cultural events—a part of the region's communal heritage.

Richer still in the deserts of the Southwest and throughout Mexico is el Día de los Muertos—the Day of the Dead—held on the first two days of November in connection with All Saints' and All Souls' Days. Anthropologists believe the festival, which is the inspiration for Tucson's All Souls Procession, stems farther back even than Samhain, perhaps three thousand years. When the Spanish conquistadores arrived in what is now Mexico, they were appalled to find Indigenous peoples mocking death. But the Aztecs, like the Mayans and Olmecs before, were not mocking. Rather, they were commemorating death; for unlike the Spaniards with their linear calendars and sense of time, the Aztecs saw death not as an end but as part of a continuum, a recurring event as natural and welcome as life itself. In the ninth month of the *xiuhpohualli* calendar (early August), the Aztecs praised the goddess Mictecacihuatl, the Lady of the Dead, a goddess who died at birth. The goddess presided over the rituals, where Aztecs displayed the skulls they kept as trophies, remembering those who passed before and could come again. Such was the cyclical nature of the Aztec calendar.

As with the Celts, the Aztecs and their celebrations could not be eliminated by the Catholic Church, though no doubt its priests and missionaries tried, and horribly so. Instead, it moved them to coincide with the existing days of Hallowmas. Like many of Mexico's religious events, el Día de los Muertos today is a mix of Aztec and other Indigenous rites and Catholic ceremony. At its core is the belief that during these days, souls of the departed return to visit the living. When they arrive, family members communicate with the souls, passing along prayers and wishes. To bridge the spirits' passage from the land of the dead, families visit graves with offerings. Orange marigolds called *cempoalxochitl* in the Aztec language of Nahuatl, meaning "twenty flowers," further attract the souls of the dead, their strong scent leading them back to the land of the living.

In America and many regions of Mexico, el Día de los Muertos is celebrated primarily through the construction of altars containing a mix of favorite foods and drink, candles, *flor de muerto*, sugar skulls decorated by family members, photos of those who have passed on, and other memorabilia. In our Tucson neighborhood of Civano, both the elementary school and neighbors participate. This year, Juliet created an altar for the first time, following instructions from Gail Arrenholz, a neighbor whose son died just a few years earlier. Gail finds healing, in part, through the creation of a large neighborhood altar on her front porch. It is a beautiful and moving sight: candles wash the home's tawny walls, casting warm light on large acrylic paintings of Gail's son and other relatives. Metal sculptures of skeletons and lizards line the walls and frame the floor, creating their own enticing shadows. Rising as a stepped pyramid, and spanning a large table, the altar features dishes of foods—nuts, raisins, chocolate bars, pastries—plus pomegranates, the fruit of the dead in Greek tradition. The pungent scent of marigolds fills the air as bright flower petals line the assemblage, a sharp contrast against green stems and linen tablecloth. Silver-framed photographs of Gail's son complete the altar. And because it is open to the community, neighbors bring photos, toys, and the favorite keepsakes of those they love and remember.

Though Gail's altar is powerful, we find a stronger connection to the simple shrine that Juliet creates for her grandmother, Nana Diana, and our dog Khloe our daughter never knew, but insists she did. We've no reason to contradict her. From her basket of scarves, Juliet selects a blue faux snakeskin as the base and places it on a small folding table in the living room. On that she stacks two boxes, one wrapped in silver cloth topped with a handkerchief of floral prints, the other sealed in silvery chintz. One of Nana's tea plates holds the offering for both: Swedish hard bread, a pomegranate, an unopened fortune cookie, and dog biscuits. Behind the plate is a drawing by Juliet: her grandmother riding a horse, rider and steed smiling broadly. Above, battery-powered candles frame a porcelain greyhound, one of two Nana gave my daughters before she passed, and the sugar skull Juliet created in school. A dozen large marigolds decorate the first two levels. On the third and final level, two photographs: Nana in her bright muumuu, straw hat, squinting into the sun; Khloe, black-nosed, blond whippet–German shepherd mix, lying on our bed in Denver.

On the afternoon of the Civano Halloween party, before a hundred or more guests arrive, we debate whether we should move the altar but decide it should remain. It's visible and could be knocked askew, yet in the few days since Juliet built it, the altar's significance has grown. I cannot walk by without remembering Nana and Khloe, though even three years after her death, I continue to think of my mother, at least, almost daily.

The colorful structure already feels entrenched in our Halloween ritual, too. Though one instance does not make tradition, the altar has the feel of family history, the makings of a new tradition and so a tie to our heritage, even if el Día de los Muertos was solely the tradition of others before this year.

Maybe that's the way heritage in America works. Everyone comes from another place, likely rich in culture and memory. Here, however, we borrow from others to make our own lives, and the lives of our children, more complete. That's not a substitute for the traditions of our parents and ancestors but, lacking visceral access to those traditions, they serve as complements. Heritage, in the end, is what we are given, what we borrow, and— woven as one—what we create.

This year, though I skulk beneath an emerald cloak, a gaudy gem at my throat, I let the visitors to our haunted garage move through on their own. When I guided them last time, the tour was more theatrical, but I spent hours in the garage and missed most of the party. Tonight I still find myself meandering in, not so much to check on the ghouls and goblins who are the neighborhood kids. Rather, I find a certain pleasure in the week's hard work, in watching the delight on my daughters' faces as they take ownership of the celebration, guiding children and adults alike, making up their own scary stories as costumed feet shuffle forward and back.

I stop at the potion master's cupboard and am cast in orange light, a skeleton hovering at my shoulder. Earlier I had set an old cookbook above the cauldron as a prop. Now I pick it up to see that it's a Swedish collection, one I found among my mother's things after she passed away. Titled *Hemmets Kokbok*, the binding is faded and cracked, the pages stained from use and damp storage. On the inside cover is my mother's signature and a recipe of her own creation. I turn the page to find that this is the forty-third edition of the book. The first was printed in 1903; this one in 1952. My mother was eighteen years old then, only eight years older than Ann-Elise is now. Sweden has a long tradition of cooking, and though I cannot read Swedish, it's a heritage nonetheless that can be passed on to our children. Tomorrow, the eve of el Día de los Muertos, seems the right day to begin.

ROUNDABOUT

The last day I saw my mother alive was June 21, 2004. She was seventy years old, but with long, white hair and skin wrapped around the bones of her hand like the translucent membrane of a bat's wing, she looked ninety. In the third-floor lobby of Atlanta's venerable Buckhead NurseCare facility, she was folded into a wheelchair, her body an umbrella draped in a brightly colored muumuu as strings of quartz and turquoise looped around her neck.

Ann-Elise and Juliet, six and three years old, recognized their Swedish grandmother, Nana Diana, and yet hesitated. As did Billie and I. We had known about her declining health, and though it had been two years since we had last seen her, she had aged, it seemed, exponentially. Less than two years earlier, she had walked on her own, moving ably though not nimbly among the tight corridors of her assisted-living unit, working late as she documented her solo road trips of the last twenty years. Now she hardly moved at all.

Hers was not solely a disease of the body—the sprawl of cancer, or the body's turning against itself as with lupus or MS. Hers was not even a disease of the mind, though she was diagnosed early in her adult life with bipolar depression and never leveled beyond a season or two on antidepressants. Instead, hers was a disease of the spirit. Confined to the cold indifference of a wheelchair, constrained to a senior apartment she could no longer maintain, and surrounded by lonely widows whose last ambition was to save her soul for a pearly-gated heaven she always rebuffed, Nana Diana was simply ready to leave. After seeing her body failing around her—even as her eyes resonated with the nautical fire of her native Baltic Sea—I believed I was ready, too.

1.

Before our house was built on the northern half of Civano, the desert was bladed and the umber earth raised five feet. Yet there remained a circle of original ground, and at its center a massive saguaro rose thirty feet above the pavement. Each morning, a cacophony of birdsong exploded from the cactus, followed by the birds bickering their way into neighbors' yards. Come evening, the saguaro's leathery skin darkened against the slow stain of dusk. In between, an uneven wash of cars whirled around the single sentinel: neighbors and construction workers, delivery vans and visitors.

Though technically a traffic circle, I thought of the intersection more as a roundabout, the British term for a crossroads at which incoming traffic yields to cars already in the loop. Modern roundabouts are different from traditional traffic circles, first used in Paris in 1906 and then called gyratories—meaning one-way circulation around a central island. Compared to stop-and-go traffic circles or more traditional intersections, roundabouts cut accidents in half while decreasing congestion and emissions as the cars keep moving.

Though ours was ringed by four stop signs, they were largely ignored, making it "nonconforming," according to city planners. But I prefer *roundabout* more because of its double meaning: a circular intersection, yet also a terminus arrived at in an indirect or circuitous way, a journey that does not end from where it launches nor follow a linear course.

One morning, cool though it was mid-September, I walked to the roundabout, dipped beneath the railing, and dropped onto the desert floor to photograph the vibrant autumn wildflowers. I remember a car cruising around my head as a sulfur-winged butterfly alighted on a desert marigold. Sparrows and starlings flew in and out of the saguaro's many cavities. A pair of fighter jets arced high overhead, a regular sortie from the air force base to the west. And 1,700 miles to the east, a nurse I would never meet found my mother limp and dehydrated, her spirit nearly flown.

2.

My mother still had an appetite on that last visit, though she was feeble. At the administrator's desk I checked her out for lunch as Ann-Elise and Juliet squabbled about who would push the wheelchair into the elevator and out to the car. When the doors slid open and a crowd of people spilled into the hallway, I decided I'd better do the pushing.

We arrived at the main lobby to the percussion of a Georgia thunderstorm, relentless, deafening, and beautiful. As I pulled around in my brother's old Volvo, I was drenched but relieved nonetheless to get out of the nursing home—happy to take my mother from that stale and sterile place, if only for a short while. I assisted her into the front seat as Billie and the girls piled into the back, and then coaxed the car up the steep incline of the exit as the wipers worked noisily against the rain. What didn't work, however, was the air-conditioning. The windshield steamed up as we perspired, the air inside the car nearly viscous even as we rolled the windows down an inch, then three. But we made it safely if not slowly to Nana's favorite restaurant, Joe's Crab Shack, ten blocks away.

For me there was no foreshadowing that this would be our last meal together. Perhaps my mother knew, as she lunged into the crab legs and fried shrimp as if she hadn't eaten an actual meal in months. And considering she hadn't ventured outside in nearly that long, I recognized that this was her first enjoyable food in weeks.

After the fractured conversation of lunch—when Ann-Elise and Juliet were too distracted by the overstimulating decorations to stay seated, when Billie was mostly silent except as she implored the girls to behave, when I found the growing heat of embarrassment for my mother who could not help but draw attention to her garish dress and all-out consumption, when my heart worked its cold vise of concern into my throat, when the restaurant's blaring music ground its way into the base of my skull, when *Goddammit why wouldn't the waitress refill my iced tea?!*—after that, I was ashamed. I was my mother's youngest son, and eating at me all that time was a broken promise I had made nearly twenty years earlier. Even before moving a thousand miles west to college and leaving my mother alone in Florida, I promised to take care of her, that no matter where I was or how she was, she could live with me. It was a pledge that I knew Billie could abide.

The care of elderly parents by their adult children is a cultural dilemma that becomes more relevant every year. In 2020 more than forty-two million households in the United States provided unpaid care for ailing parents, according to the National Alliance for Caregiving—a more than 400 percent increase since 2000. Family caregivers spend not only time—an average of eighteen hours of care a week—but also financial resources, both in money they funnel toward health care and in income lost by serving as caregivers. A 2023 report by the AARP estimates the value of family caregivers' unpaid contributions at $600 billion. In total, one in six Americans now provides care for an elderly adult. Though a majority of family caregivers feel appreciated and admit a positive sense of increased responsibility, they are also frustrated, overwhelmed, and themselves less healthy. And many—especially children who provide some level of care for parents from a distance, those who cannot or by choice do not live with their parents—carry increasing guilt.

Intentions, too, have a roundabout way of eluding us. Billie and I transferred from city to city before our children were born. We didn't have room in our small house—and would my mother really want to be confined to our tiny suburban Colorado home? Then Ann-Elise was born and she needed a nursery, her own room. And my mother was a wanderer, as she loaded her Chevy Suburban after I left home and drove around the country to "discover herself a little later than most," she once told me—moving ecstatically if not erratically from place to place on her manic highs before crashing, usually through the winters, in unbearable lows.

Sometimes she arrived unannounced at my brothers' homes, staying too long, working like a pneumatic hammer on the foundation of their marriages. Once she knocked well past midnight on the hollow door of my college apartment, her silver hair pulled back but frayed, eyes cloudy from the strain of driving under dim headlamps—the county highways tricking her, she said, on every turn. She stayed over winter break while my roommates and I traveled south. When we returned she was gone, the only sign of her visit an iridescent splay of oil in the closest parking space and a bag of cigarette butts stuffed into the trash.

Care for the elderly is no less a dilemma in Europe, where Nana Diana was born. In Germany, one in ten women—the primary family caregivers for aging parents—quits her full-time job to take care of her parents. Not so long ago, France passed a law requiring children to "honor and respect their parents, pay them an allowance, and provide or fund a home for them," the French media reports, because elderly parents, largely ignored by a society "obsessed with youth," were committing suicide at a rate of more than sixty people a week. In my mother's Sweden, responsibility for ailing parents has fallen to the state, which provides for nearly all elder care through a mix of social and health insurance and entitlement programs like paid time off for family caregivers. Even with state support—or perhaps because of it—Sweden boasts one of Europe's highest percentages of parental assistance.

Adult children live closer to their parents in Sweden and throughout Europe. In America—a nation of immigrants—children migrate. Caregiving is therefore less an expenditure of time than money. Nana Diana lived in Georgia, but her children settled in Indiana, Arizona, and California. Only her oldest son, my older brother Miles, lived nearby. For years, my brothers and I sent money to our mother. For years, Billie and I talked about how we should bring her out to live with us. For years, we watched from half a continent away as first her health and then her spirit failed.

And so Billie, the girls, and I had driven down from a vacation in Tennessee to be with Nana Diana, who had lived in the senior apartment for years and it really was best, wasn't it? We couldn't provide the kind of care she needed, the services; we didn't even live on a bus route, and who takes the bus in Tucson with its Sonoran Desert summers, anyway?

3.

At the morgue, while viewing her body—which in the end was not so different from when I had seen her only months earlier, though her eyes were closed—I could not touch my mother. I didn't know how to say goodbye, to say anything at all. The attendant didn't leave; I did not ask her to leave. But there was absolute silence, and a pallid beauty, rising.

4.

In the mid-1990s Billie and I attended our first family reunion together, at my brother's house in Indiana. As the youngest couple, with no children yet of our own, we found ourselves without a room, sleeping on a briefcase-thin mattress atop a sleeper sofa in the living room. One evening, we heard my sister Diana's voice rising from the basement, agitating like a swarm of bees. There was no door to dampen the noise. She was yelling at our mother, accusing her of denying us a "proper Christmas" when we grew up, though it was a one-sided argument. When we were young, my mother first downplayed and then lost the Christmas spirit altogether because, she explained, the season could never compare to the holidays she shared with her grandmother in Ållonö, a palace south of Stockholm at the end of a wide roundabout near the sea. The holidays of her childhood meant horse-drawn sleigh rides, live spruces hosting white candles that flickered like the faraway windows of a hillside village, ornate holiday meals cooked by full-time chefs, served by full-time stewards.

5.

One September morning, Ann-Elise, Juliet, and I scaled the concrete embankment of the traffic circle to explore the enclosed space beneath the saguaro. Down at ground level, we found three more cacti: a silver-green prickly pear with pancake-sized pads, a barrel cactus spun in curvilinear rows of red, fishhook-shaped spines, and a small grouping of pincushion, the undersized cactus with oversized blooms. In the shade of the circle we also found a young ocotillo, leafless, stalks the shape and strength of rebar spreading vaselike from the gravel floor. Fortunately, we did not see any snakes, but Ann-Elise nearly caught a black-collared lizard as Juliet watched a queen butterfly lope by just above her head.

Though we learned quickly that climbing out of the depression was not as easy as dropping in, eventually we managed it, even as the process convinced Juliet she'd stay at street level next time. Street level is likewise an important consideration for roundabouts, whose recipe for success reads like the chant of a New Age traffic engineer: *yield, deflect, flare*. Yield to traffic in the circle, deflect vehicles at the entry, and flare from single to multiple lanes to increase capacity.

6.

I was in my office at work on September 15, 2004, when my brother Miles called. Our mother was in the hospital again. "Hold tight," he said. "I'll call you back with the details." But it was more serious, he warned, than her previous stays. For her children, our mother's visits to the hospital were worrying but not uncommon. She had artery concerns that resulted in atrophy in one leg, bronchial concerns because she'd smoked since she was fourteen, mental health concerns as she periodically threatened suicide. "More serious . . ." His voice hung.

Twenty minutes later I had booked a flight to Atlanta, via Salt Lake City, that was to leave in four hours. It was an all-nighter, arriving around 5 a.m. We were not sure if she would make it through the night, and I didn't have many details. I knew she was admitted the previous day, after her nurse found her, the bedsheets drenched in sweat and blood-laced vomit. She had a virus, *the flu?* No: a bacterial infection. What did that mean?

Quickly, frantically, I sent an email to my team at work: I would be out for an unknown period of time, not checking email, not checking voicemail, unavailable. As I rushed down the hall, a coworker called after me, "Is everything alright?" The words lodged in my throat did not surface. In my bones, the same long bones I shared with my mother, I knew she was dying.

I called my brother David as I sped home to pack and say goodbye to my wife and daughters. He was driving down from Indiana and would pick me up at a light-rail station a half-dozen blocks from Piedmont Hospital, the same hospital where he and Miles were born. When I arrived home, Juliet had been crying; she had only seen Nana Diana a handful of times but had a powerful connection with her—both were sensitive, perhaps psychic. I explained that Nana was very sick, would probably die. Billie told me to try to get an hour's sleep; I had been up late the night before and likely wouldn't be able to sleep much on the flights.

In our room I blocked out the daylight and lay alone on the bed, crying quietly, when suddenly there was a calm—a knowing I could not explain but fully understood. Yes, she would pass on tonight. She was telling me that, and I was taken back to when I was Ann-Elise's age, six years old, living in Lexington, Kentucky, when my mother used to call me home as I played outside, call me home psychically; I could hear that voice clearly, in my head, sure, but as if she were mere feet away. So this was it. And she was ready. But was I?

I did not want to talk to anybody at the airport, on the airplane. Though the seat next to me was empty on the first leg of the flight, I could not read the book I brought, nor the back-of-the-seat magazine I usually enjoyed paging through. Could not listen to the flight attendant reviewing emergency procedures in the sharp light that split the airplane's windows, shattering the overhead compartments and passenger seats with their abusive patterns of blue and brown and red. Could not shut my eyes, nor keep them open.

The Salt Lake sky was dark when we arrived, and I was in the dark about my mother. How was she? I called Miles. He was alone. David had not yet arrived, would not until early morning. Diana would touch down after me. Miles was crying as he entered the room with our mother. He described her body withdrawing from itself, starting at her toes, as her feet and then legs grew cold and began to lose what remaining color they had. "She can only beat it," the doctor had told him, "if she has the will to live." We both knew she didn't. And then I was in tears again as he continued to describe the way a body shuts down, system by system. Her eyes were closed and would never open, the breathing light and almost nonexistent, heartbeat distant, slowing. I hung up and did not care that people were staring at me, may or may not have been concerned that a grown man was on his knees heaving, as if retching, as if the dark cloak of the sky had slipped through the terminal windows and placed its unceasing chill on the arc of his back.

7.

Yield. My mother was married to my father for ten years, but the man she first loved, and loved most, was someone she met in southern Rhodesia when she was nineteen. They were passionate, committed, and then this Italian man whose name I know only as Gerardo, whose story I can only tell from the memory of my mother's lament, broke. Whether he had dementia or the anti-malarials scrambled his mind, something made him unable to remember her. Like that, their lives were separate.

Deflect. When my sister was only weeks old and in her bassinette in the living room of the Miami house my mother and father built, her mother had a strong urge to pick up her daughter quickly. She did. Seconds later, a section of ceiling collapsed, crushing the bassinette.

Flare. My mother's first love was horses, and she was known widely in the field of thoroughbred racehorse pedigrees throughout her career. In Miami, though—where my sister and I were born—she volunteered when we were toddlers at a clinic for battered women, many of whom were teenage mothers. By then the marriage with my father was all but over and her blond hair had gone to silver, even though she was not yet thirty-five. By then, with the visage of a sage diva—gray-blue eyes set elegantly among Scandinavian skin and that radiant hair—she had dedicated herself to women who could not speak for themselves. She channeled her anger and passion, and an eloquent pen, into visibility for the problem that led to funding for the program.

8.

My mother died, my brother David told me when I called him once the plane touched down, while I was somewhere over Texas. Or Arkansas, perhaps. Only Miles saw her before she passed, though she was not conscious. In a way I was relieved, not only because I knew that she was finally at peace, perhaps once again with the grandmother she so loved, but also because I was afraid to see her in that near-death state. We were all afraid. Her death was a heavy emptiness my siblings and I held as we gathered together for the first time in many years. We had to let it go, even as we had all struggled, separately and together, over her care; even as the guilt consumed us. *Release it now*, her spirit said.

My mother's wake was held at the communal house of Bahá'í friends, friends who saw her alive in the hospital the evening before, who were astounded when they learned she had died. They had been talking lightly, even joking.

After the wake, and after we spent three tedious days cleaning out her apartment and storage units, my brothers and sister and I had lunch at Joe's Crab Shack. It was not a celebration of her life, as the wake had been, but rather a recognition of the roundabout way we exist, even within our own families. The gathering was the release of sadness and strength, a final parting and awkward grace, a circling back of the extraordinary life she had led, even though by the time my sister and I moved out and moved on, so much of her vigor had already been lost. We ate our fill, cracked a crab leg on the empty place setting left for her.

The next day, David and I left early, his Jeep tugging a trailer packed full with horse books and magazines for a farm library in Lexington. An hour north of Atlanta, we made an unplanned stop at a state park. We agreed that Nana Diana—who traveled from state to state and park to park as she made countless "connections" on her manic highs—would appreciate having her ashes released across a wild and rolling landscape.

Our act of subversion was trickier than expected. Sticking to the dawn shadows, we leapt the fence into the closed park and jogged a half-mile to a large hill of clover and bluegrass, thick live oaks resting heavy boughs all around. We spoke a blessing, paused to breathe the cool, humid air, and then opened the small container to the wind, which took the fine gray dust into itself. As her ashes caught the motion of the air, lingering a moment before dissipating in a white-silver plume, I caught a quick movement along the far hedgerow. I searched then for some sign: a hawk or fox or wild horse, perhaps—a chestnut mare racing among the trees like a young girl might sprint between the spruces and firs of a Swedish seaside estate. But it was only the wind bending the branches, delivering our mother, whirling out and then circling back, whispering: *You are ready.*

THE CASTAWAY

At the edge of Tucson's Barrio Viejo, a half-mile south of downtown, lies the nation's only Catholic shrine dedicated to a sinner instead of a saint. Many tales are told about the origin of the shallow portico framed by a high adobe wall, arched like an old Mexican fort. The most popular stories date to the early 1870s, when a local ranch hand, Juan Oliveras, fell in love with his mother-in-law. Caught in the arms of his lover, the young man was stabbed by the woman's wealthy husband. Or he was axed. Or he was shot—the details vary. Pulling himself out of his in-law's house, Juan staggered onto the street before making it to the edge of a barren lot, where he died. His lover wept for him, lighting candles with neighbors in the hopes of guiding his soul to heaven. They buried him where he lay, for he was an adulterer who had died before confessing his sins, and the Catholic priest would not inter the man in the church's cemetery. He was *el tiradito*, the castaway.

Today, El Tiradito—"the only shrine in the United States dedicated to the soul of a sinner buried in unconsecrated ground," according to its onsite plaque—remains a sacred and celebrated place where candles flicker and visitors leave personal messages to honor the dead, and as a means of bringing good fortune. Legend whispers, among the crumbling adobe and overhanging branches of mesquite, that the wish of a person will come true if a candle lit in the evening remains burning the next morning.

Though the original shrine was destroyed during road construction, the small lot that today houses the grotto was deeded to the city in 1927 before being named an official Tucson monument thirteen years later, when the adobe wall was built. By the late 1960s, however, urban renewal that had already claimed many of Tucson's most historic barrios threatened the shrine. A proposed federal highway would bisect central Tucson and require, according to government officials, the shrine's demolition. Outraged, residents held a series of protests, demanding that the altar and broader neighborhood be spared.

But how could a monument of seemingly little national significance convince federal bureaucrats to change their minds? The neighbors' answer: by taking advantage of federal protections and rallying around historic preservation. Years of neighborhood activism delayed highway siting while residents pushed to add the shrine to the National Register of Historic Places. In 1971 the residents succeeded: the National Register sanctioned the monument as "the only such shrine in the U.S....[and a] symbol of the belief that certain deceased individuals grant the wishes of those who light votive candles for them." When construction of Interstate 10 eventually began, its path lay six hundred yards west.

While the plaque marks the altar's historic significance, it doesn't mention the neighborhood's efforts to save the shrine. Spiritually and culturally, however, the aromatic candles, ornate ironwork, and flow of visitors attest not only to the altar's original importance but also to the perseverance of community itself.

Community can be defined as "a social group of any size whose members reside in a specific locality, share government, and often have a common cultural and historical heritage," according to Dictionary.com. Yet can community—a term that stems from the Latin words *communis*, meaning common or public, and *communitas*, meaning fellowship—itself be a "castaway"? What could it mean for the community, let alone its residents, to be an outcast—an entity discarded, unwanted? Consider the tracts of temporary trailers scattered throughout New Orleans by the Federal Emergency Management Agency following the devastation of Hurricane Katrina, which killed more than 1,800 people and caused at least $100 billion in damage in 2005. Officially designated "parks," the FEMA clusters once housed two thousand trailers and more than five thousand people. Years after Katrina, the parks still ranged from five to eighty trailers and, due to delays in posthurricane cleanup and spiking rental prices in restored apartments, accommodated those who had been displaced far longer than originally planned. In the meantime, they served as de facto neighborhoods, even if they didn't resemble the places where residents lived before the mighty storm. At the Diamond Park trailer site in Plaquemines Parish an hour south of New Orleans, for example, National Public Radio's Kathy Lohr reported that a chain-link fence extended out from a permanent gate staffed by armed guards. The fence surrounded the park, which otherwise was spread end-to-end with gravel, broken only by the trailers. If these parks qualify as community— and they may have been the only semblance of community the residents had left, for they worked hard to rebuild the playground and construct a community center—were they, like the displaced neighbors themselves, castaways? FEMA's intention, after all, was to close the parks sooner rather than later.

Or consider the city of Oak Ridge, Tennessee, established in 1942 as part of the Manhattan Project. Seven crossroads villages were seized through a "declaration of taking" by the U.S. Army Corps of Engineers, clearing the way for the vast infrastructure of what is now Oak Ridge National Laboratory. Yet from 1942 to 1945 the population of the secret city grew from three thousand to seventy-five thousand. Homes, "sometimes loosely defined," according to the lab's own historical records, popped up at a rate of one every thirty minutes.

The intention, a friendly guide told me when I visited Oak Ridge just after I began working for the U.S. Department of Energy in 1991, was that the homes built by the Atomic Energy Commission would be temporary. Fifty years after they were built, however, the square, flat-top houses that I saw remained in their original clusters, well used and decidedly neighborhood-ish. Though they had since been upgraded—wiring and water lines retrofitted, porches added and rebuilt, asbestos removed or at least buffered—the low-ceiling structures were designed for interim use. They reminded me of the small "portables" common on school campuses, some built of timber framing, resting atop concrete blocks and clad in green or gray stained plywood, with rectangular windows running the length of one or two sides, while others were built of concrete block on concrete slabs, painted white or light gray, their only distinguishing features small porches and evenly spaced if not undersized windows. Though the black oaks of Oak Ridge provided a scenic vista, and low-cut grass and tidy flower beds framed the single-story buildings, I couldn't get over the unintentional longevity of these hurried houses. Why keep them around? Why not build something more comfortable, more lasting—something like a new subdivision full of houses sheathed in vinyl siding and asphalt roof shingles that glitter like the charged particles so meticulously studied under the sweltering Tennessee sun? The guide only smiled at my bemusement, leading us then into the atomic center of that storied community.

Or what about the modern-day American suburb? Much maligned in the last three and a half decades by cultural critics such as James Howard Kunstler, whose 1993 book *The Geography of Nowhere: The Rise and Decline of America's Man-Made Landscape* quickly became both bible and manifesto in urban planning and smart-growth circles, subdivisions built since the end of World War II are predominantly segregated in their layout. Single-family homes, usually with garages in front, go here; perhaps there's a school nearby, the land donated by the developer. Stores and restaurants over there. Office complexes, charmingly referred to as office parks if enough grass and distance separate the buildings, over yonder. And industrial areas separated from everything, ever creeping beyond dark railroad tracks. The result is well known: equity across ages and income levels is lost because an automobile is necessary to move between the suburb's many factions, and mass transit options are few and far between. Logically, wide roads must be built to facilitate those cars, a resource-intensive system almost mandating single-source polluters. But given the sheer number of those auto-oriented places across the United States, is it possible that suburbs are castaways, too? Indeed, are our suburban neighborhoods—rapidly built for economy over durability, like so much else in our consumer-driven society—designed to be throwaway altogether, their castaway fate inevitable? If so, what does that say about the millions of people who call suburbia home, particularly in a postpandemic world where it's easier than ever to work remotely, completely isolating ourselves, inadvertently or intentionally?

Billie and I purchased our first house in 1993 in a suburb northwest of Denver. In the 1990s Westminster, Colorado, sprawled from a deteriorating city center into vast residential subdivisions on the plains below Rocky Flats, the Department of Energy plant that produced plutonium triggers for nuclear weapons. The two-story home we purchased was typical of new suburbs up and down the Front Range: two-car garage as the prominent feature, plywood siding fitted with planks in a cheap imitation of the Tudor style, and a sliver of a front porch. The house wasn't thrown together as quickly as those of Oak Ridge or the FEMA trailers in New Orleans, but sad similarities in quality and design remained. Nevertheless, we couldn't have been more delighted to buy our first home, to join the American dream.

The middle-class neighborhood was home to many young families, and we soon met the children next door. The daughter was a friendly girl on the verge of third grade. With straight blond hair, brown eyes, and a toothy smile, she looked much more like her mother than her father, Bill, who was of Japanese descent. We couldn't see their son's hair at all because he wobbled around in a white Styrofoam helmet. I wasn't sure if the thickly pocked shell was the result of parental overprotection or a necessity at age three given his appetite for rambunctious play.

During that first year of suburban life, Billie and I morphed into the surrogate aunt and uncle of the children. As we became closer, our front lawns commonly held the scatterings of Wiffle bats, soccer balls, and outdoor art sets. Though playing with these kids and enjoying cookouts with their parents didn't make Billie and me want to have our own children any sooner, the relationship allowed me to consider community from Bill's perspective, and ultimately my own. An attorney, Bill commuted to his firm fifteen miles away in Boulder early so he could arrive home with enough daylight to play outside with his children. I often pulled onto our street following a day at the office to find him pitching a ball to his son or playing Frisbee with his daughter and other neighbor kids. I'd swing into our garage and race over to join them. Billie commuted to Boulder, too, though she arrived home an hour later usually to find us all on the lawn, remnants of the afternoon's antics strewn across the yard. She forgave my regular oversights of preparing dinner or finishing up a project on the house because she saw the bright eyes around her, the easy happiness that comes from the earnest play of children big and small.

Bill rarely talked about work and perhaps only slightly more about politics. He was concerned about current events and the future yet had a relaxed attitude reflected not only by his uncropped hair but also by the colorful Bob Marley sticker smoothed to the rear bumper of his car. "Don't worry about a thing" wasn't just the chorus from one of the iconic reggae artist's more popular songs—it was Bill's mantra. Mostly, though, Bill won me over with his casual style of parenting in the context of suburban living. Because my interaction with my own father was sporadic, long-distance, and mostly awkward, I had no real model for fatherhood as it relates to community, let alone family. But here was a man who dedicated hours a day to his children and their friends, never seemed to lose his temper, and understood the role of raising children in an active community. That is, he welcomed the participation of neighbors in the development of his daughter and son, and likewise participated in the nurturing of other neighborhood kids. Our role wasn't to feed or shelter his children, of course, but because of the encouraged interaction, the children grew more socially adept and, in the sense of being connected to the larger whole, healthier. We did, too—sharing not only our time together but also this place, this small subdivision along the dry uplands of the Colorado plains.

"A community is the mental and spiritual condition of knowing that the place is shared, and that the people who share the place define and limit the possibilities of each other's lives," writes Wendell Berry in *The Long-Legged House*. "It is the knowledge that people have of each other, their concern for each other, their trust in each other, the freedom with which they come and go among themselves." With our neighborhood's imperfect edges and comings and goings, Bill taught me that community is less about limitations and more about engagement, encouragement, and trust. Ours was a knowledge of place not as much geographic as sensible, built from the relationships more intricately woven among neighbors than I thought possible. The very real community we shared was no castaway, even if the landscape was defined by cul-de-sacs and look-alike houses built row upon row on the slopes and swales of those windswept hills.

Does the physical design of a neighborhood therefore have less influence on its success than the interaction of its residents? Despite the documented environmental and social ills of segregated suburban life, we knew our immediate Westminster neighbors well and socialized with them regularly. We also knew the area's landscape, even if it was a landscape of suburban sprawl. While outsiders struggled to distinguish our neighborhood from other subdivisions of curvilinear streets and uniform architecture, our neighborhood held distinction for us. I recall the ribbon of wetlands that served as detention for runoff and, on grassy shallows, ground for redwood play structures. Against the wood-plank fences, shocks of cattails topped by red-winged blackbirds swayed in the wind. The blackbirds' calls mocked not only each other but also the houses of blue and tan and gray in every season except winter. In that cold swirl of white and gray, the birds were gone, but the crisp, amber cattails still shimmered, edged in ice, against the rank-and-file rooftops. Yet my academic training in urban planning prompted me to expect otherwise from such an ubiquitous place, and it wasn't until we moved to Tucson in 2000 that I learned firsthand that design can in fact make a significant difference. I learned, too, that social constructs—culture, mythology, religion—also play crucial roles in whether community succeeds. And in considering whether community can be cast away, we must also consider what it means to be a castaway—as a community and as a people.

I first visited El Tiradito on a mild evening in spring 2007. The uneven walls caught the shadowed light cast by candles in punched-tin holders and glass jars painted with the visages of Jesus and the Virgin of Guadalupe. The votive candles glowed among the adobe, and the murmuring crowd added a subtle energy. Under the gauzy moonlight, above stones and shuffling feet that stippled the dirt lot, I contemplated the word *castaway*. Is sin all that casts us out, as with Adam and Eve at the biblical beginning, as with Juan Oliveras, the lost soul, *el tiradito*? I didn't believe so, and began to think of castaway as signifying displacement rather than sin, a disconnection, not necessarily of self or even family, but of community—that vital, broader family that rallies and sustains. "My sin and judgment are alike peculiar," writes the evangelical British poet William Cowper. "I am a castaway, deserted and condemned." How easy to feel that way without the support of community, without the diversity of everyday interaction, and without a belief in preserving the ground upon which we walk, just as residents of Barrio Viejo saved the shrine and, as a result, the historic community beyond.

I visited El Tiradito Shrine that night before Easter not to pay homage to a sinner or light a votive candle, however, but to gather among friends for the Yaqui deer dance, which would last all night. That the shrine should be our meeting place before driving to the small Pascua Yaqui ceremonial site wedged beneath Interstate 10 in South Tucson was fortuitous, if not ironic. El Tiradito is a dusty half-lot lined on one side by rabbit-eared prickly pear and native velvet mesquite, and on the other by La Pilita Museum, which before its closure in 2015 shared the neighborhood's history. Located in the oldest Mexican American barrio in Arizona, not far from a park and elementary school and nestled among dense, colorful homes, the shrine is dedicated to a man's burning love, a love worth dying for. The hard work of barrio neighbors saved the shrine from the interstate. On the other hand, the Yaqui site—dedicated to a verdant mix of native beliefs and Catholic ritual no less steeped in love and spiritual ascension—was also dust-rinsed, though it just barely escaped the freeway. While residents in central Tucson fought for El Tiradito's protection, members of the Yaqui tribe, which was not recognized by the federal government until 1978, had little say in how the highway cut across their community. The government's shunning echoed the tribe's history, which alternated between savage persecution and painful neglect. When it came to the freeway, the Yaquis' was a castaway community.

Yet anyone who has attended a Yaqui Lenten ceremony like the deer dance knows that the neighborhood is rich in knowledge of place and neighbor. From the moment I arrived at the wide lot off 39th Street and 10th Avenue, I felt a sense of community that had little to do with the ill-repaired houses on adjacent streets or minimal block structures of the site itself. Though a gritty urbanism pervaded the broader area, and trucks roared by on the freeway two stories above us, the ceremonial site held an aura of focus—on the ceremonies and people and, through the deer dance itself, on the native Sonoran Desert landscape suppressed but still breathing around us.

On the surface, the deer dance is less about community than about song—the deer singer chanting against the beat of drums as the deer dancer and his ritual clowns, the *pakhokam*, dance. Combined, the song and dance weave the performers and onlookers into a trance meant to bridge this world with *sea ania*, the parallel flower world that mirrors the wild desert. In this respect, however, the dance is entirely about community, for it is "through song that experience with other living things in the wilderness world is made intelligible and accessible to the human community," write Larry Evers and Felipe S. Molina in *Yaqui Deer Songs: Maso Bwikam*. "Deer songs continue in Yaqui communities as a very real vehicle for communication with the larger natural community in which Yaquis live." Even in this urban South Tucson location, with its lack of natural landscape, here and there a velvet mesquite or sweet acacia shades a dirt courtyard, desert marigolds grow from beneath the concrete's edge, and a mockingbird sings through the night. Residents of the Yaqui community remain a part of the natural world—the Sonoran Desert wilderness that for the tribe originally stems from the Río Yaqui watershed of southern Sonora. Despite the impoverished buildings and the rush of nearby cars, I could see that theirs is a community not of castaways, but rather a community of consciousness and spiritual bounty and a deep sense of place. Theirs is not a castaway community, government neglect and prejudice be damned. Rather, theirs is a flowering wilderness, revisited and retained.

Community may be created in the blandest of suburbs, in sudden trailer towns and building complexes never intended to last more than a handful of years, and in spiritual centers at times resembling nothing more than broad dirt lots. After moving to the master-planned community of Civano in Tucson, however, I learned that while design doesn't necessarily dictate community, it nevertheless can matter greatly. For every example of successful community in the suburbs, there may be five or five hundred where community, as Wendell Berry defines it, fails because neighbors don't acknowledge that their place is shared, and celebrate that sharing. That is, the neighbors do not know one another, do not trust or share a deep concern for one another, do not experience their place holistically or spiritually.

One way to counteract the often isolating experiences of the suburbs is to create developments in which social interaction is nearly unavoidable. Over the last forty years, architects, planners, and developers have begun building and rebuilding towns, districts, and infill sites that mix houses with stores and offices with restaurants, all within a reasonable walk of each other. The movement, called New Urbanism, strives to create livable neighborhoods instead of sterile subdivisions, walkable cities rather than high-speed roadways and dangerous intersections. Planned holistically and produced by a single developer, they may build out over years or even decades, with a mix of housing types designed to be accessible by a range of income levels.

While in graduate school in Denver from 1995 to 1997, I tracked one such new development on the periphery of Tucson.

Originally called the Tucson Solar Village, the project—by then renamed Civano—promised to take New Urbanism one step further by combining physical design with quantifiable sustainability goals to create an environmentally focused village, albeit in a suburban location. The initial idea, according to Civano project manager Wayne Moody, was to "develop a whole community as a 'showcase' to demonstrate ways in which solar energy could be utilized to reduce overall energy consumption and result in a more harmonious environment." But reducing energy consumption was only one of the project's measurable goals. Others included limiting automobile traffic, creating onsite jobs, reducing potable water use, providing affordable housing, and curtailing solid waste. Perhaps more implied than quantified was the overarching goal of creating community, that "mental and spiritual condition of knowing that the place is shared," as Berry writes.

Tucson had grown as much as any western city in the previous twenty years when we purchased our Civano lot in 2000. A metropolitan area nearing a population of one million, the city ranged across a wide valley, its downtown seemingly three sizes too small. Though Denver's sprawl was broader, it nevertheless congealed around an urban vitality that Tucson lacked. But I was less concerned then about the vitality of Tucson's downtown than that of the small village-to-be on the city's southeast side.

Once Billie and I settled into our temporary apartment—two-year-old Ann-Elise in her tiny room and another daughter on the way—we planned a visit to select our new home. The developments we drove by as we followed our bungalow's construction over the next six months seemed almost desperate in their yearning for physical community: prestigious gated estates crowning the foothills of the Santa Catalina and Rincon Mountains, 1950s-era low-slung homes in midtown, and new subdivisions of stucco and red tile roofs all around. Yet I knew from our suburban neighborhood in Westminster that looks can be deceiving. Who's to say that the cookie-cutter communities of grand houses don't thrive? True, the indications were there: I recall a coworker telling me he drove to another neighborhood for Halloween, for example, because the houses of his foothills subdivision were too far apart and "everyone drives to visit their neighbors, anyway." But perhaps the residents found as much pleasure and permanence in their suburban relationships as we did with our Westminster neighbor Bill and his family?

On our commute between the apartment and Civano, I began to associate the community I expected to find—indeed, had already found even before our house was completed, thanks to regular potlucks and other social events like neighborhood movie nights—with the concept of sustainable design. Successful community therefore meant a more sustainable desert existence. But most of the neighborhoods we saw on our way to and from Civano relied on a model of intensive resource use: the long commute; the absolute segregation of homes and businesses and schools; the wasteful materials, energy, and water required to build and maintain homes in an arid environment. Though arroyos and other natural features may have been preserved, they were often walled off, fenced—discarded as if thoroughfares given over to roadside bandits. Thoroughfares they were, but of coyotes and javelinas and roadrunners, a far less worrisome gang.

The subdivisions, office parks, and shopping centers on our route largely lacked appeal, if not community. On the other hand, Civano was as distinct and promising as any community I had studied in graduate school. The neighborhood had been sited to take advantage of the desert's warm days and cool nights. Homes shaded by salvaged trees revealed inviting courtyards and porches while thin streets curved over the terrain, never ending in cul-de-sacs. And a grid of walkable streets, overlaid by trails that weave among acacia and mesquite, connected the entire neighborhood. At the neighborhood's core stood a mixed-use center, part straw bale, part adobe, with a small café, art gallery, and offices. The lots across the street were reserved for live/work townhomes: residents could operate a studio or shop downstairs while living in the space above.

The variety of homes already built on a handful of streets delighted us. Wide bungalows with metal roofs and deep porches fronted barrio-style homes of richly colored stucco and low, painted walls. Modernist desert architecture, complete with garage roofs topped by photovoltaic panels, complemented rustic courtyard homes made of recycled Styrofoam and concrete. And a series of pocket parks and larger, grassy fields offset the small lots that, like the native landscaping of the common areas, were nourished by reclaimed water.

Civano's goal of bringing people together was exceeded early on. Many residents moved to the community from cities across the country to be a part of what might be called "intentional community"—a place where people find reason to interact, or choose to interact anyway without any reason at all. Our next-door neighbors Mike and Monica, who built a casita to house Mike's elderly mother, Ruth, moved from South Carolina. A trained facilitator, he was eager to see firsthand how consensus might play a role in the building of his new community. Linda and her husband, Rick, a bearded, retired city administrator with the build and occasional temperament of a hockey goalie, migrated south from Minnesota. Scott, Deirdre, and their young daughter, Zoë, moved from Utah to build an adobe home of Scott's crafting. Rich and Susan Michal and their three daughters traveled west from Indiana; they would eventually construct a custom home of rammed-earth walls as part of Rich's architectural master's program at the University of Arizona. I recall just how sore I was from pounding earth between plywood barriers for a couple hours in yet another way neighbors came together. Even those from Tucson found the passion and opportunities for social interaction beyond expectation. Only days after moving in, residents joked that a walk to the mailbox took an hour instead of ten minutes because of the number of neighbors they'd greet along the way. I still think back on my first warm conversation with Penny Pederson, a middle-aged landscape architect and one of Civano's first residents, whose inviting, open-courtyard home was right on the way to our mailbox.

Two and a half decades after we moved in and seven years after we moved out, Civano continues to invigorate. Though the neighborhood is not without its flaws—the neighborhood center has seen more tenants come and go than residents would like, for instance, and the once-lively coffee shop closed its doors for good several years ago—Civano is a success, a built environment gem in the Sonoran Desert. So, it turns out that the community is a kind of castaway, after all. That is, even today, when sustainable design is imperative in our resource-constrained, climate-weirding world, Civano remains a radical departure from America's typical subdivisions, from places designed to build financial profit over intentional community. But it is no castaway when it comes to the knowledge, concern, and trust neighbors share, and share willingly, in an environment that by its very design fosters community.

Several years after my first visit, I returned to El Tiradito to photograph the shrine. Only a few candles burned, but a near-full moon and the sulfur light from an adjacent restaurant cast a strange orange glow over the scene. As I moved my tripod around the lot, framing the trees, the arched wall, the iron candleholders, I knelt on the ground. From this perspective, the dark wall loomed into the night sky, stars distinct despite the intensity of the moonlight. The shrine and then the ground itself seemed to stretch on endlessly, in distance and time both, before reaching back to this distinct, dusty lot in a neighborhood rich in passion and legacy. With or without the shrine's history, I felt something close to what we might call holiness. Yet *el tiradito* was a castaway, a sinner whose body was refused a church burial. The connection, I realized, was the ground itself: this sacred ground. What connects this place not only to the Yaqui ceremonial site but also to the temporary trailer parks of New Orleans, the structures of Oak Ridge, the Westminster suburb, and the newer development of Civano is sacred ground.

Like community, *sacred* is a word with a deep history—originating from the Old English *sacren*, meaning to consecrate. Sacred, then, is not a found object or place but an action, an act of creation. These grounds are sacred because neighbors, whether they trace their ancestry to the same locations or migrated in, consecrated the land. In the case of El Tiradito and the Yaqui community, the lots were anointed through ritual and religious significance, served and subsequently saved by neighbors. The other locations were consecrated not through ordained ceremony, per se, but through the active creation of community, even if in some cases the community was at first unintentional, haphazard, perilous.

What consecrated Diamond Park in Plaquemines Parish wasn't the chain-link fence, nor the trailers, but the neighbors who had no choice but to come together, to respond and build up when all seemed lost. What consecrated Oak Ridge was not the fact that it was home to secretive atomic research but that the early structures and community persisted in spite of the lab's rushed development—that in persisting, neighbors turned their temporary houses into permanent homes, their gridded streets into active neighborhoods. What consecrated the small subdivision in a suburb northwest of Denver wasn't the carbon-copy homes and wide, curving streets but the neighbors who took the time to know and care for one another. And what consecrated Civano was a physical design that fosters synergy, certainly, but also a constant, even calculated level of neighborhood interaction that results in an authentic sense of place as well as a strong sense of community.

What consecrates any place is what ultimately defines community itself: the people who share knowledge, concern, trust, and the freedom to come and go, to echo Berry once again. So, can communities be castaways? Surely suburbs, cities, and entire peoples can be displaced and disconnected. History is ripe with examples, some dramatic and some, like redlining or gentrification, more subtle. The more relevant question here, though, may be, What prevents place and the people who live there from being cast out? One answer must be the sacred. Community succeeds when people join together to consecrate place—making it essential, enduring. "The sacred is not in heaven or far away," Yaqui-Mexican American poet Alma Luz Villanueva reminds us. "It is all around us." Community is, after all, what we make it, and the making itself is the sacred.

After photographing the shrine, I remained to watch the visitors come and go. They arrived in twos and threes, young and old, some looking from a distance and others stepping close to tuck notes into the crevices of the wall—messages for deceased loved ones or wishes, perhaps, for a better tomorrow. After pressing paper into the wall, a few people lit candles, their faces bright in the quick flare of light. How rewarding, I thought to myself, to witness such community. How sacred to know that community, like the votive candles lining the fabled adobe shrine, still shines.

MY NEIGHBOR'S BIRD

The object of art is to give life a shape.

JEAN ANOUILH

My neighbor's bird perches on the wall outside my window. It is black like the buzzard, still as a heron, slick as a kestrel. In the quick corridor of afternoon light the bird's shoulders shine through the thin window and into my eyes. At night its silhouette absorbs the moonlight, half in shadow. In the morning it drinks the dew and tastes the salty air from the ancient seabed upon which our homes are built.

There is a likeness my neighbor Michael and I cannot quite name as we admire the bird in the amber light of his front porch. Glossy bands weave, feather over feather, into streamlined tail. The crested head is of a single conclusion—a sharp yet elegantly curved beak, slightly open as if panting in our Sonoran Desert heat, as if at any time the bird will spring to the wall and take flight. Unsatisfied with our first guesses, we have gathered this afternoon to identify the species it represents.

Perhaps, I suggest, it is a piñon jay, the raucous bird found not in Old but rather New Mexico, in the north, in the intoxicating juniper scrublands near Santa Fe or the thirsty flatlands farther west, in central Utah. Here, blue-black jays drink from the briny edge of the Great Salt Lake—a curse, Cochiti legend tells, placed on the children of the Santo Domingo by Old Salt Woman when the people refused to feed her. But Old Salt Woman was soon tricked by her neighbors who, offering to feed her, instead ate her flesh. They called upon Rainmaker, and he poured forth from the sky until she became the Great Salt Lake itself.

But we agree that his bird is not a jay. With its heavy frame and wide stance, it is larger, less flighty.

An iced tea in one hand and an open grapefruit in the other, Michael shares the story of his recent find: "'Papagayo,' the Mexican shopkeepers said when I bought the bird they claimed was a parrot," he explains. "I knew right away they were wrong but didn't quarrel. The bird remained on its shelf, solitary, until I purchased it." Tucked awkwardly under his arm, propped tentatively in the back of his car, Michael delivered it from the dusty commercial stall of Nogales, Sonora, to his Tucson home—the plumage an immediate contrast against quartz-white tile.

Its trip, we imagine, had been much farther from the start.

Prior to its delivery to Nogales, the bird is loaded with other animals, cages, and wooden benches onto a flatbed pickup that drives slowly, carefully, along the shoulderless highway tracking the Río Sonora from the sprawling Sonoran capital city of Hermosillo. The truck pauses to load additional merchandise in dust-rinsed towns like Sinoquepe, Arizpe, and Cananea. At each stop the driver, who could be named Eduardo, his brother César, and the brother's young wife Gabriela, pry the lid off cold cervezas and tip the bottles back to sweep the acrid road away. And at each stop they check their cargo—the furniture and stamped-tin mirrors and stoic birds. The goods are rattled but otherwise unharmed.

By early evening the flatbed arrives in the border town of Nogales, finding its way onto the cobbled lane lined with small shops and painted carts. The local disco plays a noxious song with earth-deep bass and treble far too high. Gabriela, whose long black hair offsets dark eyes, cannot stand the noise and walks past the stall, through an alley thin with open doors, brightly colored blankets, and the heavy aroma of fried corn—to a place she knows well. Eduardo and César shake hands with the shop-keeper and his son, smile knowing the long day is nearly done, and together unload the truck.

They haul furniture and wrought-iron patio sets to an adjacent courtyard, dimly lit with candled lamps that flicker along the walls. Together, the shopkeeper and his son pull the rolling metal shade that fronts their stall's window, set the locks. The four men then return to the truck to find Gabriela offering cervezas wedged with limes. They grin again as they unload the remaining goods. The birds, their most delicate cargo, come last. With a fledgling balanced on each hand, they make many short trips from truck to stall and back.

A few days later, Michael walks the crowded lane of shop fronts, past rows of hand-painted puppets and parrot-colored sombreros, until he sees his bird.

The sun dips beneath the roofline as Michael refills my tea. We speculate that the bird is a roadrunner, that lizard-catching linear racer native to our more local haunts. With its raised crest, black skin beneath streaked feathers, and long, rudderlike tail, there is a chance. Cowboy folklore has it that these brave birds seek out fights with rattlesnakes, darting past their striking heads, the trigger-quick fangs. Or, sing the campfire songs, roadrunners wait until morning's first light, after the rattler has coiled itself into daytime sleep, corralling the snake with ridiculously sharp cholla stems.

I lean beyond the porch wall to admire my own yard's cactus, the dazzling spines backlit, nearly glowing. We speculate, but decide otherwise. With its long wings, Michael's bird is not so grounded.

Prior to the birds' journey to Hermosillo, in small, angular homes overlooking the humble village of Soyopa located 260 miles south of the border, women preen the stately birds, stroke their beaks, and press smooth feathers. Here the birds are motionless, cold in an otherwise hot world not many miles from their mountainous origin. The women with names like Eréndira and Pitina help their husbands and brothers load the animals onto a flatbed truck that scrapes its way over a crumbling dirt road out of the terraced hills. Alone, the driver steers through the night to arrive in the capital as speckled roosters throw their calls against the sun. The groaning truck answers with a quick honk of its own to move them along, and to wake an old man from his bed and distant dreams.

The truck coughs to a stop at a small warehouse, where propped windows and large fan blades turn, or don't turn, beneath a sloping roof. Inside, the white-haired man who may go by the name of Sandro pushes himself up and into the morning light. He works steadily, rarely pausing, so that by noon row upon row of gleaming bird is placed on the warped but stable shelves fitted into the coolest corner of the building. He then collapses into a frayed lawn chair and pulls a warm Coca-Cola to his lips.

The birds share quarters with clay chimineas and mesquite armchairs, ironwood figurines and leather saddles. Together they wait unknowingly for their passage north.

"Águila?" Michael suggests. Eagle? The bird's stone manner and sharp eye suggest a raptor. And its ancestry may trace to the Mexica, who around 1300 CE were forced from the settlement of Chapultepec, two dozen miles north of current-day Mexico City, to an island in the middle of the region's deepest lake. Tenochtitlan was founded twenty-five years later, on the large island where the Mexica spied an eagle perched atop a towering cactus, consuming a snake. The eagle—embodying spiritual and physical strength, devouring the evil serpent—became a fitting symbol for the powerful and disciplined eagle-warriors and the persevering people themselves. Yet Michael's bird exhibits power in a subtler way—not the honed beak and talons that snare muscular prey, but rather a stoic poise and, if physical stature could reveal, an uncommon intellect behind incalculable eyes.

Centuries ago, *exploradores* traced the overgrown trails of the Sierra Madre Occidental not for the elusive gold of El Dorado but for a richly ferrous ore that was gathered, separated, and heated—then hammered into tools and weapons. In the filtered light of Copper Canyon, southwest of the Chihuahuan village of Cuauhtémoc, men chased the dark shadows of birds, spiritual guides to the heavy rocks they mined by hand and carried back to the local *herrero*, who ran his large, calloused hands over the rock to find its weakest point. Like a jaguar—its terrible force and beautiful grace—he worked the raw material into shape and reshape.

The *herrero*'s memory and myth, from childhood stories and tapestry tales, run through a young, muscular artisan as he caresses his newest bird that will soon make its journey to Soyopa and points north. Tereso is proud of his work, of the slow and deliberate method of bending the metal by hand. He slides a shield over his face, ignites the torch, and paces the brilliant flame as it cuts shoulder, wing. He lifts his mask and twists the metal slightly, pushing his full weight upon the ironwork and the wooden slab beneath. Then he steps back to let the bird cool, the sharp fumes quickly subsiding, removing his gloves so he can feel the smooth, black feathers and precise, open beak. Yes, this craft pleases him.

A quick knock at the doorframe brings him back. Lucía, a short woman in a once-white dress, smiles up at his face—solidly lined like the sculptures he creates—then comments on the elegance of the birds without removing her eyes from his. He blushes, looks to the floor, walks to an adjacent room. She follows, stroking the unfinished bird on the workbench as she passes.

The room they enter is a colony of birds perched side by side atop stained plywood shelves. Those on higher shelves will be picked up in a few days, making their way south to Torreón, Aguascalientes, and eventually Mexico City. He points to the lower shelves, finds a cart, and together they load a dozen birds. She pulls the cart from the room, smiles quickly, then leaves him. Stepping outside, he looks beyond her to a dark bird in a far pine.

Aided by a half-dozen excited children who have gathered for the chance of gum or other sweets, Lucía maneuvers the birds into a yellow Volkswagen van, then slips a small pack of Chiclets into each eager hand. With a steep rev of the engine, the van lurches forward and she heads north on the only road, a gravel-mud road, through a brief afternoon thunderstorm. She drives west over a quiet pass where the sun burns through the clouds, then down the western side of the mountain toward a small shack in Yepachic, where the metalwork flock remains that night. The next day they make the uneven trek through Santa Rosa and, by night again, Soyopa. Michael's bird, though he doesn't yet know it, is halfway to its new home.

We study the bird, lifting it from its roost on the wall as we set down our glasses. Its shape is familiar yet peculiar—not parrot, jay, roadrunner, eagle. "Raven?" we ask in unison. Could it be the darkly iridescent bird that ranges from North to South America and beyond? What, we wonder aloud, is the borderlands myth of that venerable bird?

Here is one possibility: In the thorn-scrub highlands of the Sierra Madre, Coyote is trying to capture Raven. Both are tricksters, both clever, which makes Coyote nervous. He cannot fly like Raven, cannot blend into the shadows as easily, complains to the empty audiences of the night that he is disadvantaged. The problem, as he sees it, is getting food, keeping his caches for himself.

One warm spring evening, Coyote's ears spike at the familiar yawp of Raven. She has just landed on the closest branch of an oak, nearly within leaping distance. "How may I help you?" asks Coyote, an air of annoyance in his canine voice.

"The question," croaks Raven, "is how may *I* help you?"

"Fly a bit lower so I can tell you," suggests Coyote, his sharp teeth shining, though Raven doesn't move.

"I have a proposition," says Raven. "I am hungry, like you. It is true that I have berries and beetles and a lizard now and then, but I need more."

"I can provide more? This sounds like a trap."

"It is a trap, my friend," says Raven. "But not for you. How would it be if I called to you when there was prey—prey you otherwise wouldn't know about? If in fact I help guide that antelope or young javelina to you?"

"What's in it for you?"

"Share the meal, of course. Don't run me off."

The deal was struck, and from that day on Coyote and Raven shared their meals. Today, ravens call out when prey is nearby, helping to direct animals toward the coyote. In return, the coyote lets the ravens dine on the meal, the resulting carrion.

This is, I tell Michael as we admire the silky, black raven we now agree the sculpture must be, no myth. Though the original conversation may have differed, coyotes and ravens often work together for food in the desert Southwest. It is a symbiotic relationship that evolved, perhaps, before myth itself.

It is fitting, says Michael, to settle on the raven—to imagine the artist drawing inspiration from the raven's call, the coyote's answer. Neither of us can think of another raven myth. Nor can we turn away from the long voyage of the storied bird as we contemplate our own journeys on the ancient seabed where my neighbor's bird perches, its handcrafted feathers luminous in the evening light.

A PURE COLOR

Hue:
The property of light by which the color of an object is classified
as red, blue, green, or yellow in reference to the spectrum.

1.

From the first morning, I see red. I feel it even more: fine claret
dust on my teeth, beneath my fingernails, on my skin like the
smooth scales of a coral snake. Sleeping in the teepee has something to do with it: wrapped in a tight turquoise bag on a cot
along the banks of Professor Creek, twenty miles from Moab,
Utah. I wake and wish for a cap; my exposed ears could crack
at the slightest touch. I wake and shake off the particulates that
hang in the air and in my dreams like the icy residue of fog.

The red of southern Utah is visible eyes open or closed. With
camera in hand, that scarlet hue is what I'm after. Yet there's
a broader pursuit, a central question: In the spectrum of place,
what can I learn from the hues of the land? Though I write, it is
often my camera that leads me, that captures and channels the

light and holds it. The digital lens is my regular guide to beauty, but on what paths: passion, serenity, vibrancy? And how does the experience of beauty—the seeking and obtaining—inform the landscape and our place in it?

Here, where it seems that only the Colorado River isn't red (it's milky brown or, in the evening, green tinged with indigo), the color seems inescapable. And yet it eludes me, for the light moves like a phantom across this high desert landscape: cliffs shift from vermilion to charcoal, arroyos wash from carmine to coffee. The changing light is a constant, and my desire is to hold it for the moment it takes to strike an image. In that respect I am a thief. I seek to steal the light, and in stealing so save it. Who can still such desires?

Red has long been the color of desire in Western cultures, and despite the autumn chill and thick cottonwoods along the creek, the color transports me to my home in Tucson. Our bungalow is not red but purple, the home's exterior decorated in paints labeled Putnam Plum, Concord Jam, and Ode to Purple. Contrasted against these tints, a prickly pear grows at the front of the house. Once only a trio of pale green pads, the cactus has sprawled into a spiny structure the size of a sedan. Not long ago, my daughters pointed out something odd on the plant, something white and waxy. From a distance, the growth looked like tufts of cotton caught in small patches along the cactus's spines, or like the remnants of "a spit-wad war zone," suggests entomologist Carl Olsen. It's a sure sign of cochineal, a small insect that uses its beak to spear the cactus pad and then slowly suck it dry. In Latin, cochineal means "scarlet-colored," and stripping away the wax reveals the female: bright red, baglike, a quarter-inch long.

Their history is also one of desire. According to Olsen, who studies the group of insects called scales, the cochineal was the basis for a thriving Aztec textile industry known for its bright red garments. The Aztecs called it *nochezli*, and it lived on the cactus nopal. After the conquest of the Aztecs, the Spaniards shipped bags of dried cochineal back to Spain; from there it became popular throughout Europe. Cochineal dye is found in Michelangelo paintings, in the first U.S. flags, and in the red coats of British soldiers and Canadian mounted police. Harvested today in Mexico, Algeria, and the Canary Islands, it is also used in cosmetics and food color, a natural alternative to artificial dyes.

From the frosty look of the prickly pear beneath the plum windowsill, cochineal could be harvested from our front yard as well. My daughters urge me to spray the wax from the pads. Get rid of it before it kills the cactus, they say. But I'm reluctant. Prickly pears are hardy, and though a pad or two has already fallen, I can't help but think these small beads of desire deserve a chance. While they are mostly sessile, the morning light that brings me back to Utah reminds me that desire shifts often, shimmering like the iridescent scales of a fish. The color of desire may be red, but I suspect the spectrum is not so easily divided, nor passion so clearly defined. Is it better, then, to focus less on color and more on landscape, those open spaces that likewise shift in the spectrum of memory and mood?

"Where I live," says author and naturalist Terry Tempest Williams, "the open space of desire is red." She lives one valley over. I live one state down but have traveled north less to contemplate color than to participate in a convergence of environmental writers and activists, red-faced denizens who—like Terry, like any of us concerned with the vanishing of natural landscapes and our place in them—wring their hands and then their minds in a collective desire for what we might call harmony. Or holism. Or healing. How, we ask and sometimes succeed in answering, can we counter the industry of progress with its singular conclusion of loss? Desire may be the answer, but that too may be lost in the valley's frigid morning. Or perhaps desire is exactly what I've found.

The sun has not yet risen over the vast rock formations that bulge like ancient, unlit cities. I walk toward them, my feet sweeping sand, my boots heavy with the stuff, as if the velvet ribbon of this arroyo could hold me as easily as I hope to hold it. Of course it could. Of course it has. We are never beyond the landscape, never fully able to claim it—though with camera in hand I am certain to try. A pack of coyotes calls from a distant ledge, the yipping a premature burst before sunrise. Then silence. How long can they hold it? How long can any of us hold the perfect moment before the break of day?

The sun rises and I stop. A cottontail scrambles. The sun's radiance lights the clouds in the east, though the orb has not yet breached the horizon. I raise my camera and turn to the west: a panorama of red. Sculpted, the arroyo flows and the easy metaphor is blood. But the riverbed is dry, dyed and bloodless. I think back to the cochineal, which digs in, covers itself with wax, and stays. That is a strong desire, even if humble, innate. The streambed's banks blaze with rabbitbrush and sage, foreground to tipping scarps and mesas. Burgundy then magenta then scarlet. In the distance: cliffs and spires of vermilion, rose, salmon, garnet—too many reds to count, more than my camera can claim or decipher. The rabbit rushes across the wash and I turn, lens whirring into focus, but miss the shot. It slows then and transforms: to juniper, to hill, to ruddy bluff. To the mesas and the sky beyond, red and—like an old desire made new—redder still.

2.

If red is desire, then psychologists like Morton Walker, author of *The Power of Color*, tell us that blue is serenity, cool both in temperature (based on the frequencies and literal temperature of its light wavelength) and identity, finding its way onto a majority of business logos, business suits. I admit less interest in blue as the corporate color of choice than as the color of landscape. And here I'm initially drawn to the discrete blue, like A. R. Ammons in his poem "Corson's Inlet," in which he compares the tiny blue flowers of a weed to a carapace of crab to a snail shell—all as "pulsations of order."

I think of pulsations not so much of order as of connectedness, transcendence. A deep link to the unconscious and the Earth—to aggregate grace and spirit that is the color blue. Yet it was a recent experience that bridged the color between landscape and self, a kind of passage embodied in the salty thrash of seawater, the struggle with flippers and mask and snorkel. I had never before snorkeled, and I struggled to relax, to float in a state of what I call *amniosis*. If such a word existed, it might mean "You get my drift." Or: I am adrift.

Still, the hook of the tube and the tasteless layer of rubber between teeth and cheek were alien. Head down, nose pinched in the mask, my breathing felt unnatural—frantic and forced. *Force yourself to be steady*, I remember thinking. *Imagine scuba diving: the whole body submerged, the full atmosphere of comfort strapped in a canister on your back, weights on your belt. The sinking in nautical light to darkness.* This was nothing, relatively; this was only snorkeling in a protected cove off Isla Coronado in the Sea of Cortés.

Only inches below the water, maybe ten feet above the brilliant ocean floor, panic was nonetheless my first reaction. I strained to keep my head down, to force the taste of saltwater from my snorkel so I could breathe unhindered. Though I saw blue I could not absorb it. But slowly the tension subsided, lost to the bay's mild currents and the weightlessness of my surroundings. Above, the azure sky was cloudless, only a moderate breeze from mainland Baja California Sur and the town of Loreto, flanked by the Sierra de la Giganta, blue and brown-blue as they faded into afternoon. Below, white sand tinted the water aquamarine, nearly green. Green, like blue, is an abundance in this garden of the desert's sea—the great inverted peninsula, rich in rare sea life. Yet in the vast blue, I also saw red. Like tranquility responding to desire, the ocean is a blue that relies on red. "Water owes its intrinsic blueness to selective absorption in the red part of its visible spectrum," say chemists Charles Braun and Sergei Smirnov. "Because the absorption which gives water its color is in the red end of the visible spectrum, one sees blue, the complementary color of red." Serenity as the complement of desire? Had my tranquility arrived because of the struggle, the hard desire, that came from forcing myself to relax? Perhaps any transformation to a higher state—a landscape internal or external—requires a challenge. Here at least, there is no equilibrium without change: no blue without red.

Yet this wasn't why I was here. Rather, the scrutiny of terms like *sustainable development* and *new urbanism* brought me to Loreto Bay, to the site of one of North America's largest resort developments at the time. No development exists out of context, of course. No development can call itself sustainable without an intrinsic connection to landscape. As with plants and animals, human communities must seek a certain symbiosis, a mutual success—a complementariness?—among the built and natural environments. That may mean regenerating the estuaries, planting organic gardens, pulling energy straight from the wind and sun. It may mean creating new schools, calling on alternative architecture, crafting a plan to support the Indigenous in place.

When the words and catchphrases run their length, however, what is left is image; and at the core of image: color. What this new community seeks is not a blue coolness but a rich relationship to place exhibited in the vibrant tropical hues of red and yellow and orange. Yet blue is all around: the sky and the sea, and also as a visual manifestation of trust and duty—associations Walker credits to the color blue—that must accompany any successful development. Trust between neighbors and among built and natural systems. Duty to actively enhance the landscape and the people who live and work on it. Neither is easy, though both are essential.

The chartered yacht to Isla Coronado was a side trip, a lucky tourist jaunt between these technical sessions. At Loreto Bay, I swam among a hundred dolphins, spied moray eels in the tidepools, and found myself voiceless in the synchronized fin sweeps of stingrays. Floating in the water of the turquoise sea, I could have been drifting anywhere: in the amniotic fluids of the womb, perhaps, or above the pearl of the Earth. "At a few hundred kilometers altitude, the Earth fills half your sky," says astronomer and author Carl Sagan, "and the band of blue that stretches from Mindanao to Bombay, which your eye encompasses in a single glance, can break your heart with its beauty…that relentless and exquisite blue."

Under that relentless, exquisite blue, the rhythm of the waves, draw of the current, and click-thrumming of the reef worked like a drug. I had felt this way only once before, under the influence of valium. Then I was certain I was a jellyfish, buoyed without a care in the peaceful sea. Here, I was attuned to the trio of angelfish beneath me, the curious triggerfish, those colorful wrasses weaving in and out of the coral. If only my wife and daughters were with me to experience this equilibrium. If only I had my camera, protected in a clear plastic case. But I am not certain the lens would have captured the full spectrum of the scene, the light refracted and reflected, returning the image I thought I'd seen. And I am not certain I would have tried in such an absorbed state of mind.

3.

The absorption of light by the landscape, and all physical matter, is deceiving. "The color of an object is not actually within the object itself," says physicist Tom Henderson. "Rather, the color is in the light which shines upon it and is ultimately reflected or transmitted to our eyes." The red rocks of Utah and piercing blues of the Sea of Cortés are not fundamentally red and blue, though their atomic structure may absorb light of certain wavelengths—certain colors—so that the frequencies of other colors are not revealed. It is a dance at the atomic level I struggle to comprehend, just as I strained to breathe mask-down in the sea. Yet the significance does not escape me: color is neither inherent nor absolute. If beauty is in the eye of the beholder, then color is an algorithm among the eye, the object, and the energy between. It may be as appropriate to define color as emotion or character or spirit, then, as to label it by the frequency of its wavelength— the physical hue and intensity of light that is the perception of color. Indeed, it may be more appropriate.

Take green: the color of healing, of freshness and nature, says Walker in *The Power of Color*. The origin of the word itself, *groeni* from the Old English, is related to the verb *growan*, meaning "to grow." Green as in verdure (from the Old Norse *visir*, for "bud, sprout") and, in more recent etymology, as in vibrancy: "vigorous, full of life." Green not as physical representation of color—only a perception, after all—but as embodiment of a state of being. And of distinct landscapes: the idea of landscapes?

In the Sonoran highlands of southern Arizona—where last summer I climbed the dry snake of a trail into the shadows of Sabino Canyon—green is the color of the desert. From spreading fleabane to waxy creosote, from airy brittlebush to palo verde, and from pineapple cactus to saguaro, here, in the foothills of the Santa Catalina Mountains that rim Tucson's northern edge, the desert is green: green thorns and branches and knotted trunks. Green shadows. Green flesh.

"If your knees aren't green by the end of the day, you ought to seriously re-examine your life," says Bill Watterson, author and illustrator of *Calvin & Hobbes*, the popular comic strip that subtly critiqued American culture and commerce. So beside the path, after scanning for rattlesnakes, I kneeled and pressed my knees into the desert soil, atop the minimal plants whose swollen buds were wrapped in leaves as dark as jade or, just as often, the light silver-green of chromis, the flash-finned tropical fish.

We also flash. One summer afternoon, seven inches of rain fell in the blue fir and pine forests of the Catalinas' highest peaks. Collecting, rushing through the canyon, and blowing out the road.

Flash flood: flash-forward: a U.S. Forest Service public meeting, following two months of input from neighbors and activists, was convened to determine whether the canyon's road should be rebuilt. And if so, whether the tram that accommodates passengers of all ages, at six dollars a ticket, should continue to run. The concerns, on one hand, were tram noise, pollution, the unsightly string of red and white cars against brilliant desert peaks. On the other: access, comfort, knowledge (perhaps) in the guide's magnified voice.

I wanted to lend my own words, if not my images, to the lush and spiny mix. So I voted no tram but supported the road. That's access and a bit more comfort. Knowledge? Bring a guide—human or field—and learn about the cactus wren and coyote, javelina and desert hare the old-fashioned way. Observation. Patience. The silent conversation with the land that is not possible in or from any machine. Seek there the color that is within oneself—the landscape, the vibrant spirit, may in turn absorb or else reflect. In either case, the light and its viewer have changed.

On my knees, I was tempted to slide my hands over the ground, to grasp the rocky soil and succulent plants. But in the Sonoran Desert, you're a fool if you try. The cholla, vibrant green with yellow, inch-long spines, is deceptive. Backlit and from a distance, the branching cactus looks soft. But the spines are barbed. They won't release without pliers and, generally, no small amount of pain. And then more anguish, for they carry an inflammatory—a mild poison that stiffens the wounds and slows the healing.

A risky landscape, then, in the deceptive green. And usually an arid landscape despite the verdure. Yet what I now fear is not the deception, nor the absence of water. What I fear is encroachment, one subdivision after another leaching into the canyon, so that green becomes something else altogether: the red of tile roofs, tan of stucco, black of asphalt. These must be the concerns of the neighbors of Loreto Bay as well. What representations, like the blue of trust and duty, does green confer in the salvation of the canyon? Not commerce, I hope, as in greenback; nor the green-eyed monster of envy. Choose instead resilience, vibrancy.

Despite my better judgment, I touched the ground that day, my fingertips finding a saguaro seedling beneath mesquite. It may have been a week old or a year, but no older. In time—in 150 or 200 years—it will grow to be nearly fifty feet tall and weigh six tons, thick arms sprawling. White flowers will bloom in May and then drop, followed by the fruit of June, glistening. The sweet flesh is red: like blood, like desire. Sharp contrast against green.

4.

If there is a contrast between color and landscape, and in that contrast a thread of connection between people and place, I may not be able to hold it. Words and photographs can fail, for they too are only perception. Perhaps, then, a new vision is needed? Perhaps we should trust the eyes of another form of art—the ability to transform color and in fact create it anew? "Some painters transform the sun into a yellow spot," says Pablo Picasso. "Others transform a yellow spot into the sun." And still others—those seeking the landscape's most saturated hues—are themselves transformed: one season barren and windblown, the next aflame in saffron and gold.

It is early March on the dunes of Sonora's Pinacate Desert, six miles south of the Arizona border. Early spring following a glorious winter of rain, when forgotten rivers raced in eddies of ochre and bronze. An early morning march through the waist-high sunflowers, black eyes and yellow petals; through the tangled evening primrose now closing for dawn; through the viole(n)t blooms of verbena. Through and above it all, the horizon bends to white. All frequencies of light, all wavelengths are scattered, and the landscape can absorb no more. Among the flowering dunes that seem endless this morning, I too feel white. But not colorless, technically achromatic because white has no hue. Rather, white as the combination of all colors of the visible light spectrum.

Moving among the flowers, my camera captures image after image of the dewy scene, a rarity here in Mexico's largest desert, where the dunes bloom on average every decade or less. Though I am filled with the full spectrum of colors, delighted to the brim, there is a hue brighter than all others, and it calls to me in its Spanish name: *amarillo*. Yellow.

After a photograph taken on my knees, my head dowsed in the petals, I realize I cannot go on. I cannot go on for all the yellow. I don't need a book of color psychology to understand that it is the color of praise and promise and hope. In a word: beauty. And it consumes me: the wide field of sunflowers, the burning disc of the sun, the golden tint of my own skin. Everything brilliant and blazing and yellow. Yet everything ephemeral, for in two weeks the temperature will arc into the nineties or higher, and the flowers will fade and fall, the dunes regaining the wind-carved cleft of the landscape.

Everything ephemeral. That's not what we're taught but what we learn in studying the land. Or stopping to watch, camera to eye or otherwise. Who can grasp the scale of geologic time? The mauve Sierra Pinta across Mexico Highway 2 were not even hills a hundred million years ago. Who can question the arid wisdom of Pinacate's maar craters, those mile-wide calderas formed between 150,000 and five million years ago, when rising magma collided with groundwater in atomic-force blasts that created a moonscape of black pumice and red-walled cliffs? And who among us can lend an Earth-old voice to the great and terrible changes of our own age?

"The people who live in a golden age usually go around complaining how yellow everything looks," says the poet Randall Jarrell. Yellow not as praise but tarnish. Yet all I see over these miles of sloping dunes is yellow, blooming even if short-lived.

The poet contends that people complain about things no matter how good they've got it. Or said another way: they cannot appreciate the colors in the landscapes, and therefore the landscapes themselves, if we can even see them at all. Yet all around us is beauty. It is easier to see, perhaps, in the red canyons of Utah, blue shoals of the sea, green scarps of the Sonoran Desert. Or the flaring yellow wildflowers of Pinacate. But it takes neither a photographer's eye nor a dramatic vista to realize that beauty shines across all our landscapes. To see the beauty, to focus the light to a brilliant white, can be a considerable task, at times more frustrating than the crafting of a poem that seeks its own certain beauty. So perhaps we begin just by stopping. Maybe none of us can go on until we resist, refocus, and reconsider. Or maybe in stopping we need only absorb, find our complement in the landscape, and accept that we too may complement the landscape rather than oppose it?

In Pinacate, I came across a throng of blister beetles—black crossed by copper—on the wind-worn edge of the largest maar crater. The insects crawled and swarmed. They transformed the landscape—moving in fervor to find a mate, to take their brief inheritance of time and push on. Push forth without pulling away. The beetles reminded me of the cochineal, whose waxy threads litter the prickly pears of my yard in search for mates. Science tells us of this drive for progeny, and that much is clear. Still, it seems there is a deeper drive in each of us; something along the lines of the color yellow, if I had to name it by hue.

The blister beetles couldn't stop in all their focused frenzy, but I could. Looking up, I saw that the edge of the caldera was bronze in the afternoon light. Here and there, chollas glowed amber against the volcanic soil. Green-leafed ocotillos wore caps of scarlet blooms, yellow-centered, and the bees were delirious in their own frenzied work among these eclectic desert plants. Looking down into the crater, I saw iridescent buzzards circling five hundred feet above the poppy-covered floor that emanated in rings of yellow and orange. It was a strange scene, full of odd colors and odder shapes; but whoever said beauty meant popularity, conformity? Each landscape is unique. Each color can be newly revealed—humans can see up to ten million of them—and beauty strikes at every opportunity.

There is a strange property of light, too, in Pinacate, leaving me silent along the edge of this caldera, or in the morning's intoxicating dunes, or among the yellow-green senita cacti that glow like candles from a black desert floor. It is a light that feels exact, like the definition of hue itself: "a pure color, one without tint or shade." If I could paint that light, striving for the dabs and strokes of Picasso, I might find the canvas is inside me as surely as out. There, the landscape begins with red and blue, green and yellow. Here, it concludes in desire, serenity, vibrancy: a certain beauty, ephemeral but pure.

PHOTOGRAPHING THE RESPLENDENT TREES

The Visual Elements of Photography

Texture · Focus · Color · Framing and
Composition · Light Quality · Angle of View

AMON CARTER MUSEUM, FORT WORTH, TEXAS

TEXTURE

How the surface of an object appears to feel or actually feels;
shown in photography by the way light falls on an object and
through value changes.

Though the wind has always shaped the West Texas landscape,
I hadn't anticipated its gusto the night I made camp in the
Guadalupe Mountains. I arrived late, my brain and limbs stiff
from the four-hundred-mile drive. Only a crooked path lined by
cholla and piñon separated the pullout from the campsite. But in
that cold distance, I reconsidered. While an evening in my tiny
Honda would no doubt be an exercise in contortion, a night in a

nylon tent buffeted by the riotous wind looked even less appealing. Once I pinned down the parachute of my tent and mastered the spindly contraption of the poles, however, exhaustion won out, and I slept.

The following morning the campground was quiet even as the wind rushed above the canyon. A thick ribbon of silver clouds sped over the mountaintops like an animated diorama of the Gulf Stream, skimming the craggy caps of El Capitan and Guadalupe Peak, at 8,700 feet Texas's highest point. Though I'd seen the silhouette of the mountains against the dazzling sash of the Milky Way as I pitched the tent, I hadn't realized their drama. Now I was held not by the clouds—though it was hard to pull my eyes away from the body of their velocity—but rather by the pale cliffs buttressed by hills of oak and Texas madrone, split by canyons of maple and ash, the leaves a tattered weave of scarlet and saffron on this late October day.

An assignment for a University of Arizona landscape photography course prompted my visit to one of the most diverse mountain ranges in the desert Southwest. But the federally protected region that spans northwestern Texas and southeastern New Mexico had tempted me for years. Famous for its exposed fossilized reef, Guadalupe Mountains National Park is also a favorite of western leaf peepers: the Guadalupes harbor the Southwest's largest congregation of hardwoods. Bigtooth maples grow alongside ash and oak to form a layered canopy of flashy autumn leaves lining deep limestone canyons.

My task wasn't simply to photograph the mountains and trees in peak foliage, but to show the place in a way that both documented the landscape and presented scenes in unique and surprising ways. My goal was to break from the long-lived (and long-loved) manner of capturing landscapes in the common, even stereotypical photographs found, for example, in large-format books and panoramic calendars. That is, I sought an evolution of my own photography, as craft and art—building from the techniques of the classroom and the guidance of my mentors. In thinking critically about how I composed photographs, I therefore found it necessary to explore the reasons behind my passion for photography. Do I seek the experience of taking the picture, or do I prefer instead the end result that is the presentation of the photograph itself? Are those pursuits mutually exclusive, or is there something larger involved? Why do I invest so much time, energy, and money in a hobby that has increasingly possessed me, and happily so? Or, as landscape photographer Frank Gohlke writes, "To say that I am offered the possibility of a picture is true but inadequate; what begs for explanation is why a tactually, chromatically impoverished scrap of illusion like a photograph should exert such a persistent hold on anyone's behavior, maker or viewer."

Camped along the golden foothills of the Guadalupes on that first chilly morning, I found that the landscape provided the rich texture, like my daybreak photograph of two trees intertwined, for these questions and my own subsequent search. In the photo, the gnarled branches of a gray alligator juniper twist around the smooth trunk of a Texas madrone. The madrone's limbs are creamy in the soft light, delicious except the charred gash that centers the photo and is framed by the chaos of the juniper's aged branches. In the background, the muted hues of yellow, red, and green form a tapestry of autumn leaves, further emboldening the branches of the foreground. Though the photograph may be an illusion, its texture lures me deeper. Though photography may be the pursuit of illusion, the journey itself is no less real.

FOCUS

The sharpness or clarity of subjects in the photographic image; photographers use aperture and limitations of the lens to create sharp detail, soft edges, or both—this is called selective focus.

Though I moved to Tucson in 2000, I didn't visit the University of Arizona's renowned Center for Creative Photography until 2009. The center opened in 1975 with the archives of five American landscape photographers—most notably Ansel Adams and Harry Callahan—and now houses more photographic work than any other museum in the United States. Unlike traditional museums, the center allows select visitors to request viewings of individual photographs through its print study program. Curators arrange matted prints in a viewing room, the photographs placed at eye-level and lit as if in an art gallery. Prints may not be handled, but a close viewing reveals a sharp difference between the ubiquitous calendar reprint of Ansel Adams's *Moonrise, Hernandez, New Mexico*, for example, and the intricate print that Adams himself first developed in 1941.

A recent viewing of the prints of Adams and other American landscape photographers led me to think about the idea of cliché in photography. *Cliché* is a French term originally used in the 1820s by printmakers to represent a stereotype plate: a block containing a common phrase that could easily be inserted into the printing press instead of placing individual letter blocks with each use. By the 1890s, cliché became a word to critically describe language, "a usually pejorative general term for a word or phrase regarded as having lost its freshness and vigour through overuse (and therefore suggesting insincerity, lack of thought, or laziness on the part of the user)," according to the *Oxford Companion to the English Language*.

I don't consider Adams's photos clichéd, even if the successful marketing behind the prints leaves them commonplace. But photographs that mimic the dramatic vistas and sweeping, silvery style of Adams's prints might be considered stereotypical nowadays, at least by those seeking a newer way to photograph American landscapes. And that mimicry is what I hoped to avoid in my photographs of West Texas.

I was drawn to the Center for Creative Photography through the landscape photography course taught by center director Britt Salvesen and Frank Gohlke, the university's Laureate Professor of Photography and a senior research fellow at the center. Best known for his large-format prints that mix the built and natural environments—grain elevators of the Midwest, Massachusetts's Sudbury River, his childhood home of Wichita Falls—Gohlke is an engaging teacher with a keen eye for landscape and place. To him these terms have different meanings. "A place is not a landscape; places are contained within landscapes," he writes. As we explored the concepts of landscape and place through photography, I began to form a better sense of how to frame the scenic vistas of the Southwest, relying heavily on a wide-angle lens to capture the desert's wide-open sky. In the photos I shared in class, I hoped to show the majestic essence of place—not the full landscape, of course, but some striking representation.

"Well—," Gohlke said during a meeting to discuss my final project, in which I proposed the trip to the Guadalupes. His voice trailed off, yet I knew he wanted to say something else. He was reluctant, perhaps hedging on whether he'd hurt my feelings. I urged him on; twenty years older than most of the students in the class, I hoped my constitution was twenty years stronger as well. "Your photographs are too clichéd," he finally said.

He handed me an issue of *Arizona Highways*, the touted travel magazine known for its superb photography. "Don't be like this," he said, pointing to a dramatic picture of the Vermillion Cliffs, clouds sweeping over the red rock formations like the wings of angelic swans.

At first I blanched. I wasn't offended that he criticized my photos. Already I was seeking new approaches to my work, which still slid comfortably into the panoramic landscape views so common in *Arizona Highways*. What troubled me instead was that, clichéd or not, I found the photos in the magazine, Sierra Club calendars, and the like to be stunning. I had seen dozens of pictures of radiant desert mountains above fuchsia fields of verbena, for instance, but if the photos were dramatic and well-crafted, I liked them anyway.

Clichés can also be valuable. "Proverbs, because they are mnemonic formulas, help people pass on elements of oral tradition without needing or seeking to be novel or clever every time," notes the *Oxford Companion*. "Comparably, many common expressions derive from classical cultures and much-admired texts, and have become part of the language because they have long been highly valued, and acquire as a result a kind of proverbial status." These common phrases were admired, in fact, because they were unoriginal to begin with—they were familiar to their audiences and fostered a sense of belonging. Couldn't beautiful but clichéd photographs be familiar and therefore valuable to their audiences, too?

Audience plays a key role when considering the photographs of *Arizona Highways*. The purpose of the magazine is to sell Arizona, and whether macro or panoramic, the photos all represent a vivid focus on the natural and cultural diversity of the state. Even if the pictures are not stereotypical, their goal is to entice people to come to Arizona, to fondly visualize and remember its stunning landscapes. The audience for nature calendars and large-format books similarly seeks the iconic representations of place—unforgettable images of natural scenes undoubtedly photographed and presented many times before, yet still appealing.

Yet in its photography submission guidelines, even *Arizona Highways* urges against the clichéd: "Be original and creative in your composition and approach to common subjects, and avoid visual clichés like saguaro silhouettes at sunset." Paradoxically, the first image to appear on (and the background throughout) the magazine's website is a crooked ridge of saguaros silhouetted at sunset.

Nevertheless, considering my photography in the context of cliché enabled me to refocus, represented by a photograph of an oak branch against a boulder I took in the Guadalupes. The small lobed leaves, gold tinged with scarlet, seem to float against the unfocused gray background. And though the details of the bunched branch are sharp—a single green leaf jutting beyond its yellow sisters, the contrast of wine-red twigs beneath the leaves—the shape, shadows, and coloring of the rock ultimately draw my eye beyond the foliage so that the picture becomes two images: branch and boulder. Taken separately, each is distinct, a singular resonance that could hold its own frame. Together, however, the images create a balance of focus that is anything but clichéd—as if the composition, rather than the photographer or viewer, selects its own focus.

COLOR

Artists use color to achieve many effects, including a sense of mood, place, and time of year; it can also move your eye around a composition and create a sense of space on a flat surface.

I shouldered my camera bag and walked west into Pine Springs Canyon, cleft from the eastern edge of the Guadalupe Mountains. By the time I reached the first hill's shallow summit of oak, yucca, and prickly pear, I had snapped three dozen photos on my digital, multilens camera: first the quick corridor of the clouds, then the striated cliffs, then the dead and twisted limbs of an alligator juniper shining like chrome in the morning light. Behind me the flatlands of Texas spread for a thousand miles or more, that slow slope into the Gulf of Mexico. Before me, however, flat surfaces diminished: a split boulder as big as a bear, or the wiry shafts of knee-high grass. In between, the trail edged the rim of an arroyo so that every now and then the top of a solitary crimson maple stopped me cold. I was unsure whether I'd see brighter foliage farther in and closer at hand. I framed another dozen photos, just in case.

During the first mile of my hike, I paused at the sudden buff-colored shifting on a nearby knoll. I heard the breaking of a branch before the noise and movement vanished. Though I raised the camera to my eye, a voice in my head urged caution: I remembered the sighting of a young mountain lion in my neighborhood just the week before, and recalled a cougar recently shot by wildlife managers in Madera Canyon south of Tucson for stalking hikers. Don't run and don't crouch low, I said to myself. Back away slowly, arms raised in my best imitation of a walking tree—formidable and, with luck, inedible. But I couldn't level myself, couldn't find the patience I knew was necessary to frame the shot. "Hey!" I yelled, my absurd attempt at authority echoing across the canyon. An instant of silence and then the crashing of rocks as two deer leaped from the dark scrub and bounded into a thicker copse, their white tails arcing out of sight. I watched them trail off before I breathed again.

My destination was Devil's Hall, the terminus of a four-mile trail that wasn't as much strenuous as tricky. The path wound through a limestone canyon, cairns marking the way. The first half tracked the grasslands of the higher foothills. Then the trail dropped to a wash—its smooth rocks white from the calcified fossils—while the steep but weathered walls of the canyon closed in. Though the stream was dry when I passed through, it could rage during summer and winter rains. Branches and dislodged trees splayed against the creek's curves and mammoth boulders, building up until a wall of water would flush them downstream.

Once in the arroyo, however, my fears dissolved. Not only did I forget about mountain lions, but I became lost in the myriad colors. Reaching a bend in the streambed, I stepped into a stand of maples every hue of fire, and some beyond. The trees leaned over the wash, which meandered in direction and width. Though the canyon floor was stippled with fallen leaves, the trees still held full canopies. I spent the next hour taking three hundred photos.

Where the trees framed a view of the jagged peaks to the south, the clouds split to reveal blue sky and a new light that outlined the crispness of every branch. Once I reached the natural stone staircase that rises at the canyon's narrowest point—Devil's Hall—I turned again and again, intoxicated not by the thinning air but by the views: amber leaves on ashen walls, scarlet leaves above white boulders, auburn leaves against a sky of tungsten and azure.

If I was drunk from the autumn colors on the hike of the first day, I was downright dizzy on the second. I could not attribute my altered state to the fall foliage, however. Instead, I blamed the long trail up Guadalupe Peak, the steep switchbacks that left me out of breath, the intense sun as I climbed higher. Though I hiked for hours on that bright morning, I never reached my summit destination. Regardless, the view from the eastern slope, though not as broad as from the ridge a thousand feet higher I'm sure, was grand. Short of the final vista, I had nonetheless trekked far enough to frame subjects far from ordinary. I photographed the wide views, keeping the shining road in the frame rather than cropping it out as I would have done before. And I photographed closer views: purple cactus spines on waxy green pads, the dimpled vermilion berries of Texas madrone.

Hiking back down, I considered why, beyond the excuse of a class I greatly enjoyed, I chose to travel hundreds of miles east to photograph this landscape. The phrase that echoed in my mind was *to see and to resee*. Friends who know my passion for photography have asked whether the camera distorts my view of place—whether I miss something because I'm constantly looking through the viewfinder. My answer surprises them: the camera instead enables me to see much more of the landscape and, depending on the lens and other factors, to view the landscape from multiple perspectives. How so? I pay more attention to my surroundings with a camera in hand because I seek a composition that reveals not only the place itself but also its context. "A well-made photograph directs us past the history of its own creation to the histories of everything in it, of the things in themselves and of how they came to be where they are," says Gohlke in his photography collection *Accommodating Nature*, which was commissioned and published by the Amon Carter Museum.

It may seem that only those photos containing distinct human elements meet Gohlke's criteria for well-made photographs. Yet even in deep wilderness, my best photographs reveal histories, though notably more ecological than human, for they are the slow and elegant histories of the mountains themselves. One photo from Pine Springs Canyon in particular is framed by orange maples at the curve of the limestone wash. Large white boulders, cracked yet smooth from tumbling through the canyon, stack pell-mell beneath a pocked rock as big as a house. Jammed between the rock and a bigtooth maple, the stripped trunk of a thick pine balances: the arroyo's giant driftwood caught at the canyon's turn. Surrounding each boulder, beneath each limb old and new, lies a quilt of autumn leaves.

Beautiful in its own right, the scene is rich in the histories of seasons, years, and millennia. The fallen leaves of the previous few weeks will wash away in winter rains and summer floods, as they have season upon season for a thousand years or more. The large trunk that once stood on a ridgetop will also, some summer, be cast farther downstream. And as over the past hundred or thousand or million years, the rocks will continue their slow roll down the canyon; the fist-sized cavities in the large rock will broaden from wind and sun and rain; the maples will grow and die and fall, saplings reaching up in their absence. And the mountains? Formed more than 250 million years ago as part of the Capitan Reef in the Permian Ocean, they've been subsiding ever since.

Without my camera in hand, a stroll through a desert arroyo may take twenty minutes. With my camera, it is likely to take an hour or more as I scan the intricate leaves and rocks, the broader panorama—composing each photograph over and over before clicking the shutter. By switching lenses, I further adjust focal points, depth of field, image breadth, and more, allowing me to view a scene in a variety of ways.

Paying close attention to and therefore spending more time in a place is not the only reason I photograph. Just as important is the finished product—the photograph itself, which in my digital world is transferred from the camera via a thin memory card onto my computer. Once on the monitor, I adjust brightness, contrast, saturation, and the like, with the goal of reseeing the place through the photograph and sharing the image with others, usually online. That's a different process than print photographers like Gohlke undertake: there are no chemicals to mix, no darkrooms to maintain. Yet I hope the outcome is comparable: an image that contains not just the framed elements of the particular landscape but also the complexities, histories, and emotion of the place and, to no small degree, its photographer. I strive to capture and share the dynamic spectrum—the myriad colors—of place.

FRAMING AND COMPOSITION

Framing is how a photographer presents a subject by deciding what to include in the picture frame; the photographer then composes the image to draw a viewer's attention to the subject in a way that best expresses the artist's idea of it.

Although I was eager to broaden my photographic perspective, not to mention my skills, I didn't necessarily agree with Gohlke's damning of *Arizona Highways*' dramatic photos. What he called clichéd I considered simply a matter of taste. Here were sublime photographs of the rugged desert landscape, framed in such a way as to accentuate the powerful crux at which rock meets cloud, on one page, and the curve of a cerulean stream that flows in a valley so glowingly beautiful it is almost beyond comprehension, on another. How could my teacher not also swoon in the view of these wild landscapes, these stunning photographs?

This far into the course, I should have been able to answer the question even before asking it. Early in our readings we studied cultural geographer J. B. Jackson, whose philosophy that "landscape is a human creation" greatly influenced Gohlke's work. In 1975 Gohlke was selected with eight other artists to exhibit in *New Topographics: Photographs of a Man-Altered Landscape*. The exhibition was "an instantaneous revelation to the photographic community," according to Amon Carter senior photography curator John Rohrbach. "By attending to the mere look of places in all their mundane being, they were celebrating not beauty or artistic genius, but photography's ability to record," he writes. Gohlke's panoramic photographs of Mount Saint Helens following its 1980 eruption show that beauty and artistic intent still matter, but even at that time, Rohrbach says, "Gohlke was rejecting a widely accepted definition of landscape as a picturesque emblem of beauty, balance, and stasis that had been held since the Enlightenment. His vision heralded the land as active and filled with unpredictability."

Before my trip to the Guadalupes, Gohlke loaned me the magazine, a special issue on photography. As I turned the pages, my awe and excitement waned as I saw that, with the exception of cultural artifacts like missions or mesquite fences on picturesque ranchlands, the photographs distinctly kept out the idea of landscape as a human creation. I still enjoyed the photos, and envied their making, but I couldn't help but think of the dichotomy in my own work: I write about the passions of culture and our human place among the desert but photograph the desert mostly devoid of humans. I've understood and appreciated for years—at least since living in Denver and studying urban and regional planning in the 1990s—that humans are an intrinsic part of the landscape. Yet the photos I most enjoy and try to emulate are those of unspoiled natural landscapes. Even Ansel Adams's *Moonrise, Hernandez, New Mexico*, one of my favorites, relegates the small pueblo of Hernandez to a static (though essential) element of the landscape's foreground.

Robert Adams, who like Gohlke exhibited in *New Topographics*, explores the photographer's drive to document landscape in his essay collection *Why People Photograph*. One conclusion suggests that photographers work on a kind of visual subconscious level and not in the pursuit of an ideology or even, perhaps, aesthetic. "One does not for long wrestle a view camera in the wind and heat and cold just to illustrate a philosophy," he writes. "The thing that keeps you scrambling over the rocks, risking snakes, and swatting at the flies is the *view*. It is only your enjoyment of and commitment to what you see, not to what you rationally understand, that balances the otherwise absurd investment of labor."

Without a whit of rational understanding, I became interested in photography the summer between my sophomore and junior years of high school, when my father purchased an Olympus OM-F before I embarked on a two-month trip around the world. The camera was paired with a manual-focus 35mm lens. While entry-level 35mm cameras today come equipped with autofocus 18–55mm lenses that allow some degree of telephoto zoom and panoramic perspective, the constraints of a fixed-width lens sharpened my ability to compose a photograph, even as I struggled with aperture, shutter speed, and a stiff, lead-lined travel bag stuffed with film cartridges.

Our first destination was Reykjavík, Iceland, and almost immediately I set out to photograph Hallgrimskirkja, the landmark church that soars above the quaint Scandinavian capital. I made it only as far as the field across from our hostel, where I knelt down to capture the church's gray tower against a backdrop of ice-capped mountains and a high foreground of grass. It remains one of my most successful images, as if the sober tower grows from the feathery field itself. As the trip continued through northern Europe, across Russia, and into Japan, I photographed historic buildings and interesting architectural angles—row-houses in Copenhagen, Saint Basil's Cathedral at Red Square, the vibrant orange gate of Kyoto. Much to my later chagrin, I photographed few of my traveling comrades, and surprisingly little of the wild landscapes, even though we traveled for days on the Trans-Siberian Express without seeing a town or even a homestead.

Back in the United States, I put away my camera, except for the occasional family reunion, until I graduated from college and moved to Colorado. By then I was a raging environmentalist, fresh off the works of Edward Abbey and Aldo Leopold, under the influence of the enticing if not always legal antics of groups like Earth First!. Yet I also worked for the U.S. Department of Energy and had to quell my radical environmental leanings, at least during the workday. The long commute between suburban apartment and spruce-dotted office park compounded the pressure of keeping my environmental opinion to myself. The result: a renewed interest in photography, coupled with a series of trips to the great vistas of the West. I moved between color and black-and-white film, shooting panoramic landscapes in such locations as the Grand Tetons, Rocky Mountain National Park, and the Canyonlands of southern Utah.

In Colorado, I often traveled with a college buddy who likewise was a budding photographer. Yet when I moved to

Maryland the next year, my interest in photography sloughed off like the technicolor autumn leaves of local sugar maples. Though I continued snapping a few photos here and there when my wife and I returned to Colorado a year later, the come-and-go hobby didn't morph into the sometimes absurd passion it is today until we moved to Tucson, when friend and neighbor Scott Calhoun convinced me to join him on a trip into Mexico's Pinacate Desert in 2005. Among the elbow-high sunflowers whose green knees knocked sand verbena, evening primrose, and a dozen other showy flowers on Pinacate's sculpted dunes, I joyfully succumbed. The day we returned to Tucson, I purchased a new camera, a Canon DSLR, and a spectrum of new lenses to adorn it. As my passion and expertise grew, the landscapes of my compositions increasingly kept people out; there appeared to be no room, and no need, in the frame. Why, I said to myself, include people and the mundane when they just clog the view?

On a ledge overlooking the desert grasslands of West Texas, however, I framed a shot that begins to convince me otherwise. In the photograph, the trail to the summit of Guadalupe Peak is edged on the left by clumping junipers before dropping to the mountain's base. Grass along the left edge of the trail flares in the morning light. Beyond that: the east, and a sky white in the morning sun. To the right, high grasses, mesquite, and prickly pear echo the new day's glow so that the viewer is compelled to keep going, to climb toward the lush brightness. Yet the chalky trail—bisected by timbers that serve as steps and prevent trail erosion—lies in shadow, the crumbled limestone almost blue. A reason, perhaps, to turn back? Just the opposite: the cool trail stitches the radiant mountainside, inviting the viewer into the scene. Indeed, the composition would mean little without the trail. It is separate neither from the mountain nor from my experience of the mountain, despite efforts I would have once made to exclude it.

LIGHT QUALITY
The source, amount, and direction of lighting in a photograph.

Upon my return from the Guadalupe Mountains, I tallied nearly a thousand photographs. Where those images ended, my memory clicked in: an owl dipping like a net through the faint stream of bats at Carlsbad Caverns, a glossy king snake gliding the trail at McKittrick Canyon, the heavy cap of mountain clouds as night brewed over the campsite. Like those clouds, my mind swirled, creating a strange weather of ideas around the challenge of capturing surprise and originality in a landscape largely devoid of human objects. That may be Gohlke's approach—to seek out the ordinary landscape of humans, a landscape made unordinary by his elegant eye—but it couldn't be mine. Instead, I found the most success where I turned the subject upon itself by mixing my choice of lenses. Instead of the wide-angle lens that would capture the mountain's breadth, I mounted a telephoto lens to hone in on a cliff washed with the contrast of yellow ash and emerald pine. Rather than the macro lens for every close shot, I switched to the panoramic, bringing to light both the object and its broader context, whether a lichen-laced rock or the hazy Texas plains beyond the mountains. After reviewing the photos, however, I realized that I hadn't fully explored the question of why I photograph—even if I did (mostly) succeed in avoiding cliché.

Returning the favor of Scott's spring wildflower emergency to Pinacate, I called with an autumn leaf emergency. Two weeks beyond the Guadalupes' peak, the leaves of Garden Canyon deep within the Huachuca Mountains of southern Arizona should be at their prismatic prime, I told him. Scott agreed, and with my younger daughter, Juliet, we loaded into my car and headed south. Like the Guadalupes, the Huachucas provide a delightfully craggy habitat for trees found in few other places. With its perennial stream, Garden Canyon is overgrown with bigtooth maples, Arizona sycamores, scrub oak, and here and there the rare Apache pine. We sought southern Arizona's most coveted fall foliage, and we hoped that the clear skies above us wouldn't let the mountains live up to their Apache name: *huachuca*, thunder.

In the Guadalupes, reaching the canyons required formidable hikes. Accessing Garden Canyon required a different type of exertion: permission from the U.S. Army. The only road into the canyon is through Fort Huachuca, a historic garrison spanning the eastern side of the mountains. Though the base's signal command and military intelligence tasks may be secret, the target ranges that line the road to the canyon are in full view. Fields chiseled from high Chihuahuan Desert offer practice for pistols and assault rifles, grenade launchers and even larger weapons. Scott, Juliet, and I passed them all in my Honda once the guards logged our identities, and though I found myself tempted to stop and photograph the well-kept ranges that foreground the mountain's wilder slopes, we kept to the road lest the army rescind its decision to let us in.

Though the sky was cloudless, the chinooks seemed to follow me from Texas. My low-slung car crept over the dirt road that climbed the steep canyon, but we swayed less from the ruts and my sudden maneuvers to avoid large rocks than from the gusting wind. Halfway up the road we saw that the sycamores had lost most of their foliage—only the lower branches held firm to the baseball mitt–sized leaves, yellow and yellow-brown, that dangled from elegant white limbs. I drove as far as I dared, thinking of a previous car's busted oil pan from a similar trek, and then parked.

Hiking up the hardscrabble road, we spied a few trees of ruby and gold but otherwise found only waning sycamores and browning oak. Then we rounded a curve to view something unexpected. As a professional gardener, Scott is familiar with the plants of the desert Southwest. Yet the grouping of thin roots swaying from the underside of an adjacent scarp was new even to him. Was it moss or some hairy lichen? Maybe, I suggested, it was bear fur. At that height, a bear could have used the sharp granite to scratch its back, he agreed. We approached, bemused. Then I touched the fibrous mass—and sprang back, nearly toppling my daughter. In an instant the congregation of daddy longlegs erupted, hundreds of arachnids scuttling away from my touch almost as quickly as I yanked back my hand. A few moments later, the harvestmen crawled back, nuzzling into each other so that only their threadlike legs remained exposed.

I was reminded of my encounter with deer on the trail to Devil's Hall—the heightened moment of the unknown, when the light turns crystalline regardless of the weather. I was reminded, as well, of the joys of the unexpected and of the superb moment of uncalculated risk that make the experience of landscape photography fulfilling, even before focusing the lens. "The odd thing for me," says Gohlke in *Accommodating Nature*, "is that the network of relationships in my photographic work does not seem to originate in a stationary point of view, even though at some moment in time a stance must finally be chosen, a choice that constitutes the eventual picture." Motion, like narrative arc in prose, indeed seems an essential component regardless of the subject.

Do I photograph, then, to keep moving? The answer must be yes, though even that is not the complete answer. To access the photograph I don't yet know I'll take, I must seek it out, moving through a place and in the process finding the right emotion both for me and the landscape. Likewise, I seek the light that best engages the subject while setting the photograph's tone. Early morning and the last rays of day are natural windows, but even midday—such as our journey into the Huachucas—can surprise and reveal. One of my first photographs from the trip, for example, is of a trio of Arizona sycamores towering against a mountainside of granite and pine. Stripped bare from the wind, the trees rise like bleached antlers against a cobalt sky. Though the yellowing leaves of the foreground catch the midday light, creating an intricate pattern of shadows, what captures my attention is a single oval cloud—its edges blurred—just cresting the mountain. Bisected by the center sycamore, the cloud itself represents movement, or movement stilled. I have moved, and so has the cloud; yet in the print the cloud remains forever motionless. Is a part of me likewise now still? Thinking through the moment of the photograph—recalling place and time through color and light—I recognize that I am always moving: the spinning of the galaxy, the rotation of the Earth, the sway of family and landscape and place that draws me out with camera in hand.

ANGLE OF VIEW

The position from where the photographer takes a picture; angle of view can also express emotion or mood and give the viewer a sense of being big or small.

The last time Scott, Juliet, and I set out to photograph the landscape, we reveled in the early spring glow of southern New Mexico's Organ Mountains. Scott and I moved delicately yet also deliberately through a desert thick with ground-dwelling yucca, prickly pear, cholla, and whitethorn acacia, our shadows leaning across the landscape as the sun set behind us. Staying until dark, we tracked our own trails, as we often do—in part to chase our distinct visual whims and in part to avoid capturing the same images. Juliet followed behind me as I loaded my memory cards with those happily clichéd photographs of the mountains' rhyolite cliffs, the sapphire sky, the enticing shapes of the succulents and flowering shrubs. Picking our way back to my car, we were exhausted but delighted in the afternoon's successful outing. As I drove the vehicle from the dirt roadside, Scott switched his digital camera into image view mode and clicked through his photos, pausing occasionally to show me a particular favorite, the three-inch LCD screen lighting the car's interior. After he stowed the camera I shifted into higher gear and, rounding a wide curve, promptly lost control of the car and crashed.

The dust cleared and we assessed the situation: the damage was notable but not disabling to the car's body, or thankfully to ours. I considered whether my car's slide into the high dirt embankment was the direct result of my earlier photo-taking or the fault of poor driving. What now seems more relevant was the altered state brought on by the photographic excursion, not unlike my sense of bliss at Devil's Hall: not a sustained state, but a heightened conscious and subconscious connection to the landscape brought on by my efforts to photograph it. "The axis of sight, as it swings around its center, supplies the amplifying force to a photographer that the limited range of instruments and materials cannot—the imaginative analog of mechanical advantage," writes Gohlke.

A quarter-hour after our discovery of the daddy longlegs at Garden Canyon, I still sought that axis of sight, that psychic bridge brought on by the beauty and sublime calling of place.

And I sought, too, a more definitive response to the question of why I photograph. So far, however, we were disappointed in the fall colors and bruising wind of the Huachucas. Finally, though, we spied a small break in the trees that revealed an airy hall thick with orange maples. We could have easily walked past the gap that seemed to tumble open like a broad and leafy kaleidoscope. But our eyes were keen, even against the wind.

Peering in, I saw a crooked stream drop in a series of small waterfalls. The dark ribbon divided the canyon, and here and there sharp gray boulders rose from the ground that was otherwise thick with leaves. At the edge of the stream, the rocks appeared smooth and often lighter in color—not pale like those of the Guadalupes, but limestone still, worn by water and wind. As in the whitewashed canyon of Devil's Hall, I felt my head begin to spin and cupped my daughter's hand to keep from whirling away. I may as well have been one of the bronze leaves scuttled by the wind for my sudden lack of grounding.

Scott launched into the woods, his camera out and tripod extended in one slick move. But I kept Juliet's grasp as we picked our way in, until deep among the trees. Not only had the wind let up, but the leaves stained the light. Instead of the harsh hue of the road, a soft saffron filled our eyes even as the rush of the stream filled our ears. And there was Juliet's laughter, too, as she scrambled to the water's edge, poking and pulling back, testing the cool flow against the dry carpet of leaves.

I unsheathed my camera and began my work, if composing photographs here could be considered labor. After all, I'm not paid for my photography like Scott, who finds landscape and botany photography a steady source of income. I doubt he would call it work, either, even though Robert Adams notes the "otherwise absurd investment of labor" that it can be. "Almost always, I find fieldwork exhilarating," Scott says. "For me, the intersection of botany and photography is endlessly fascinating; I see photography as a way of documenting the florally ephemeral (and sometimes compromised) American landscape." He then tells me that the Pinacate dunes we photographed four years ago are now under invasion from Sahara mustard, and "the flowers and vistas we recorded may never look like that again."

Thinking of Robert Adams, I considered once more my maxim from the hike down Guadalupe Peak two weeks earlier: *to see and resee*. In *Why People Photograph*, he recalls why he started photographing: "to see if I could find, by pictures, an emotional equivalent to the churches" he found so appealing from his time in Germany. Through my camera, I seek to see and then see again, like Adams, not just a place, but an emotion that triggers a visceral response for photographer and viewer alike. I seek a connection to place and the broader landscape both conscious and subconscious, yet still grounded. In photographing the resplendent trees, I entered a relationship with place made all the more intimate by taking photographs and then sharing the prints.

My favorite photo from that series is a vertical shot of the stream where the water widens and stills to a deep blue, the forest's canopy opening above. Fallen leaves in hues of ochre and orchid run the length of the photograph's left side, ending at a submerged stone. In the rest of the photo, water reflects sky— indigo reflecting dark branches, each limb a black seam on the stained glass of the water. Given the picture's angle of view, the tree trunks and branches appear upside down, and only the leaves provide context as to the breadth and depth of the water, or the size of the trees. I recall taking that photograph without my tripod—which I had already packed away—because the composition struck suddenly. Though I didn't know the photograph would turn out as well as it did, I was aware of the emotion of the place, a moment when photographer synced with landscape—a moment stilled, retained, shared. And I was aware of Juliet, who guided us back through the woods as Scott and I trailed behind her. She moved lightly among the airy branches of the maples, the curled and papery leaves falling onto her shoulders, her long hair and the autumn sky radiant, a composition in the making.

AFTER

After the fall, I was frozen. But my shock—the suspended second or hour or millennium, for time was everything and nothing, the dim room a universe collapsing in on itself—was infinitesimal compared to the horror on my daughter's face. And her cuts and blood. And the glass, its silver shrapnel scattered around her eleven-year-old body. And her body, angular yet sprawled, the swimsuit she had just put on to dash out to the pool pierced, like her flesh. And her flesh, cut to the bone—the exposed bone on her shin as white and smooth as agave root. And how she lifted herself up almost immediately, stood there swaying as if rooted in place. And the silence of her shock after the awful crash: no scream accompanying her plunge through the wide, transparent door that divided dark living room from dazzling sunroom—the thick, untempered glass scything the air as it severed my daughter. And my daughter: fallen, and somehow risen.

"Call 9-1-1!" I yelled, finally unfrozen, before running to my daughter and her breathless *Oh my god oh my god oh my god*. Her sapphire eyes stared through me as the shock took and then released her, her body collapsing across the door's threshold and into my arms. I lifted her from the glass as the other parents rushed to our aid, helping to hold her, to soothe her, to tourniquet her leg and compress the punctures on her arms and chest in clothes stripped from their own bodies—gauzy blouse, gray T-shirt—their swift actions miraculous as my daughter and I trembled together. Then I noticed the dark-haired boy, a fellow cast member from her children's acting troupe, a boy I did not know but who—himself trembling—held up her leg, his eyes full of fear and beautiful determination.

"You're going to be fine, sugarbug," I said to Ann-Elise. "You're doing so well, sugarbug." Reassuring us both, I hoped, before and after the paramedics rushed in, their blue uniforms in sharp contrast against the chrome rails of the gurney, my daughter's linen-white face beneath a bob of sandy hair, the blood blooming like scarlet peonies through the cloth above her wounds. Was I then yet thinking about my daughter's recovery—before I had called her mother or raced the ambulance to the hospital or returned that evening to collect my daughter's things from the unfamiliar house hosting her final cast party? Had her grief yet set in? Was there any spark of hope on a horizon that was suddenly as dark as ashen sky?

After the eruption, Mount Saint Helens left a seemingly devastated landscape for miles around the southwestern Washington volcano. More than 230 square miles of forest were buried or blown down or burned, temperatures in the pyroclastic flow reaching 1,500°. A massive landslide traveling fourteen miles down the North Toutle River scoured everything in its path and buried the river itself to an average depth of 150 feet, the resulting mudflows extending even farther, disrupting commercial shipping traffic on the Columbia River fifty miles to the west. A dark column of ash and dust rose fifteen miles high, spewing volcanic rock called tephra around the mountain—its collapsed summit now some 1,300 feet lower—and depositing ash across seventeen states once the toxic plume reached the stratosphere. One hundred eighty-five miles of roads and fifteen miles of railroad tracks were destroyed or severely damaged. In nearby Spirit Lake—once a sublime, resort-dotted getaway nestled in a forest of old-growth Douglas firs—a wall of water more than eight hundred feet high washed over an adjacent ridge as the mountain's debris avalanche crashed into the lake, which settled some two hundred feet higher in elevation and nine hundred surface acres larger, a sprawling mat of those massive, charred fir trunks now floating atop the poisonous stew.

Fifty-seven people died in the blast, the eruption continuing for nine terrible, awe-inspiring hours. Of course, the numbers were much higher for animals. Scientists estimate that five thousand deer, fifteen hundred elk, two hundred black bears, and fifteen mountain goats died, notes author and biologist Eric Wagner, whose book *After the Blast* details efforts by researchers to understand the landscape's ecological recovery following the May 18, 1980, eruption. "Most died when the lateral blast cloud swept over, crushing them under the falling forest, striking them with flying stones, or picking them up and hurling them bodily through the air," he writes. "Others succumbed in the hours that followed, their pelage burned and their lungs seared by hot volcanic gases, or they suffocated in the thick ashfall and were buried under nearly three feet of tephra."

But I knew little of the mountain's destruction thirty years later—one year after Ann-Elise's fall through the plate-glass window. In 2010 I was invited to join a handful of other writers and artists for the Mount St. Helens Pulse, an every-five-years gathering of scientists sponsored by the U.S. Forest Service's Pacific Northwest Research Station and Oregon State University's Spring Creek Project. I had done little research on the volcano prior to my arrival that late June except what I could easily find online. Indeed, until the invitation I'd hardly considered Mount Saint Helens at all. Yet the eruption is part of our American landscape lore, even in my long-dormant volcanic landscape of the desert Southwest, where I am surrounded by the remnants of ancient activity. Just north of our home in Tucson, for instance, Picacho Peak rises an abrupt 1,500 feet from the desert floor, a geologic fault of tilted, eroded rock interlaced with rich veins of lava some 22 million years old.

Unlike the scientists, who were gathering to check their plots and, in some cases, find the next generation of researchers to take over their many years of work, and unlike most of the other authors and artists, who came as nature poets and environmental essayists and landscape artists, my creative interests leaned toward the built environment. That is, I wanted to know what this posteruption landscape could teach our built landscapes about recovery—from disasters both natural and human-caused. How, for example, does wholesale trauma turn to trust and rebuilding? How do we tap community resilience in the face of devastation?

After the fire, Patrick Dibala had no choice but to leave his home. On September 7, 2020, winds reaching seventy-five miles an hour swept through central Oregon's McKenzie River Valley, knocking a tree into high-tension powerlines. The resulting spark ignited a wildfire near the hamlet of Rainbow that funneled west down the valley—a literal firestorm—ultimately burning more than 173,000 acres and destroying more than 700 buildings and

several communities. The Holiday Farm Fire scorched entire forested mountains for twenty-seven miles on both sides of the river,
and burned for nearly a month. Patrick's home near Blue River
was not one of those that was lost, though he told me that the
heat from the wildfire melted the vinyl surrounding his windows
and cracked another while the fire otherwise incinerated every
building, pumphouse, vehicle, and piece of machinery around.

"Our house survived because, just the day before, I climbed
our trees and lopped off the lower branches," he said to me on
an unseasonably warm day in July 2023, pointing to his white
house, the only building standing among the only thriving trees
in the clear-cut field before us. That burned and logged field rose
to a burned and unlogged hillside, its second-growth Douglas
firs charred, dead but still standing, a spritely understory of bigleaf maples, fireweed, and invasive Scotch broom greening the
ground in contrast to the black trunks and deep blue sky. "I'd
cleared most of the other trees thirty or forty feet out from our
house years before, and I'd been watering the grass every day. We
were lucky."

The business he and his wife opened in 1993 in Blue River
was not so lucky. Like every other building in town, Christmas
Treasures burned to the ground. Only a brick chimney, an indis-
tinct pile of rubble and ash, and half a dozen sooty concrete Santa
sculptures remained. I met the man who himself looked a bit like
Santa, a cheerful red face and short-clipped white beard beneath
khaki ballcap, just south of the nearby Blue River Dam and Lake.
I was viewing the burnscape from the roadside, where I held up
my iPhone to identify the calls of songbirds. As he walked past,
he asked what I was up to. I had arrived three days prior for a
weeklong stay at the H. J. Andrews Experimental Forest. My
first evening I was serenaded by a pair of Swainson's thrushes as

I walked a gravel road among a tangled stand of moss-draped Douglas fir, hemlock, red cedar, maple, and yew. Theirs were the only birdcalls I could discern. On the burned edge of the recovering forest, however, my Merlin app identified nearly a dozen birdsongs: Western tanager and common yellowthroat, black-headed grosbeak and cedar waxwing, MacGillivray's warbler and white-crowned sparrow, house wren and Swainson's thrush, spotted towhee and lazuli bunting. I only saw a bird or two, and wasn't close enough to identify any of them by sight, but their emphatic calls were a welcome lushness I had not expected on this traumatized landscape.

"A number of people watched the fire, scared out of their wits, from right over there," Patrick said, pulling me away from the birdsong as he pointed to the parking lot at the dam's edge. Behind the azure water of the reservoir, high this year thanks to one of the wettest winters on record, rivulets of dead but standing trees striped the otherwise green mountains, likewise victims of the 2020 fire. "They thought they were going to die."

"It all started on an evening like any other," he continued, "except the wind, and our power was out, which happens." Power outages caused by fallen branches are common during high winds in the McKenzie River Valley. Though utilities often cut power during severe windstorms to avoid exactly what happened farther up the valley—a live wire going down and sparking a forest full of tinder-dry undergrowth—local utilities had not deenergized systems in the fire area until early the next day. "I was on the porch, sipping whiskey, you know, when I got a text from my son that they were evacuating. I got up and walked around the house. It was dark out, but I could see the orange glow of the fire over that ridge," he said, pointing to the charred hillside to our east.

Seeing the fire crest the ridge, he ran to his nearby rental house and alerted the residents, who left immediately. He saw that his other neighbor was home, but she refused to leave, calling the evacuation "only a precaution." She changed her mind quickly, Patrick said, when he urged her to step outside, the flames growing higher. "I jumped into the car with my wife and we drove into town, but so much was already ablaze," he recalled. "The store was still there, so we grabbed some paperwork, a computer maybe, and raced back to the house. My wife looked up. 'How could there be helicopters?' she asked. But then we realized they were embers, swirling down all around us." By that time, the route north on the U.S. Forest Service road that runs between the reservoir and the Andrews Forest was backed up with others who sought their own escape. They had no choice then but to drive southwest, back toward the flames and their now-burning store. They reached Highway 126, turned west, and then, as Patrick told me, "we seemed to be traveling with the fire, smoke and ash as we went, along with everyone else, bumper to bumper." With flames in their rearview mirror, they stuck to the winding two-lane highway that edges the river and finally, frantically, made it to the Willamette Valley and Springfield and safety.

The Andrews Forest sustained damage from the fire as well. Approximately 400 acres burned several weeks after the initial, two-day windstorm from the east diminished and more seasonal, less intense winds from the southwest kicked in. That's when the fire turned back on itself and, in late September, burned up and over the mountainside on the Andrews's southern edge, where fire lines dug by hand and bulldozer were repeatedly jumped—until, finally, they weren't. Though most of the trees in the Andrews burn area survived, the Holiday Farm Fire wasn't fully contained until smoke from the fire cast a pall over the area—reducing the overall temperature—and wildland firefighting crews could finally turn their full attention to the Andrews, which was the last area to extinguish. The rest of the valley, which includes the damaged but still-standing home of environmental writer Barry Lopez several miles west, seemed lost. "The land around us as far as we can see looks flayed," Lopez wrote on Facebook on November 5, 2020. "For ten miles in both directions along the river from us, all that stands where a whole community once lived are bare chimneys. The devastation for some is catastrophic and irreparable. This part of the western Cascade Mountains was declared a National Disaster Area in September. The severity of the fire is widely thought to be the direct result of a climate change event."

I didn't have to prompt Patrick for his opinion on the climate crisis. He offered it up freely, mentioning the burned timber he harvested on his eight acres of land, the trees he replanted in April 2021, 40 percent of which failed in the deadly heat dome two months later, when temperatures reached 110°, 30 degrees above normal. "I guess it's all on account of climate change," he said. "How will we survive?"

After the fall, in the blunt brightness of the emergency room, I stood with Billie beside our daughter's gurney. The doctors and nurses moved swiftly to attend to Ann-Elise in the chaos of that place. Despite the crush of the noise—the tings and tones and alerts of the machines she was connected to, the groans of nearby patients, Ann-Elise's frightened babble as she swam in and out of consciousness—the doctors and nurses worked cautiously yet quickly. The surgeon drew out shards of glass like precious gems, then stitched her shin and knee knowing they'd have to reopen the wounds the next day to fish out the tendons and deeper glass. The tendons in her leg had recoiled once severed, snapped like a powerline in a windstorm, so that they curled beneath her flesh, her foot now limp, no spark of movement possible.

When her eyes opened, her pupils were contracted, a wild animal in sudden light. "Mommy, Daddy, where are you?" she asked.

"Right here," we said.

"Why is the car moving?" she asked.

"We're in the hospital," we assured her.

"Why is the room moving?"

"It's not moving, honey."

"Who is that? Where are we? Where are you?" And then her heartbreaking sobs before she'd lose consciousness a few minutes more and, again, "Mommy, Daddy, where are you?"—the anesthesia her bitter friend.

In the curtained cubicle next to us a man moaned and flailed and then fell silent. Surgeons scrambled as the lead doctor screamed for silence. Nurses slipped in and out of our stall, the ER suddenly quiet except for the frantic murmuring of the doctors next door and the constant beeps of who knows how many heart monitors. Then the biker, who flew in the last light of the afternoon before tumbling to the asphalt, moved no more.

I could not sleep that night in the chair next to Ann-Elise's bed, once she was moved to her own hospital room, as much to ward off my own nightmares as hers. By morning I believed only in the precise schedule of nurses, the persistence of fluorescent lights, and the doctor we met the day before. Cool as a leading actor, the orthopedic surgeon warned me that the day's operation could fail—if the tendons retreated beyond mending or the nerves did not properly respond, he said, she might lose the foot's function. He then took my hand, mentioned his daughter of the same age, and pointed me to the lounge where visitors gathered in twos and threes, waiting out their loved ones' diagnoses, huddled in their own theaters of victory and defeat.

It was not her leg wrapped and immobilized, nor the tubes draped like tendrils from her body, nor even the black stitches on her head and shoulder, her wrist and thigh. Rather, it was her bruised eyes and cracked lips that warned me of the arduous recovery before she woke from her second surgery. I took her hand as her eyes found their focus. She did not recall the nightmares, but her pain was intense—"Nine on a scale of ten," she breathed, as the nurse increased her dosage and the pain fled to her head and she vomited through the afternoon. Yet the surgery had succeeded—with a splint in place, followed soon by her first cast, she could begin moving again through the hospital, through our house, through a summer now lost, yet another season of childhood severed by the swift blade of one hand or another.

But the scythe of her fall continued to cull long after my daughter's return home. She endured her wheelchair and then her walker and the physical therapy along the way, but she faltered under the bruised plume of darkness as her nightmares returned. Each evening she tumbled into that foreign house, adrift in the shadow line between dark room and bright, the glass shattering and resealing, her body folding and unfolding—the fall and pain real until she woke in a panic, drenched in sweat and tears. And when her fellow actors and their parents visited, their eyes held tears too as they recalled her plunge, for they knew more about her accident than they saw, and they saw more than they said. Ann-Elise also knew how close the call had been—a puncture this way or that in her chest, the cut above her eye just a half-inch lower, the wrist slit a slight bit deeper . . .

But she lived, and if she didn't thrive right away, neither did she wilt. Wheelchair bound, she learned on our family reunion in San Diego two weeks later that special wheelchairs with wide, royal blue plastic wheels are available for cruising across the sand. Back at home in Tucson, I'd race her down the sidewalk, swerving past puddles following monsoon rainstorms, cornering like a barrel racer, until she had worked up the strength and determination to push herself along. After three weeks the orthopedic surgeon cut away her cast, exposing the flesh and black wound that curved across her pale shin like a centipede—each stitch a violet leg, each segment a stain of dead skin or angry scar. She turned away despite the doctor's guarantees that the cleft would fade, words spoken as he plucked the stitches from ankle to knee and spun her second cast in wild pink.

If we do not understand that fairness dissolves when healing comes to court, then we learn it fast, for the task of recovery is often tougher than the injury itself. I did not ask her if the pain of that first step was worse than her fear of pain. I did not know if her faith would shatter like untempered glass, shards of doubt lodging in tissue and bone. My hope was that she would step through not unscarred, of course, but otherwise unscathed, leg teetering but still standing, hands locked around her silver walker, head and eyes raised in bold conviction. That she would take that first step, painful as it no doubt was, and then another. Perhaps recovery is that way—the flight to forget fuels the fight to push forward, and forward again.

After the eruption, the first scientists to visit Mount Saint Helens didn't know what to expect, beyond bleakness. And with one or two exceptions—a single fireweed shoot somehow poking through the moonscape of pumice below the volcano's crater, or the small, dark rubble of a gopher's mound atop the tephra of a scorched and needleless fir forest—that's what they found.

Going into it, they figured that the mountain and surrounding area wouldn't recover for a century or more, and when it did, that recovery would come from the edges. But almost immediately they knew they were wrong. "Right off, all of us smart ecologists realized we didn't have the correct working hypothesis," says Jerry Franklin, an ecologist with the U.S. Forest Service who with other scientists visited the blast zone just after the eruption, the crater still steaming, the ground unsettled.

"The fireweed that Franklin saw not only changed the ways that he and other ecologists approached the eruption and the landscape it created, but also led to new ways of thinking about how life responds to seeming total devastation," writes Wagner in *After the Blast*. Fred Swanson, the tall, mild-mannered Forest Service ecologist and research geologist who served as our generous guide for the 2010 Mount St. Helens Pulse, agrees. He was with Jerry Franklin on that first helicopter ride, and has studied Mount Saint Helens and other volcanoes from that day forward. "My preconceptions of how volcanic landscapes behave in the aftermath of an eruption were blown away like the top of Saint Helens, and I've been reconstructing my understanding ever since," he told us as we piled into the van that took a dozen excitable writers and artists on that first morning's tour around the mountain.

"In overwriting the landscape, Mount St. Helens had presented ecologists with what was in effect a huge natural experiment," writes Wagner. That natural experiment revealed that life in the blast zone has emerged rapidly, though certainly not comprehensively. It returned, in a way, but mostly it already existed in tiny semblances here and there—protected from the blast by snowbanks, brought forth in new soil pushed up from surviving pocket gophers, dropped in on a spider's floating web. The landscape's repopulation wasn't primarily from the edges of the blast zone inward—though there was some of that, exemplified by the nesting horned larks and chicks we saw with ornithology doctoral student Elise Larsen on our last full day on the mountain (the birds are not otherwise native to the region; the open, rocky expanse provides new opportunities). Rather, species recolonized the most impacted area—the so-called Pumice Plain—through tiny oases of lupine communities that had, over the thirty years since, grown together not completely but still substantially. And by then, a few silver firs, huckleberry bushes, red alders, and willows had started to take hold on the plain, particularly where it met Spirit Lake, which was by then anything but poisonous.

The vast mat of scorched firs—weathered to massive logs of driftwood after floating the lake for three decades—remained atop Spirit Lake, and though interesting when viewed from the Pumice Plain, was downright bewildering, mesmerizing even, when seen up close. We hiked the switchback trail down to Spirit Lake from the pullout on the ridge above. Though no tall conifers yet grew, the alders and maples were vigorous, providing some shade for our sunny start, while at our feet pearly everlasting, Indian paintbrush, and penstemon colored the trailside. By the time we reached the lakeshore, a mat of gray clouds had covered the top of Mount Saint Helens, though from the far edge of the lake we could still see the Pumice Plain and Loowit Falls at the volcano's dark base. Before the hike, Fred had spread out a map of the vicinity, demonstrating how the blast with a force five hundred times that of the Hiroshima atomic bomb had reshaped the lake and surrounding ridges—the "blowdown," the trees still standing but burned to their cores, the lake's outlet to the river dammed under countless tons of debris. At trail's end, he set us loose to experience that power firsthand.

But in the cooling weather and mild breeze, I felt more harmony than fury.

I pushed myself atop one of the larger floating trunks and found I could balance my way across the mat—not too far out, for the mat regularly drifts from one shore to another. Fred forbade us from swimming, and urged extra caution should we accidentally find ourselves in the water. The logs were too large to easily climb if one of us fell in, and they would be unforgiving if we got trapped between them. The temptation to explore this disaster-formed barge of several thousand logs was too great for most of us, however, and I'm happy to report that though we lingered for hours, none of us fell in.

As I settled onto a broad log close to shore, I considered our assignment as visiting artists. Our charge was not only to learn from the researchers and observe the natural experiment Mount Saint Helens presented—researchers demonstrating their techniques and reviewing their long-term results at stop after educational stop, viewpoint after stunning viewpoint, hike after delightful hike—but also to artistically interpret the mountain's recovery, to share its story through literature and art. And that interpretation began with a blunt conclusion, impressed upon us by every scientist we spoke with: what is happening at Mount Saint Helens is not recovery. It is *renewal*, for the landscape will never return to its former self, even over centuries—and as the most active volcano in Cascadia, erupting on average every 150 years, it never has. That's a powerful personal lesson in resilience, too—how we not only heal following a traumatic event, but also how we are changed along the way; how we can never return to our former selves. And it's an important lesson for humans more broadly as we consider how to rebuild communities following natural disasters, particularly in light of a rapidly changing climate. Should we attempt a return to the way our communities were built previously? How has the devastation transformed us, made us stronger, given us the wisdom (or imperative) for evolving our places in spite of the patterns, structures, and efficiencies of our former ways?

After the fire, the town of Blue River is rebuilding. Yet planners, developers, builders, and ecologists must recognize these built and natural communities are forever changed. Residents have no choice but to adjust. Patrick Dibala said as much to me as we looked across the charred trees along Forest Service Road 15: "I never thought it would happen to us. I don't think things can go back to normal."

Fred Swanson knows there's never truly been a *normal* in this volatile landscape, and though Blue River is far from Mount Saint Helens, the entire Cascades Range is volcanic, full of repeating destruction and renewal if one takes a long enough view in time. Indeed, his research shows that while some Douglas fir stands in this region have burned on average only every four hundred to five hundred years, others have burned as frequently as every one hundred to two hundred years. Still others in what he calls "refugia" can live to be as old as eight hundred years, untouched by fire. As a scientist, he finds that change fascinating—it is, after all, his life's work. But as a resident of the Willamette Valley and long-time researcher at the Andrews Forest, he recognizes that with increasing temperatures, wildfire is more likely than at any other time in recent human history. He also realizes that how humans prepare for and respond to environmental change will determine, ultimately, whether humans survive. One response Fred has long called for is using stories to effectively and broadly communicate the outcomes and urgencies of scientific research—and who better to tell those stories than writers and artists? That's why, as part of the Spring Creek Project, he invited us to Mount Saint Helens, why he is working with photographer David Paul Bayles to document renewal following the Holiday Farm Fire at the Following Fire website, and why he has invited me (and many others before me) to a residency at the H. J. Andrews Experimental Forest.

For years I had pined to visit this long-term ecological research site, a 15,800-acre forest encompassing the Lookout Creek watershed in the Oregon Cascades. Data has been collected, curated, and archived at the Andrews since 1948—and will be collected far into the future. Though research has spanned such broad categories as forest management, streams, watersheds, and wildlife, the "most emblematic long-term experiment," as Fred says, is the log decomposition study, a two-hundred-year experiment of 530 decomposing logs each five and a half meters long placed at multiple sites around the forest. Initiated in 1985, the study incorporates four tree species that, it turns out, decay at different rates, ranging from (relatively) fast to slow: Pacific silver fir, western hemlock, Douglas fir, and western red cedar. Studies on the decomposing logs include forest respiration, carbon sequestration, and microbial and insect ecology. The results of these studies have "influenced the science of carbon dynamics at local to global scales and management of dead woods as an ecosystem component," according to U.S. Forest Service literature. The science has created its own term, *morticulture*, coined by recently retired Oregon State University biologist Mark Harmon, whose seminal research at the Andrews demonstrated that leaving dead trees in the forest replenishes soil, provides habitat for numerous species, and creates a more diverse, resilient forest ecosystem.

Though Fred couldn't join me during my visit to the Andrews in July 2023, former Spring Creek Project director and fellow Mount St. Helens Pulse participant Charles Goodrich led me on my first visit to the log decomposition study site, one of several "reflections" spots for artists now that the forest is also designated a Long-Term Ecological Reflections program site. We hopped into his Prius from the Andrews Forest headquarters and drove several miles to reach the site off one of the many Forest Service roads that bisect the forest. It had been several years since Charles himself had been to the site, but his memory proved true as we parked at a small pullout past a single-lane bridge and found the overgrown trail.

Immediately we were immersed in the dense forest, a soaring, sun-dappled overstory of Douglas fir, western hemlock, and western red cedar above vine maple, bigleaf maple, moss-draped Pacific yew, dogwood, huckleberry, sword fern, and too many other plants—and shades of green—for me to name. The difference between this leafy, mature forest and the burned forest only miles away was dramatic. As we hiked, Charles tested the red huckleberries by touch before declaring them not quite ripe enough to eat. "I made a promise long ago never to pass up a huckleberry treat," he said with a smile, his gray goatee blending to white, green eyes beaming. We stepped over fallen hemlocks and maples and ducked under gargantuan trunks of downed Douglas fir, rich in moss and insects and spiders, before he stopped me abruptly and said, "We are now entering the sanctuary."

Here the trail opened onto a soft floor of moss and conifer needles surrounded by old-growth Douglas fir, some easily ten feet in diameter at the base. On the ground, dozens of moss- and lichen-covered logs splayed, many topped by large, white PVC pipes used to collect exhalations of carbon dioxide from

the decomposing logs. Here and there a standing tree wore a tarnished metal tag, and faded pink flags marked other study specimens. The setting was altogether magical, though less fairy tale
than scientific tale, for the mark of investigation was all around
yet did not diminish the verdant beauty of this research-centric
old-growth forest—a sanctuary indeed.

Charles opened the book he'd brought along—*Forest Under
Story: Creative Inquiry in an Old-Growth Forest*, which he co-ed-
ited with Fred Swanson and Nathaniel Brodie—and read aloud
Jerry Martien's poem, "return of the dead log people," a tradition,
I gathered, when he introduces someone new to the log decomposition study site. The poem got me in the right spirit, particularly as the ancient yews cloaked in the moss called old man's
beard seemed to circle us like a scene out of a J.R.R. Tolkien
book. I half expected them to walk toward us, becoming Ents,
the mythic tree people of *The Lord of the Rings*. And though
they didn't move, Charles did share their plight of the 1980s
and 1990s, when the small, drooping, slow-growing tree was
poached widely across the Pacific Northwest for its bark, which
proved to be the only natural source of Taxol, a drug used to
treat breast, lung, and ovarian cancer. Now designated as "Near
Threatened" on the IUCN Red List of Threatened Species, the
ruby-and-chestnut-barked tree—which is slow to rebound from
poaching and other disturbances, including fire—is no longer
sought after for pharmaceutical purposes because a less costly
synthetic drug has been manufactured. Charles and I agreed
that, instead, we much preferred one of the Indigenous uses for
the tree: the Puyallup, Klickitat, and Cowlitz peoples selectively
harvested yew to craft bows from the strong wood, which they
then strung with animal ligament. We also acknowledged the
irony of the bark's use as a medical treatment when other parts

of the tree, and particularly the seeds in their bright red arils, are highly toxic.

The day after my conversation with Patrick, I returned to the log decomposition study site alone. I brought more poetry to read—Anne Haven McDonnell's powerful *Breath on a Coal*—before reflecting on fire and morticulture in the context of landscape renewal. Such a sacred place seemed like it could and should last forever; the forest was too peaceful, with only the low buzzing of flies and high-pitched call of a Pacific-slope fly-catcher interrupting my thoughts, and delightfully so. But as the unseasonal heat of the previous few days reminded me—leading the Forest Service to increase the fire risk from high to very high, placing additional limitations on forest use—no place is immune from the risks of damage or decay, if not outright destruction. Yet with education, smart planning, and good storytelling, can we not reduce that risk and, when a catastrophe does befall us, build back more wisely, where building back makes sense?

Even then, if we somehow get it all right, I wonder too about grief and hope. I don't really believe that time heals all wounds, but it does take time to properly grieve and restore ourselves after trauma, and even then we must be prepared for the unexpected trigger that can throw us back into deep grief, or the next traumatic event itself. How we pull ourselves up—more difficult than climbing onto a rolling log drifting atop a cold mountain lake, no doubt—may indicate how we find and keep hope.

"There is always hope," says Aragorn in Tolkien's *The Twin Towers*, as Helm's Deep prepares for siege. But is there? Patrick, despite his cheery face, seemed hopeless at times as we spoke, asking what we'd do if we lost our water, how we'd feed ourselves, where we'd go—not exactly rhetorical questions. Here, then, I think of another quote, by Barry Lopez, before he passed away three and a half months after the Holiday Farm Fire: "I would ask you not to give in to the temptation of despair." But how do we not give in, in a world of radical environmental and geopolitical change, the climate crisis upon us?

Folk singer Joan Baez may guide us there: "Action is the antidote to despair," she says. Ann-Elise put one step forward, then the other, until she could walk again, until she could run. Researchers worked with politicians to permanently protect—and study long-term—Mount Saint Helens, establishing the Mount Saint Helens National Volcanic Monument on August 27, 1982. Patrick planted and then, when nearly half of the trees died from extreme heat two months later, replanted again the following spring. A forest ranger in Willamette National Forest's McKenzie River Ranger District told me the Forest Service is evaluating "assisted migration"—planting more drought-tolerant, eastern Cascades conifers where the forest burned on the west side of the range in light of increasing temperatures. Which is to say: we take action.

Six years after the fall and thirty-five years after the eruption, I returned to Mount Saint Helens. Ann-Elise, then seventeen years old, joined me. Though some of the participants in the 2015 Mount St. Helens Pulse had changed—a few scientists by then retired, a new generation of students eager to conduct research, several different writers attending for the first time—Fred Swanson still led the site visits, and Charles Goodrich once again joined us as the Spring Creek Project liaison. They were both as sage and encouraging as before, a lovely combination to lead our new, or in some cases renewed, explorations. The journey for Ann-Elise following her accident had often been rocky. Her scar had lightened but persisted, as did a large area of pain and numbness on her leg and foot, though she otherwise regained full mobility. I wondered, however, if the trauma had resulted in longer-term psychological challenges still to be resolved. Or perhaps, like so many of us at that age, she was simply a stubborn, rebellious teenager, a dose of anxiety added in for good measure. More recently, she had also been afflicted with an undiagnosed illness that limited what she could eat and, many mornings, how long she could keep it down. My hope in bringing her to the volcano was both to get her out of the routines and ailments back at home and to foster her passion for science, for she had spent the spring volunteering at a wildlife rehabilitation center in Tucson and planned to major in biology when she attended college in the fall. What better place could there be to immerse her in science than Mount Saint Helens, under the tutelage of some of the world's premier disturbance ecologists?

Following our three-day drive from Tucson, Ann-Elise and I settled in among the many other campers at the Tower Rock U-Fish RV Park in Randle, Washington. Located halfway between Mount Rainier and Mount Saint Helens, it was the only campground spacious enough to host the Pulse, which seemed larger in 2015 than 2010. After raising our tent just across from the campground's stocked pond, we learned that "U-Fish" applied mostly to a pair of resident ospreys, who every evening just before sunset dived from their perch on a Douglas fir, more often than not snagging a silvery trout as they skimmed the water with talons at the ready before rising and returning to a tree. Though this scene was perhaps commonplace for many of the biologists at the Pulse—and frustrating for the campground owner, who complained about losing fishing revenue—my daughter and I cheered, if quietly, every time the raptors scored a fish. Ann-Elise had worked with several injured birds in the spring, including a chatty raven, and a family of Swainson's hawks saved from the local air force base, but water-loving ospreys are rare in the desert Southwest.

At the campsite we also explored a trail to the nearby Cispus River, where Ann-Elise dipped into the rushing water tinted by glacial silt, delighted in this unfamiliar landscape—despite an earlier run-in with stinging nettles. "Dad, I found a raptor feather!" she called from the streambank, holding her new prize high. Could this wild welcome be a precursor of a new and more empowering time, as she transitioned from her own injuries into a renewed self? Was a dose of nature all she would need—one more action to feed her hope?

Because Ann-Elise and I had a smaller window on this trip, just three days compared to the full week of the Pulse, we participated in only two site visits: Spirit Lake and the Pumice Plain. At Spirit Lake—the log mat as fascinating for my daughter as it was for me—I realized just how out of shape I'd gotten in the past five years, as I huffed on the slow hike back up to the ridge. "Move it, Dad!" Ann-Elise said each time I paused, teasing at first and then more earnestly the higher we climbed. Clearly her injury hadn't negatively impacted her cardio, as she trotted up the steep trail as if it was even ground.

While Spirit Lake was formative in my first Pulse, the Pumice Plain with its surreal lupine bloom and unobstructed view of the volcano's icy, ashen crater was transformative. I wanted Ann-Elise to experience the magical place I hiked with poet Derek Sheffield, essayist Elizabeth Dodd, and Mount St. Helens Institute director Jeanne Bennett; the place where special access must be granted; the place that changed not only the perspective of ecologists Jerry Franklin and Fred Swanson after they first touched down but that revolutionized disturbance ecology altogether.

On my first visit, Jeanne had driven us to the Pumice Plain in her Subaru Outback on the thin and, by all appearances, crumbling dirt road that skirts a mountainside. With a sheer drop-off, gashes and boulders to evade, and a slight slope toward the edge, the milelong trek was slow and unnerving. One wrong turn and the car would tumble a thousand feet; there would be no recovering from that trauma. In 2010, when she drove in, my eyes were locked forward to quell my acrophobia. Perhaps trusting our two feet more than four tires, Derek, Elizabeth, and I decided to walk the thin road back. In 2015 I was in the driver's seat, my Subaru Forester carrying not only Ann-Elise but also Derek, who like me returned for his second Pulse, and Andy Gottlieb, a poet from Southern California attending for the first time. On the drive from the campground we'd had to pull over for Ann-Elise to vomit, her stomach upset once again, the cause still unknown despite an endoscopy two weeks earlier. "I'm alive," she said, almost reluctantly, when she slumped back into the car. I placed my hand on her shoulder in what I hoped was a comforting way and said what I meant, "I'm sorry," recognizing that was little relief for the illness and anxiety that blanketed my daughter.

Before passing through the gate that restricts access to the Pumice Plain, ecologist Charlie Crisafulli stopped each vehicle, a more serious look in his eyes than I had seen before, urging extreme caution. Like Fred Swanson and Jerry Franklin, Charlie had built his career as a researcher at Mount Saint Helens and was the nucleus of the vibrant, widely dispersed volcano ecology community centered there. I don't recall his exact words, but in effect he said, "Don't fuck up." I do recall, once on the road, that very real drop-off and very noticeable slope, and I recall looking in the rearview mirror to see Andy praying, though I'm not certain he is a religious man. No one spoke a word as the Forester crawled around the mountain and out onto the broad, gravel parking area, where we all finally exhaled.

Already I could see more impressive growth around the Pumice Plain since 2010. Still largely devoid of conifers, more shrubs had moved in, though as Charlie shared, the resurgent elk population was keeping the plants in check more than might otherwise be the case. Wolf reintroduction, anyone? Though we couldn't spot any elk—the herd now larger than preeruption times thanks to easy foraging on the open plain coupled with a lack of predators—we did spot, high up on the volcano, mountain goats, their white coats like bright embers against the dark gray mountainside. Ann-Elise smiled despite her obvious discomfort and, I could tell, growing frustration.

As we checked our backpacks for the day's excursion, Ann-Elise informed me that she wasn't up for a hike. "Dad, I can't," she said flatly. "I'm not going."

"Do you want to try eating something?" I asked. Sometimes she could eat shortly after her nausea to gain back her energy, if not her spirit. Ann-Elise had grown up with food allergies, so her options had always been limited. Still, we had plenty of carb-laden, wheat- and egg-free treats with us, and I suggested a couple of options. But by then her mood had turned to agitation—she was still a seventeen-year-old, after all, and I was still her annoyingly concerned father, the satellite whose orbit was suddenly too tight.

"No," she said, arms now crossed. "Just go."

"Sugarbug, we're going to be here a while and we can't head back until the convoy is ready," I said. "Please, eat something. You'll feel better." Here I was reminded of Professor Remus Lupin in J. K. Rowling's *Harry Potter and the Prisoner of Azkaban*, offering chocolate to Harry Potter as a quick fix for the malaise caused by the soul-sucking dementors. On the sunny slopes of Mount Saint Helens, however, there were no dementors, and chocolate was no remedy for this malaise. In the end, Ann-Elise held fast to her pledge to stay, a scowl on her face as I walked away with Derek, Andy, and a handful of researchers and other writers. I offered to leave her the keys so she could sit in the Forester with the air-conditioning running if necessary, a little concerned she might try the road on her own, but she refused even that.

By the time we returned, two and a half hours later, the day had warmed up and Ann-Elise had mostly cooled off, the nausea now gone but her temper still simmering. Worried that she had stayed in the parking lot the entire time, missing out on this rare chance to immerse herself in one of the most unique (and youngest) environments of North America, I asked if she had explored a bit, trying the trails beyond the parking lot, seeing the lupine and Indian paintbrush in all their glorious bloom, watching the dust and ash blow off the top of Mount Saint Helens like the posteruption steam many presumed it to be.

"Yeah, a little," she said, a cinder of regret in her voice as she listened to our traveling companions rave about the songbirds we saw along the moss-edged rivulets that trickled down to the willows at the edge of Spirt Lake. "I saw the mountain goats again, and the lupine. But mostly I hung out with the ravens," she said, pointing to the large black birds hopping along a row of boulders at the edge of the parking area.

Mountain goats and corvids aside, I knew the missed opportunity here, not only for her to learn from the scientists who explained what we were seeing along the hike, but for us to experience the volcano together. I wanted so badly for Ann-Elise to feel as transformed by this evolving landscape as I had been, for her to discover as much about herself as she might about this traumatized place. But I knew, too, that wasn't for me to magic up. In her journey of recovery, her pursuit of renewal, only my daughter could decide what steps she would take to outpace her pain, what paths she would explore to find her true self, and what actions to take as her own antidote to despair.

"The forest has one rule," writes Alison Hawthorne Deming in response to her time at the H. J. Andrews Experimental Forest: "start over making use of what remains." Might that apply to people as well as landscapes? Are we not, after all, all starting over in one manner or another following every traumatic event, taking steps and missteps along the way, adjusting as we go? Sometimes abruptly, often slowly, we use what remains to renew and rebuild—after the fall, after the eruption, after the fire. And before whatever transformation comes next.

CODA

Less than a month after I finished my residency at the H. J. Andrews Experimental Forest, the Andrews burned again. This time, the fire—which was ignited by a lightning strike on August 5, 2023—began in the experimental forest itself, on Lookout Mountain, and was the most severe blaze the forest has experienced since it was designated for research seventy-five years ago. The Lookout Fire burned for two months, charring more than 25,700 acres, both in and east of the Andrews. Though the experimental forest's headquarters and surrounding area were spared, many old-growth sections burned heavily, including three of six log decomposition sites, among them the site Charles

Goodrich and I visited over the summer. In total, two-thirds of the Andrews's 15,800 acres burned.

Researchers are only now returning to the forest—where it is safe to do so—finding their plots and instruments and years if not decades of research in ashes—or not, for the fire burned hotter in some areas than others. Because the Andrews is an experimental forest, the fire's impact will now turn many researchers' focus to the forest's response and renewal. "I don't know anywhere on the planet that has had so much long-term data," said Andrews Forest lead principal investigator Matt Betts, as reported in a September 2023 *Seattle Times* article. "And now it has had a major fire, so I think it is unprecedented, some of the findings that will be coming out."

But first, the researchers must process the personal trauma of the fire. "I don't feel devastated, but I may still be in shock," Fred Swanson told me just before Thanksgiving as he paraphrased a line from a poem to express his mood: "'I always knew this day would come, but yesterday I did not know it would be today.'"

"People are processing stages of grief and trying to dial in on the grief-to-hope gradient," he continued. "Grad students may be the hardest hit because the tree climbers have an especially close relationship with individual trees—trusting their lives to them."

I think back on the beauty and recent history of the log decomposition site I visited only months ago, "the sanctuary," as Charles called it. While the instruments will need to be replaced, and the trees and shrubs and other forest beings regrow or return, there is hope not only in the regenerative nature of the forest but in the decades of data collected from the site and, indeed, across the experimental forest—data that can help guide the landscape's renewal here and in temperate forests around the world. I think back, too, on Alison Hawthorne Deming's wisdom: "The forest has one rule: start over making use of what remains." What remains changes the place, and us, forever. At the H. J. Andrews Experimental Forest, the transformation has already begun. As scientists, as humans, we watch and listen and learn.

PALO DE MUERTO

Here, we, where the white wood stands,

together we meet,

together we will talk about this animal.

FROM AN UNTITLED YAQUI DEER SONG

BY DON JESÚS YOILO'I

1.

This animal that is a god, or God. This god that is ever-present, or ever-distant. This god that is in all things created—the wilderness, the moon and sun, the pulsing galaxies beyond—or the god that is the Genesis and the Exodus, no longer a god. This god that is a universe, at once in and of everything, or the god that is a machine, our machine, an enterprise of self-replicating technology, the temple and its congregation of inventors. This god in the indigo eyes of my daughters, or the god of plague and terror and genocide. This god of indifference.

2.

The dark shape of an eagle moves across the stretched-glass sky, high enough to leave a vapor trail, then orbits back toward Earth. The earth is the rich desert of northwestern Mexico, below the granite hills of Hermosillo, Sonora. Though not wealthy in the context of industry or market, the landscape here offers a gilded mix of plants, a lush portfolio of flowers and trees and succulents. The organ pipe cactus, for instance, grows in gray-green columns, often jointed, two dozen arms rising twenty feet or more. During summer nights, blooms appear at their tips: gold-centered flowers that share their dividends with bats, doves, and more. But Sonoran plants are sharp and, like the animals, sometimes poisonous. They are weary and withdraw in the heat of the day. And they are enigmatic, able to withstand six-month summers—dormant, as if dying or already dead.

On the thorn-scrub plains that slide into the Sea of Cortés, there is one such mysterious plant: palo de muerto. Stick of the dead; tree morning glory. For much of the year the silvery tree is leafless, its branches shining like white tributaries against the azure sky, the trunk a lit stream among cardón and mesquite. But as the midsummer rains sweep across Sonora, the palo de muerto explodes into an emerald plume of leaves that drop—sensitive to the waning light, the cooling night—just four months later. Over the mild winter, clusters of white flowers bloom at the ends of branches. The flowers last longer than the leaves, opening in the morning so that each tree sparkles like a constellation, as if the whole theater of the sky awoke in the humble branches of a tree. It must take all day for the ruby-centered stars to find their way back, visited in the meantime by hawk moths and hummingbirds. And when they fall, the deer eat them, stealing the light before noon, so that the astronomers are right: everything, ultimately, comes from the stars—a brilliance that fills us all.

3.

As a boy, a recurring vision held me before I slept. In a trance of half-slumber, I lifted from my bed, rose into the night, and glided beyond the blue sphere of the Earth. The body leaving the body, I remained a boy's form—my own pale arms and legs— but had no weight. Each evening I prepared myself by slowing my breath, fixing my eyes behind dull lids, willing my spirit's separation. Skin tingled as energy pulsed, as muscles tightened and then released, my spirit breaking free as the body subsided, exhaled, deflated, perhaps never existing at all.

Absent time and distance, I drifted through an astral world until finding a silver channel, a vast pane of light that divided the night like a crucifix into quadrants. Below the horizon, the sky loomed dark and barren. But above the arms of the cross, a dusky window brightened into day on my approach. I floated over the threshold and into a vast wilderness heavy with water and life, then landed in a massive tree, moss draping, vines as thick as pythons. The primeval jungle was nearly unbearable in its vibrancy—the mad songs of birds and frogs, deer leaping among the fronds, jaguars racing, the plants themselves riotous in their green joy.

For many years I associated those visions with my spirit, and in that sense they became my true identity just as they became a nightly elixir that numbed me to the chaos of this world and delivered me to the next, if only briefly. But what was this place, and how did I find it night after night, exhausted to dreamless sleep upon my return? Was it heaven or the garden before the fall? Where was my family then and yet to come?

4.

An animal tunnels beneath the lime-white roots of a young palo de muerto, the same roots once eaten by the Yaqui of central Sonora. It may be centipede or millipede, wood rat or gopher snake. The roots are thick and bulbous, like sweet potatoes, and the meat soft, like balsa. Wild burros and livestock graze its argent bark during drought. Sometimes they eat the entire trunk and the white tree falls—a stream run dry, a constellation inked out.

I am troubled by my own fall and uncertainty of beliefs and experiences: the passing of faith as Billie and I raise our daughters in a secular home. How do parents of differing beliefs teach their children to, if not have faith, then at least have hope?

Billie once believed that God created the world and then drifted away. When she was young, her single mother dropped her off at church every Sunday before heading to work. Billie attended by herself, of her own will, curious in the faith and community and convinced, then, in a benevolent God. Yet by the time she was twelve, she stopped attending services because she no longer believed. Her mother worked multiple jobs, often late into the night. At the edge of poverty, Billie could not understand how a god could allow her family and indeed most of the world to "struggle so endlessly." An atheist most of her life, she now believes that God and religion simply do not matter. "What matters," she says, "is being a good person."

5.

A mourning dove calls from a single desert tree: *coo-wah coo coo coo*, the soft echo of emptiness. The tree, an acacia, leans out of the dry lawn of Whitmore Elementary School, where in fourth grade my leg broke. Playing a game of pickup football, I was tackled from behind. I woke paralyzed, it seemed, except my head, which swayed back and forth beneath the glaring sky, the pain extreme but empty, building and releasing, breaking in uneven waves from the snapped femur that bulged like the enflamed bud of a desert lily. There was no red blossom; the bone had not torn my flesh. A crowd of students gathered, the teachers huddled, and paramedics rushed in. My mother appeared. A visage of white-blue moon stained the afternoon, then disappeared behind the shape of a man who sliced my tan corduroys to reveal the white bulb of the broken bone just beneath my skin, glorious and sickening.

I woke hours later at Tucson Medical Center, my left leg lifted in traction, the swelling gone but a pin drilled into my fibula, below my kneecap, then tied to a system of pullies that kept the two halves of my femur in place. In the bed next to me, a Mexican boy named Jesús heard my groaning as I heard his. Jesus? I had never known the name of Christ used for another person.

After traction and the four-hour surgery that placed me in a hard, spread-eagle cast; after the nurses demonstrated how to bathe me and turn me; and after the wild ambulance ride where the driver thought a little excitement might do me good, I came home. After that, I saw the angel.

I heard him first, in the hallway outside my bedroom, where the door was open. Calling, I thought it was my sister, but there was no reply. In a hooded cloak the color of manila paper the figure moved past the doorframe, gliding through the hallway and soon out of sight. His face was hidden and didn't look my way, but the specter had the height and, if possible to tell beneath the muted outline of the cloak, the build of a man. I should have been scared or otherwise paralyzed, but was neither. It is not quite right to say there was a sudden calm—a warm blanket, the sweet scent of citrus—yet a sense of the serene overcame me. So I didn't tell my mother until the evening.

"Your guardian angel," she said, unworried, full of a faith akin to spirituality more than religion. Though not a Christian, nor a member of any organized religion, my silver-haired mother held a strong belief in the supernatural, in the presence of her own psychic senses as much as a "higher power" she called God. Years later, when I struggled with the idea of a singular, Christian God as a student at a parochial high school, she had sensible answers of no doctrine other than her own. "God wears many masks," she said, "and He uses those masks, those religions, to reach people of different faiths." Heretical from a Christian point of view, but acceptable from her global perspective. "Each is holy in their own belief" was her mantra, an eloquent outlook especially from a woman who grew up Lutheran, in Sweden, under the cloak of state religion.

My guardian angel? Saint Jerome, the ecclesiastical wanderer who died in Bethlehem in 420 CE, interpreted many passages of the Bible to mean that each person has a guardian angel to lead them to the kingdom of heaven. "How great the dignity of the soul, since each one has from his birth an angel commissioned to guard it," he wrote. Sentenced to a full body cast, did I now need a guardian angel? Maybe, though my struggles were greater in the coming months, during rehabilitation, as I learned how to bend my knee, how to walk again.

The most difficult days, however, came several years later, when like my mother I found myself alternately depressed or manic, sad or ecstatic, a boy sometimes suicidal—the product, we hoped, of the chemical imbalances of adolescence. That may explain the timing of the second and final sighting. At our next

Tucson home, not far from the adobe ruins of Fort Lowell and along the banks of a wide arroyo, I entered the townhouse to see the angel, rising. His unwinged back moving from me, the figure climbed the stairs and turned at the landing to enter my room. I followed, finding the room bright with morning light but otherwise vacant.

6.

For much of my life, I have considered myself spiritual, though not religious. The difference has less to do with etymology than architecture. The word *spiritual*—pertaining to the spirit or soul—derives from the Latin word *spiritus*, meaning "breath." The origin of *religious*—having or showing belief in and reverence for God or a deity—is less clear. Though also Latin, its source could be *relegere*, "to read again"; or *religore*, "to bind fast," as in a bond between humans and the gods; or even *religiens*, "careful," the opposite of *negligens*.

Religion classes at parochial schools and conversations with pious parents cast religion as a high-walled, unwavering bastion—a monolith where decisions and judgments were handed down from on high, where despite the teachings of love and forgiveness, the dogma was accusatory and full of wrath. Ornate ceremonies fit my view of this citadel; not a part of my early youth, they were foreign and uncomfortable. I could not stand the cold vulnerability.

Then as now, spirituality represented freedom in unordained faith—an integral though indefinable sustenance from a power beyond the self, beyond the world, yet wholly connected. Religion, on the other hand, continued to mean faith engineered from rites and observances; doctrine and practices set and largely unalterable.

There was a time, however, when I was "saved," when I fully accepted Jesus Christ as the son of God, my personal savior. I preached to my friends and mother and nearly drove them mad. Only months into freshman classes at St. John Lutheran High in Ocala, Florida, the change was swift—and necessary. Before that, as a naïve (though sarcastic) boy in the shadow of my older, partying sister, I drank alcohol every weekend and envied her wild lifestyle, not yet aware of the effects on her body and spirit. I cheated on the occasional test, didn't care if I lied, hung around with the proverbial wrong crowd.

After my conversion—a simple moment when I lingered alone after class one autumn day, a moment when my new exposure to Lutheran teachings suddenly dissolved the walls so that acceptance flowered from within—I stopped drinking and cheating. And though my sarcasm remained (it was, after all, the language of youth), I strived to follow the Scriptures, to love and be loved, and spread the word. Those may have been enlightened days, but they didn't last. Only weeks later, I slid out of the Christian faith, deciding Jesus was a prophet, certainly, but not the son of God.

Why the sudden departure? For years I blamed it on the hypocrisy so rampant at school and, it seemed clear, throughout the Christian faith. But that was only a symptom. Better to say: it didn't stick. In the end, I could never subscribe to the idea of original sin, that infants are born in sin, spiritually if not morally cursed, and only through baptism could find sanctity.

What of the millions of others, in different religions and otherwise, who are never baptized? What of my own children? Are they condemned to a fiery afterlife? "Yes," according to the Southern Baptist who drove me to high school after my sister moved to Los Angeles. "They are going to Hell, which is why our life's work is to save their souls." She undertook Bible study while steering the old Buick, eyes scanning the primer more often than the road, scaring the hell out of me and perhaps taking heaven, too.

What remained after my falling out was the desire to be lawful, and more importantly to be "good," a concept derived in part from the teachings of the New Testament—love one another, practice forgiveness—and in larger part from the tolerance and compassion of my mother, the steady influence in my spiritual progression even as she promoted my enrollment in parochial schools for the quality of their biased education. I didn't drink again until I turned twenty-one, studied instead of cheated, worked hard at being compassionate, likable. Other beliefs crept in, too. I adopted my mother's polyreligious doctrine—the holiness in each of our faiths, so long as no one is hurt—but didn't dwell on the details. That openness allowed me to create my own belief system, one without ritual or history but strong in purpose.

The Dharmic idea of karma, in this life and the next, took hold. Unlike the threat of eternal damnation or immediate retribution, I adopted the idea of positive reinforcement—that good deeds, while not individually rewarded, both define and direct us. Cause and effect: a seemingly scientific formula with cosmic results. And like my mother and those of Hindu and other faiths, I adopted a belief in reincarnation, assuming that after we die, our souls pass to a sort of heavenly holding tank, a lovely, gardenlike wilderness full of friends and family who also have died (an echo of us always remains in that place, I supposed), before evolving into a body capable of higher spiritual thought; until eventually becoming not just a part of God—"We are individual drops of water in the ocean of God," another of my mother's sayings—but actually becoming God. That is the purpose of life, I believed: to evolve spiritually.

"I always knew there were people like you," said a college sophomore after I told her my thoughts on reincarnation, "but I never thought I'd actually meet one." From a small Alabama town with a quaint Baptist church and a sheltered faith in the literal Word, she was taken aback, and likely appalled, because she never returned my calls after our first date.

Where is God now? I wondered. Never believing that God simply vanished after creating the Earth or the cosmos, I saw holiness all around me, yet only in our natural places—the swift springs at the source of a subtropical river, for example, or the airy halls of the longleaf pine forest just outside my door. The question became, What is God? The answer was logical, inasmuch as logic plays a role in any spiritual belief: God is nature and nature is God. I began to think of myself as a druid—not a cleric of nature spirits, but a worshipper of nature in the church of bluejack oak, the cathedral of old-growth pines. I was a member of the congregation of the great outdoors.

What, then, of humans? Are people a part of nature, and therefore a part of God? My mother thought so, believing strongly in interconnectedness, the indecipherable linkages between people and the universe—whether people choose to recognize them or not. Yet I saw people as separate. Civilization and technology were, if not antithetical to nature, then at least artificial. Constructed. What else could explain deforestation, strip mining, damming the wild rivers? War and famine. Why would God destroy God?

Looking back, I see the immediate conflict—people apart from nature, and, therefore, apart from God, yet whose purpose in life was to evolve into God. The conflict has not resolved, though one possible bridge is Indigenous cultures. Even large environmental organizations like the World Wildlife Fund recognize, after decades of initiatives to the contrary, that wildlands are most successfully preserved not absent of Native peoples but because of them. They are an intrinsic part of their natural habitats, which begs the question, Shouldn't we all be part of our natural habitat? Let's consider children, whose innocence and curiosity inherently link them to nature so that natural habitats become an integral part of who they are. At what point, though, is the linkage lost, and why?

7.

The coyote will not eat crushed mesquite beans from my hand, though my daughters and I coax the wary canine from beneath a knot of mesquites outside our Tucson home. Do my children see God in his umber eyes, in the heavy-branched native trees, in the Rincon Mountains vermilion in the coming dusk? We've had conversations about religion—Juliet's best friend is Mormon, and asks my daughter about her relationship with Jesus almost daily, though her parents are not evangelical and have never approached us about their faith—but not *the* conversation, the "Does God exist?" query. If prompted, I might default to my answer about the tooth fairy and Santa Claus: they are real so long as you believe in them. But I do not classify God with the tooth fairy or Easter bunny or Santa Claus. Even as I struggle with my own faith, I favor a deist approach—that there is a central spiritual force in our world and the worlds beyond that operates on and above science and reason; that the force, the unending energy, binds us to place; that, after all, "each is holy in their own belief." How, otherwise, can we respect Indigenous— or even our own—beliefs?

The Yaqui believe in a dual world, a universe of parallels—this desert landscape and a "mythic, primeval place called...*sea ania,* flower world," write Larry Evers and Felipe S. Molina in their book *Yaqui Deer Songs: Maso Bwikam*. The worlds are bridged by the deer dancer and the men who, in support of this sacred performance, sing the deer songs. The songs themselves "tell a continuing story of life and death in the wilderness world of the Sonoran Desert." And they bring forth the voice of *saila maso*, the deer who is exalted among all others in the flower world, in the afterlife, to the east.

The palo de muerto represents *sea ania*, the flower world—at least to me, a man who is not Yaqui, whose knowledge of Yaqui ceremony and beliefs is limited, and who has rarely seen the tree. It's a dangerous comparison, though, because it comes without authority, a kind of socioreligious anthropomorphism, if not appropriation. Yet it's a metaphor that works: the clustered flowers that shine as if from another world, and the deer that eat them after they fall. The branches like silver antlers, and the resurgence of leaves and life with the summer rains. The tree is not a portal, but a symbol—an allegory for my own otherworldly pursuit. God as nature, nature as God: the ancient wilderness here and beyond.

If nature is God, then God is inherently neutral—neither good nor evil. Yet, like Billie, I strive to be an involved, inspirational, and encouraging parent and community member, to treat others with fairness, to use compassion and empathy at all times. How to graft the disparate branches? While I agree that nature cannot intrinsically favor good or evil—even as humans seem to exhibit the full spectrum—I must believe in the overall good of self, the possibilities of good in the world, if I want to seed hope in my daughters. And hope is the essential seed. I am not certain of hope's relationship to spiritual evolution; maybe they are the same. Maybe hope is the vine that climbs beyond the flower-tipped branches.

8.

This animal beneath the white tree is me, and the trail is of my making. Billie and I have followed our own paths—she without parental guidance, I with insight from my mother. There seems to be a difference. Without her mother or father raising her in faith—religious or otherwise—Billie has none. No faith, that is, in a force or transcendent spirit beyond the self, though it's clear— as a teacher and idealist—she has faith in herself, in education, in family and community. "Be good," she says. It's the *being* that counts, not the tallying of deeds to be scrutinized at a pearly gate.

Yet my visions as a child—the strangely tangible faith I sometimes miss, sometimes decline—lead me to believe that even when we do not seek it, even when our parents and the wider community do not immerse us in it, spirituality has a way of finding each of us. Grace seeks us as much as we seek grace.

Perhaps, then, matters of faith may be learned but not actively taught. Perhaps by our actions and conversations alone, which are more than mere indifference, our children also find their own way, a path that encourages discovery through the world around us—the lofty flight of an eagle and low song of a dove, the skittish lope of coyote and quick curve of centipede. And perhaps curiosity—its own kind of *sea ania*, the flower world both within and beyond—is enough.

When we first saw the palo de muerto on the bajadas below Hermosillo, my daughters knew it wasn't dead because, against the low winter sun, the flowers flared. "Like an angel," said Juliet, who traced the tree's outline against the tinted glass of our car. "Like an angel," I echoed, considering the soul's guardian—an angel, an illusion, the deep-seeded self?—as we journey through this life, and the next.

CREDITS AND ACKNOWLEDGMENTS

My thanks to the editors of the following publications, where several of these essays first appeared, often in an earlier version: "The Sum of All Species," *Mid-American Review*; "Calendars of Sun and Moon," *Weber Studies* (now *Weber: The Contemporary West*); "Satellite," *Platte Valley Review*; "Songbird," *Hawk and Handsaw: The Journal of Creative Sustainability*; "The Bells of San Borja," *Pilgrimage* and reprinted in *Telling It Real: The Best of Pilgrimage (2003–2008)*; "My Wildflower Bromance," published as "Chasing Wildflowers in El Pinacate y Gran Desierto de Altar," *Terrain .org*; "The Biter on Tap," *Copper Nickel*; "Roundabout," *r.kv.r.y. Quarterly*; "The Castaway," *High Desert Journal*; "My Neighbor's Bird," *Dark Sky Magazine*; "A Pure Color," *Wildbranch: An Anthology of Nature, Environmental, and Place-based Writing*; "Photographing the Resplendent Trees," *ISLE: Interdisciplinary Studies in Literature and Environment*; "Palo del Muerte," *The Chalk Circle: Intercultural Prizewinning Essays*.

Funding, travel, or accommodations for some of the research and writing of these essays was made possible in part by the Arizona Commission on the Arts, Grace A. Tanner Center at Southern Utah University, Pacific Northwest Research Station (U.S. Forest Service), Spring Creek Project at Oregon State University, Tucson-Pima Arts Council, and Zion Canyon Mesa. Thank you.

There are many people I am grateful to for their support, insight, and friendship in the making of this book, first and foremost among them Alison Deming, my MFA thesis advisor, longtime *Terrain.org* supporter, friend, and champion; and Scott Calhoun, a character in more than a few of these essays and a fine character otherwise, not to mention a close friend, confidant, reader, writing group co-conspirator, and so much more. Alison and Scott, thank you.

My thanks also to my other writing group friends over the years: Lisa Levine, Jana Dawson, and Judyth Willis. Judyth, I miss your beautiful energy.

The ideas for many of these essays were seeded in the mid-1990s, when I was in the graduate Urban and Regional Planning program at the University of Colorado Denver. My thanks to Marianne MacDonald, Michael Holleran, Raymond Studer, Christopher Koziol, and Tom Clark, terrific program faculty, as well as Daniel D. Chiras, a member of my thesis committee, and Linda Hogan, who let me join her graduate environmental essay course in Boulder. And poetry, too, underlies many of these essays, so I am grateful to the two most influential professors during my undergraduate degree at Auburn University, outstanding teachers, editors, and poets both: Miriam Marty Clark and R. T. Smith.

Several of these essays were first drafted when I was in the Creative Writing (Nonfiction) MFA program at the University of Arizona, which offered a sacred time and space for which I am grateful. I am especially thankful for the faculty's insight and support during that time, particularly Fenton Johnson; the wonderfully curmudgeonly Richard Shelton, may he rest in peace; Ander Monson; the beautiful spirit Aurelie Sheehan, may she rest in peace; Judy Blunt (as a visiting professor); Franke Gohlke and Britt Salvesen with the Center for Creative Photography; and the aforementioned Alison Deming. Just as integral to the development of many of these essays were my classmates, who seemed okay with having a dad ten or fifteen years older than most them as part of the intimate cohort we became, particularly Riley Beck Iosca, Nishta Mehra, Aisha Sabatini Sloan, Karinya Champoux, DW, Patrick Burns, Jessica Wilson, Amy Knight, Jennifer McStotts, Kristin Winet, Lisa O'Neil, Chet Phillips, Kirk Wisland, Nathaniel Brodie, Jaren Watson, Kati Standefer, and Megan Kimball. And let's not forget Brother Ben Quick and Joshua Foster, whose insights and friendships mean the world to me.

Other writers and editors who have also helped guide these essays, for which I am grateful, include Scott Russell Sanders, Kathryn Miles, W. Scott Olsen, Tara Masih, Florence Caplow, Susan A. Cohen, Jake Adam York (rest in peace, my Auburn brother), Allison Adelle Hedge Coke, and Juan Morales.

I am especially grateful to Elizabeth Dodd and Derek Sheffield—for our time together on Mount Saint Helens, their amazing editing, their volunteer work with *Terrain.org*, and our nourishing friendship. Thank you. And thank you, Andy Gottlieb. And to other *Terrain.org* compatriots whose writing, editing, and thinking have helped guide my own writing, thank you: Jennifer Case, Pam Houston, Doug Carlson, Janine DeBaise, Melissa Sevigny, Taylor Brorby, Rob Carney, Joy Castro, Kurt Caswell, Debora Fries, Renata Golden, Julian Hoffman, Hannah Fries, Erik Hoffner, J. Drew Lanham, Jessie Lendennie, Carly Lettero, Eric Magrane, Nick Neely, Janisse Ray, Galina Tachieva, and Lauret Savoy.

Other thinkers and writers who deserve my thanks for conversations or insights that in one way or another have influenced the essays in this collection begin with David Rothenberg, whose keen insight has always been a gift, and also include John Price, Michael Branch, David Gessner, Laura-Gray Street, Jennifer

Sahn, Christopher Cokinos, Joni Adamson, Nicole Walker, Ken Lamberton, Margaret Ronstadt, Ken Pirie, Ari Patrinos, Jeanne Bennett, Logan Hebner, and Patrick Dibala.

As robust a thanks as I can muster goes to Charles Goodrich and Fred Swanson. Colleagues, friends, changemakers, I am grateful that you brought me to Mount Saint Helens—which was life-changing—and even more grateful for your long friendship since.

Special thanks to Bruce Kirschner for taking me under his wing at Western Area Power Administration (and for teaching me how to be a decent facilitator and mentor, how to brew, and so much more); to Bill and Kim Hayashi for being such wonderful parents and neighbors and community-makers; to Colorado compatriots Carolyn and Joe Dooling, Todd Ziebarth, John Morris, Catherine Cunningham, Matt Wiewel, Pete and Sarah Crozier, Cheryl Hennessy, and Jason and Shannan Reese; to Utah colleague Danielle Dubrasky; to University of Arizona writers and friends Liz Warren-Pederson and Pila Martinez; to University of Arizona guardian angel Merrilee Holmes; and to Civano neighbors and friends Dan and Ingrid Weber, Rich and Susan Michal, Ted and Jana (again) Dawson, Scott (again) and Deirdre Calhoun, Duane and Pam Bateman, Mike and Monica Eng, Patrick Whelan, Todd and Anna Craig, Jerry and Dorothy Wheeler, Rick and Linda Hanson, and Michael and LaDawn Austin.

For their support, flexibility, professionalism, and so much more, my sincere thanks to the team at Trinity University Press: Tom Payton, Sarah Nawrocki, Bridget McGregor, Lee Ann Sparks, Daniel Simon, and especially to my wonderful editor, Steffanie Mortis Stevens.

Finally, this book would not be possible without my family—brothers Miles and David Buntin, sister Diana Newton, father Ed Buntin, and my mother, Diana Ann-Marie Estelle Gunilla von Schinkle Bancroft, whose amazing spirit left us far too soon. And there would be nothing at all to write without the loving support of my wife, Billie Harris-Buntin, and our daughters, Onyx and Juliet. Thank you for letting me share our stories: I am grateful beyond words—though there are, I realize, plenty of them here!

SIMMONS BUNTIN is the author of two books of poetry, *Riverfall* and *Bloom*, and the coauthor, with Ken Pirie, of a collection of sustainable community case studies, *Unsprawl: Remixing Spaces as Places*. He is also the coeditor, with Elizabeth Dodd and Derek Sheffield, of *Dear America: Letters of Hope, Habitat, Defiance, and Democracy*. He is the founder and editor-in-chief of *Terrain.org*, president and director of the board of Terrain Publishing, and director of marketing and communications at the University of Arizona College of Information Science. He lives in Tucson, Arizona. Access resources for the book at simmonsbuntin.com/satellite.

SATELLITE

Essays on Fatherhood and Home, Near and Far

"A field guide to a father's love."
—Janisse Ray

Simmons Buntin

www.ingramcontent.com/pod-product-compliance
Lightning Source LLC
Jackson TN
JSHW082055181224
75517JS00003B/2